Amartya Sen

Key Contemporary Thinkers Series

Amartya Sen

Lawrence Hamilton

polity

First published in 2019 by Polity Press

Polity Press
65 Bridge Street
Cambridge CB2 1UR, UK

Polity Press
101 Station Landing
Suite 300
Medford, MA 02155, USA

ISBN-13: 978-1-5095-1984-2
ISBN-13: 978-1-5095-1985-9(pb)

A catalogue record for this book is available from the British Library.

Library of Congress Cataloging-in-Publication Data

Names: Hamilton, Lawrence, 1972- author.
Title: Amartya Sen / Lawrence Hamilton.
Description: Medford, MA : Polity, 2019. | Series: Key contemporary thinkers |
    Includes bibliographical references and index.
Identifiers: LCCN 2018040025 (print) | LCCN 2018052297 (ebook) | ISBN
    9781509519880 (Epub) | ISBN 9781509519842 (hardback) | ISBN 9781509519859
    (pbk.)
Subjects: LCSH: Sen, Amartya, 1933- | Economists–India. | Welfare economics. |
    Social justice. | Economics–Moral and ethical aspects.
Classification: LCC HB126.I43 (ebook) | LCC HB126.I43 .S467 2019 (print) | DDC
    330.15/56–dc23
LC record available at https://lccn.loc.gov/2018040025

Typeset in 10.5 on 12 pt Palatino
by Toppan Best-set Premedia Limited
Printed and bound in the United Kingdom by CPI Group (UK) Ltd, Croydon

The publisher has used its best endeavours to ensure that the URLs for external websites referred to in this book are correct and active at the time of going to press. However, the publisher has no responsibility for the websites and can make no guarantee that a site will remain live or that the content is or will remain appropriate.

Every effort has been made to trace all copyright holders, but if any have been overlooked the publisher will be pleased to include any necessary credits in any subsequent reprint or edition.

For further information on Polity, visit our website:
politybooks.com

In memoriam John Hamilton

Contents

Preface

There is something neatly apt about finishing a book on Amartya Sen on the day the world celebrates Labour Day or International Workers Day (truth be told, on the United Kingdom's watered-down 'May Day' version) and a couple of days after Karl Marx's birthday (Marx at 200). Marx is much more of a forebear for Sen's ideas than many admit – including Sen himself; and Marx, Sen and Labour Day all celebrate the powers and solidarity of workers the world over. A great day to end a period of great labour, though not easy, as it is a beautiful spring day out there – the warmest May Day on record – and I am stuck inside. Moreover, today is supposed to be about leisure, something that has inspired Marx and Sen's thinking though, of course, the sheer volume of their writings attests, in all likelihood, to very little leisure time.

It has been a privilege to write this book. It has also been really hard work. This is the case for two main reasons, the one positive and the other negative. The positive reason is, of course, that trying to distil the main ideas of someone who has published so many groundbreaking works in such varied fields is quite a task. I hope I have done some justice to the work of Amartya Sen's prolific and original contributions to so many areas of inquiry into the human condition. The negative reason is that, as Sen himself notes when discussing the work of John Rawls, 'every summary is ultimately an act of barbarism' (*IJ*: 53). I hope that on the scale of literary barbaric acts this one is not too bad.

At first glance, the informed reader may ask herself how a book on Sen does not include a chapter on 'development' or 'famines' or 'gender'. The easy answer would be to say that they are covered throughout, as dictated by Sen's own way of dealing with them in relation to the subjects covered by the book's chapters, which, although true, sounds a little like a cop out. The more correct answer is that I cover all of these topics at some length in the main introduction and in the first chapter; though, given Sen's interdisciplinary approach, the answer that sounds like a cop out is, in fact, closest to the truth. As will become obvious, all three of these topics are constant areas of concern and inspiration for Sen's work, and so they also make appearances throughout the rest of the book.

As regards 'development' in particular, I take it to be so central to understanding Sen's ideas as a whole – including the later ideas on justice and democracy – that it constitutes a helpful mechanism of 'entry' into the colossus of his corpus, which is why a large part of the substance of the introduction covers Sen's approach to development. As I argue there, development (and its deprivations) is what animates most of Sen's work. The book is thereafter structured around five main themes: choice, capability, freedom, justice and democracy. These are the titles of the substantive chapters. I have chosen this structure for both intellectual historical and pedagogic reasons. As regards the former, if rather loosely, these themes map the development of his thought over time. As regards the latter, the way in which I have laid out the chapters introduces the reader to the extraordinary breadth and depth of Sen's work and allows me to highlight two things: his most important ideas and a few possible lines of criticism. In other words, the chapters build on one another, so it does make sense to read them in the order they appear. However, they are also completely self-contained, so a reader with a particular interest could easily and productively dip in and out of chapters as required. Needless to say, given their subjects, they also cover some of the most important topics in economics, philosophy and politics.

So, in very brief outline, in chapter 1, I focus on choice, how Sen engaged with and transformed social choice theory and critiqued many of the main assumptions in welfare economics, including 'utility', 'revealed preference', 'rationality', 'poverty', 'inequality' and 'welfare'. I also discuss his innovative work on famines under the general rubric of deprivation. In chapter 2, I dissect the conceptual schema for which Sen is now most famous: his 'concern for capabilities', as he now likes to put it (Meeks 2017, 2018). I suggest that, taken together, 'functionings' and 'capabilities', as Sen conceives of them, constitute a marked conceptual improvement for assessing well-being, the quality of life and standards of living.

This is particularly true as compared to the main contending rivals over the last century: the notion of 'utility' central to welfarism and utilitarianism, the concept of 'primary goods' propounded by John Rawls and the idea of 'resources' submitted by Ronald Dworkin. The important focus on agency within Sen's capability approach, for a number of reasons, leads felicitously into a discussion in chapter 3 of his account of freedom and the role it plays in his ideas. I position it vis-à-vis the broad spectrum of competing theories of freedom, and suggest that it provides the basis for a unique, fourth conception of freedom as power. This, in turn, given the centrality of freedom in his account of justice, makes for a smooth transition, in chapter 4, to his work on justice. Again here, as Sen himself does, I compare his view of justice, aimed at resolving instances of injustice rather than providing a blueprint for an institutionally ideal society, to various other accounts, particularly that of John Rawls, but also a wide variety of western and non-western views. I submit that, while his 'idea of justice' never escapes the confines of the North Atlantic analytical philosophical tendency to view justice in the artificially reduced form of 'distributive justice', it marks an important departure. Nevertheless, in a similar way to his treatment of the topic of the fifth chapter – democracy – we are left wondering whether impartiality, public reason and deliberation can achieve as much in the real world of politics and economics as Sen supposes.

Acknowledgements

First and foremost, I would like to thank Amartya Sen for carefully and brilliantly pushing every boundary he has come across and for putting up with my stumbling early criticisms as a graduate student more than twenty years ago. He has grace. I have gratitude.

I am also indebted to a number of teachers, colleagues, friends and students for reading and commenting on parts or all of versions of this book and discussing some or all of the topics covered in this book. These include Thomas Aubrey, Candice Bailey, Jude Browne, John Dunn, Ze'ev Emmerich, James Furner, Raymond Geuss, Sophie Harbour, Tim Karayiannides, Duncan Kelly, Stephen Louw, Mairéad McAuley, Gay Meeks, David Moore, Moshibudi Motimele, Ayesha Omar, Laurence Piper, Ramakwe Nicholus Pule, Ian Shapiro, Nicola Viegi and three very helpful anonymous reviewers sourced by Polity. Everyone I have worked with at Polity has been excellent and efficient; together, they are a model of the patient, informed and polite editorial team. However, George Owers deserves special mention. He has been an absolute pleasure to work with: he approached me with this idea, cajoled me at all the right times, allowed me to miss a few deadlines, and yet stuck firm when necessary. He read the entire manuscript really carefully, returning his marked-up version with so many helpful insights it was as if I had had four academic readers. He is a member of a small and dying breed of editors that still read every word you produce. Polity should cherish him, as I am sure they do. I am also indebted to audiences in Accra, Cambridge, Cape Town, Johannesburg, London, São Paulo and Tokyo, who have heard me talk about topics covered in this book and offered help and criticism, not all of which I have been able properly to respond to, but all of which have made me think harder. The usual disclaimer applies.

Many thanks, too, to my colleagues in the Department of Political Studies at the University of the Witwatersrand (Wits) and the Department of Political and International Studies (POLIS) at the University of Cambridge, for allowing me the space to get on with this project and for constant inspiration. I am also extremely grateful to Wits, Cambridge, Clare Hall College, Cambridge, the South African National Research Foundation, the Newton Fund and the British Academy for their institutional and financial support. The last three in this list can also be credited for providing me the research space and financial support that allowed me to take on and complete a project of this kind. It comes in the form of the SARChI/Newton Research Chair in Political Theory that I hold and they fund (grant number 103137). Without it, I would not have had the time and opportunity to offer back to the academic community (and beyond) something I hope will be of use. Amartya Sen's ideas are of enormous importance across the globe, but many of them are also challenging to comprehend. If I have enabled the process of their understanding, significance and application – via elucidation and constructive criticism – this little book has been worthwhile. We are all therefore also indebted to Robin Drennan, Wits's Research Manager, and his team for their managerial skill, patience and no-nonsense attitude in the complicated process of implementing this Bilateral Chair I hold; no easy job! I have also been very fortunate, both before and during the early days of my new Chair, to have been blessed by a number of exceptional departmental and Chair administrators and research assistants. Many thanks Suzy Adcock, Candice Bailey, Alexandra Barry, Catherine Cebindevu, Thoko Jean Chilenga, Rae Israel, Dan Jones, Rita Kruger, Moshibudi Motimele, Thandeka Ndebele, Gillian Renshaw, Ricardo de Sao Joao and Cerys Thomas for everything you have done to keep my work environments (and me) running smoothly.

The range of researchers and graduate students that constitute my Chair, both at Wits and Cambridge, is like a family to me, but it is my real family that I must thank the most. Mairéad heard more about Amartya Sen than she may care to think about and also read a lot of what I tried to write about him with great patience and insight. Lorcan, Cormac and Lanark are too young to fully comprehend why a 'book' could keep their father so busy for such a long time, but they are at least happy to hear it is finished. Sadly, my father passed away at the beginning of this project, so he is gone forever, something I and my kids cannot quite comprehend. I dedicate this book to him.

Finally, I would like to thank *Government and Opposition* for allowing me to reuse some material from my article, 'A Theory of True Interests in the Work of Amartya Sen', *Government and Opposition* 34(4) (1999). Parts of the middle of chapter 2 and a small section of the main conclusion are loosely based on this article. Parts of the book's main conclusion also originate in two other articles of mine: 'Justice and Real Politics: Freedom, Needs and Representation', in C. Boisen and M. C. Murray (eds), *Distributive Justice Debates in Political and Social Thought: Finding a Fair Share* (London: Routledge, 2016); and 'Amilcar Cabral and Amartya Sen: Capability, Freedom and Resistance' (forthcoming).

Key Texts

CS: A. K. Sen, *Collective Choice and Social Welfare*, expanded
        edn (London, Penguin, 2017 [Holden-Day, 1970]).

OEI: A. K. Sen, *On Economic Inequality*, expanded edn with a
        substantial annex by J. E. Foster and A. K. Sen (Oxford:
        Clarendon Press, 1997 [Oxford University Press, 1973]).

EW: 'Equality of What?', in Sterling McMurrin (ed.), *Tanner
        Lectures on Human Values, Vol. 1* (Cambridge: Cambridge
        University Press, 1980).

PF: A. K. Sen, *Poverty and Famines*, in *The Amartya Sen and Jean
        Drèze Omnibus* (Oxford: Oxford University Press, 1999
        [International Labour Organization, 1981]).

CWM: A. K. Sen, *Choice, Welfare and Measurement* (Harvard University Press, 1997 [Basil Blackwell, 1982]).

RVD: A. K. Sen, *Resources, Values and Development* (Oxford: Blackwell and Cambridge, MA: Harvard University Press, 1984).

CC: A. K. Sen, *Commodities and Capabilities* (Amsterdam: North-Holland, 1985).

WAF: A. K. Sen, 'Well-being, Agency and Freedom: The Dewey
        Lectures 1984', *Journal of Philosophy* 82(4) (1985): 169–221.

SL: A. K. Sen, 'The Standard of Living', in G. Hawthorn (ed.),
        The Standard of Living: The Tanner Lectures on Human Values
        (Cambridge: Cambridge University Press, 1987).

OEE: A. K. Sen, *On Ethics & Economics* (Oxford: Blackwell, 1987).

IR: A. K. Sen, *Inequality Reexamined* (Cambridge, MA: Harvard
        University Press, 1995 [Russell Sage Foundation, 1992]).

CW: 'Capability and Well-being', in Martha Nussbaum and Amartya Sen (eds), *The Quality of Life* (Oxford: Clarendon Press, 1993), pp. 30–53.

PO: A. K. Sen, 'Positional Objectivity', *Philosophy and Public Affairs* 22(2) (1993): 126–45.

DF: A. K. Sen, *Development as Freedom* (Oxford: Oxford University Press, 2001 [New York: Knopf, 1999]).

RF: A. K. Sen, *Rationality and Freedom* (Cambridge, MA: Harvard University Press, 2002).

IJ: A. K. Sen, *The Idea of Justice* (London: Allen Lane, 2009).

Introduction

Amartya Kumar Sen is one of the world's leading contemporary public intellectuals. He is probably the world's best-known economic, social and political theorist since the Second World War. Although his primary academic recognition has been in economics, for which he was awarded the 1998 Nobel Memorial Prize, he has also made significant contributions to a myriad of topics within philosophy, social theory and politics. His work on social choice theory is seminal, his capabilities approach changed the way we think about human well-being and the quality of life, and his contributions on freedom, agency, the standard of living, justice and democracy shake to the very foundations many of the theoretical edifices we have constructed around how best to conceive of our lives together.

The sheer volume of his published work is something to behold. He has published more than two dozen books and countless academic articles, so many that most of his 30-page curriculum vitae is made up of a list of his publications. His books have been translated into more than thirty languages. However, it is once you get beyond this edifice that you realize that the quantity of output is eclipsed by its quality. The consistent excellence and polite erudition of his contributions are inspirational. Most of his published work is not just good. It is groundbreaking. Very few, alive or dead, have produced so much of such significance.

Sen is an economist by formal training, but he is also one of the world's leading social, moral, legal and political philosophers. Besides his fame for discipline-defining contributions to social choice theory, welfare economics, development and our understanding of famines, among others, he is less recognized for also contributing to and, in some cases, completely transforming the way we think about, for example, public health and medicine, population and the environment, gender and feminist economics, education, and Indian economics, society, culture and politics. The list goes on. A mere list, though, would take away from a very important component of his work: always with elegant charm and grace, he has transcended the standard categories, gently chiding those who have felt too comfortable in the received opinions and traditions of their disciplines.

In other words, while Sen's many contributions to human understanding are rooted in economics, they are far from confined to it. This is the first goal of this short book: to introduce the reader to the full breadth of Sen's work in philosophy, economics and politics. The second objective is, simultaneously, to be selective, that is, to focus in on his most important ideas and their development. In other words, as a mere introduction to Sen's ideas, this little book cannot hope to cover the entirety of his massive corpus, even in introductory outline. If the reader feels short-changed, I can but beg indulgence. The final aim of this book is to assess the legacy of his thought, outline the debates surrounding his work and propose a novel critique of his political theory.

Sen is justly famous for his 1998 Nobel Prize in economics, though he is also the recipient of many other global awards (Sen 2015: 276; and more since). This highest of accolades, the Nobel Prize, was awarded for his pioneering work in social choice theory, welfare economics, poverty indexes and his empirical studies of famine. Yet his tendency not to be bound by traditional academic boundaries is often not celebrated as much as it might be. Its importance is manifest in two main ways, which also reflect two of his most breathtakingly courageous academic moves. First, despite his training in the mainstream of strait-laced post-Second World War economics, in exemplary fashion he grasped the opportunities provided to him and schooled himself in the main currents of contemporary philosophy. This gave him a much broader and more capacious view of the assumptions of the 'dismal science' of economics, the main shibboleths of which would be his targets for years to come. In other words, in line with two of his greatest forebears and two of the political economists upon whom he draws most, Adam Smith and Karl Marx, he has done all he can to understand the main problems and issues in economics from the perspective of a broader ethical concern: improving the quality of life of all. Second, especially in his work on famines, but also right across his many contributions in other areas, such as development, freedom, justice and democracy, Sen has always immersed his reader in his deep and broad knowledge of theory, while never tiring of supporting his claims and arguments with relevant empirical facts. Needless to say, the Nobel Committee was well aware of both of these points: 'Amartya Sen has made a number of noteworthy contributions to central fields of economic science and opened up new fields of study for subsequent generations of researchers. By combining tools from economics and philosophy, he has restored an ethical dimension to the discussion of vital economic problems' (Nobel 1998).

While it would be fair to suggest that Sen is first and foremost a man of letters (and numbers), he has also been involved in a number of practical projects that have changed the way the world thinks about and carries out a number of important and pressing matters, particularly as regards development. In fact, it is his work for and criticisms of large international bodies such as the United Nations (UN) and the World Bank (the Bank), and many others besides, that has broadened his appeal and fame, along with his associated practical contributions to, for example, global attempts to eradicate poverty and reduce inequality. These interventions are the fruits of a number of collaborative academic and political interventions. These include theoretical and applied writings on poverty, inequality, famine and development; a central role in the creation of the UN's Human Development Index (HDI) and his role, alongside the founding role of Mahbub ul Haq, in the birth and nurturing of the UNDP's Human Development Reports (Sen 2000); the foundation of the United Nations University World Institute for Development Economics Research (UNU-WIDER), which recently celebrated 30 years of research excellence; and his various (sometimes controversial) roles in a number of higher education institutions in India. These and many other practical achievements have helped reconfigure how most international development practitioners go about their craft.

Not least of all these practical achievements has been the practical effects of his work on, and his willingness to engage with, the Bank. Thanks to Sen, part of what I describe below as having characterized the top-down failed development projects of the Bank for many decades is now no longer true of how it proceeds. While not exactly fully embracing all his recommendations, it has at least started to focus more on education and various other components of how best to enhance the quality of life of individuals in the developing world. At long last, the Bank has realized that while this shift in focus from growth to measures of individual quality of life may not have immediate, quantifiable returns, as compared to the way that, say, building a factory produces a quantifiable return, it is possible to see substantial returns, especially if you change your evaluative profiles and weightings to make them look a little more like what Sen proposes (cf. Chang 2003; Williams 2014).

Sen has provided new ways of conceiving of development, as well as new tools for measuring it and its component parts: famine, poverty, inequality, growth, freedom and so on. So, while some of Sen's most important and telling contributions have been theoretical, many more have been practical, and most of his theoretical moves have been developed with at least one eye on their implications for pressing economic or political matters of the moment. Moreover, especially of late, the public intellectual in him has come strongly to the fore as he has critically engaged with the political leadership of the United States of America, the European Union and India, as I discuss in greater detail in chapter 5.

It will not surprise many to hear that Sen's impressive contributions to a variety of fields is grounded in excellent early training and matched by a stellar academic career. He was born in 1933 in Santiniketan in West Bengal, India, on the campus of Rabindrath Tagore's Visva-Bharati University. Rabindrath Tagore, probably India's most famous literary figure and musician, who founded Visva-Bharati University, himself gave Sen his name (Bengali অমর্ত্য ômorto, literally 'immortal'). Growing up in these university campus surroundings and with academic parents and grandparents, some with close ties to Tagore and to public service (his mother was a close associate of Tagore and his father, a chemistry professor who also held various public service posts), it is not surprising he excelled at school, university and beyond. He went to a Bengali-medium school (Patha Bhavan, also in Santiniketan), where, as he puts it, he was 'deeply involved with the study of Sanskrit, on one side, and with mathematical and analytical reasoning, on the other' (Sen 2015: xxviii). The study of Sanskrit – the intricacies of the language and its literature – enthralled him. For many years, Sanskrit was Sen's second language, after Bengali, and he could read classical, Vedic and epic Sanskrit. This fascination with the language and literature of Sanskrit also balanced and complemented his acumen in mathematics. Both of these important skills have been readily apparent ever since in his academic work, often side by side in the same volume. His grandfather, Pundit Kshiti Mohan Sen, was a great Sanskrit scholar and, although Sen did not need much encouragement, was also helpful in firing his enchantment with the literature of Sanskrit, from the famous Bhagavadgita, actually only a small part of a grand epic, the Mahabharata, the plays of Kalidasa, Shudraka, Bana, through the 'clarity of reasoning' of Gautama Buddha, who moved Sen so much, to the mathematics and epistemology of Aryabhata, Brahmagupta and the Bhaskaras (Sen 2015: xxix–xxxi). Hardly surprising then that a little later, at Presidency College, Calcutta, he earned a first-class BA in economics with a minor in mathematics. In 1953, he moved to Trinity College, Cambridge, where only two years later he earned a second first-class BA in economics, topping the year list. While still officially a PhD student at Cambridge (though he had finished his research), he was offered the position of professor and head of the department of economics at the newly created Jadavpur University in Calcutta. He served in that position from 1956 to 1958. Thereafter, he taught and held professorships at the Delhi School of Economics, Oxford, the London School of Economics and Harvard, before being elected Master of Trinity College, Cambridge, in 1998. In 2004, he returned to his Harvard position as Thomas W. Lamont University Professor, and Professor of Economics and Philosophy.

Sen's work is, of course, the result of a razor-sharp and capacious mind combined with an enormous capacity for dedicated hard work and commitment to a cause. This prodigious output and commitment to hard work may not have always sat easily with his enduring love of cricket, at least in its five-day test match version. It has not stopped him, however, from giving amply of his time as an inspiring teacher and supervisor, something to which a long line of academics and development specialists will happily attest.

This book has no pretensions to be a comprehensive work of intellectual history or a biography, but two things are worth noting about the background to Sen's famous academic career. First, he is a product of India at independence, where the upper echelons of society were well equipped by a combination of eastern and western learning to handle the rigours of his subsequent Anglo-American academic trajectory. In fact, if the number of top global economists produced by the Delhi School of Economics alone is anything to go by, this is a gross understatement. This post-independence milieu was a veritable hothouse for the growth of a diverse and large number of academic and political leaders. Second, Sen is also a child of the Bengal famine and Indian Partition. He experienced at first-hand as a nine-year old boy the horrors of the Bengal famine of 1943, as he did a little later the horrors of communal violence of Partition. In a number of places in his academic and non-academic work, he tells the story of how, during the sectarian tensions and violence that accompanied Partition, a Muslim man, a poor day-labourer, was attacked by a gang in his mainly Hindu area. The man was still alive as he stumbled into Sen's childhood home; the now slightly older boy helped organize to have him sent to hospital. Unfortunately, he did not survive. Not only does Sen use this story to illustrate his oft-repeated and convincing point about the dangers of sectarianism and dogmatic community and identity-based thinking, but also that, despite his wife imploring him not to go into Hindu areas in this period fearing for her husband's life, this poor man felt impelled to do so as he was the breadwinner for his family and could get work nowhere else. The harsh realities of economic underdevelopment – economic unfreedom – coupled with sectarian violence left the man with no real choice and culminated in him losing his life and his family losing their loved one and breadwinner (Sen 2006a, 2015; and many more besides).

From very early on, these experiences and the elective affinity Sen developed with the famous Cambridge Marxist economist, Maurice Dobb, put him at odds with the highly theoretical and dogmatic utilitarianism of most economists he came across in Cambridge, including that of his formal supervisor Joan Robinson. His earliest research work – his PhD thesis, which led to the publication of his first book (Sen 1960) – displayed all of his mathematical expertise alongside a need to escape the confines of mainstream welfare economics in general and development economics in particular. Most obvious, even from early on, was an enduring belief in developing an approach to development economics that moved beyond the assumptions of utilitarianism and the idea that economics was a singular science – with a concrete set of analytical tools – that, once mastered, could be applied anywhere any time. This early work was directly concerned with how a society chooses possible models or paths of development – that is, plans for development – from within an 'underdeveloped economy'.

Having grown up in a developing world context, a number of Sen's subsequent theoretical and empirical moves would be driven by the unique demands of development. This abiding interest in questions of development is evident in the more than fifty articles he has published on the topic, from as early as 1957, via his justly famous *Development as Freedom* (*DF*), published in 1999, which presents an overview of Sen's thinking on development, while pulling together a whole tapestry of themes familiar from his earlier work, alongside the various volumes on development in India he has published with Jean Drèze (Drèze and Sen 1999 [1989], 1999 [1995], 2002, 2014), and beyond. This predominance of the central problems and challenges of development is apparent in his thinking more generally, despite the fact that he has also contributed to so many other fields and that, *en passant*, he has pursued very deeply a number of seemingly unrelated theoretical problems. Social choice theory and welfare economic theory was, for example, at the forefront of what he did at least from the publication of his *Collective Choice and Social Welfare* (*CS*) in 1970 up until what might be called a full 'return' to development economics marked by the publication of his 'Development: Which Way Now?' (Sen 1983c; see also Sen 1989, 2000). This is not to suggest that all of his arguments around choice, capability, freedom, justice and democracy are not also applicable to a whole range of questions and issues in developed contexts, as he is at pains to stress repeatedly (see *DF* for just a few examples). Rather, my point is that it is obvious that the main inspiration for his work is the terrible effects of a series of deprivations on human lives most evident in less-developed contexts.

Sen has stayed away from many of the more virulent ideological battles that have characterized development economics, but he has a firm and clear position on how best to approach the economics of development. Alongside his important contributions regarding how best to understand famines, Sen is most famous for developing a substantive, broad view of development based on his conception of capability, or what he prefers to call his 'concern for capabilities'. This is important for a number of reasons. First, he presents a philosophical alternative to the utilitarianism that underpins so much of economics, something that is discussed at length in the first two chapters of this book. Second, he delivers an alternative development objective, where development becomes 'a process of expanding the real freedoms that people enjoy' (*DF*: 3). This transforms the 'evaluative space' for determining development issues. As Sen puts it, 'for many evaluative purposes, the appropriate "space" is neither that of utilities (as claimed by welfarists), nor that of primary goods (as demanded by Rawls), but that of the substantive freedoms – the capabilities – to choose a life one has reason to value' (*DF*: 74). This is an important advance on a number of narrower views of development proposed by those who identify development with the growth of gross national product (GNP), or with the rise (or maximization) in personal incomes, or with industrialization, or with technological advance, or with social modernization. As he argues, all of these can be very important as means to expanding the freedoms enjoyed by members of a society. But freedoms and quality of life depend also on other determinants, such as social and economic facilities for education and health care as well as political and civil rights. If freedom and quality of life is what development advances – if that is the goal of development – 'then there is a major argument for concentrating on that overarching objective, rather than on some particular means, or some specially chosen list of instruments' (*DF*: 3).

This alternative development objective not only informs a wide range of issues, from markets to gender, democracy to poverty and freedom to justice; it also meets head-on an enduring problem within the theory and practice of development: paternalism. From a variety of different ideological perspectives, development has been unable to escape a top-down method of proceeding, where ideas and institutions from afar are given licence to dictate to the poor how best to develop without reference to their needs, values and conditions. Sen's starting point is different. As he puts it in *DF*, his approach to development as freedom investigates various contributions 'to enhancing and guaranteeing the substantive freedoms of individuals, seen as active agents of change, rather than as passive recipients of dispensed benefits' (*DF*: xiii). It is worth quoting Sen at length on this point.

> In terms of the medieval distinction between 'the patient' and 'the agent,' this freedom-centred understanding of economics and of the process of development is very much an agent-oriented view. With adequate social opportunities, individuals can effectively shape their own destiny and help each other. They need not be seen primarily as passive recipients of the benefits of cunning development programs. There is indeed a strong rationale for recognizing the positive role of free and sustainable agency – and even of constructive impatience ... I am using the term 'agent' ... in its older – and 'grander' – sense as someone who acts and brings about change, and whose achievements can be judged in terms of her values and objectives, whether or not we assess them in terms of some external criteria as well. (*DF*: 11, 19)

Sen's theoretical and practical proposals based on his version of capability value the agency of individuals in and of itself – as constitutive of a life worth living – and because they tend to produce better overall effects in development projects. This is the third important contribution that Sen's approach to development provides. As will become obvious in this book, agency in general and the requirements for it lie at the very heart of most of Sen's work.[1]

The substantive link between agency and freedom is outlined and discussed in the first three chapters of this book. For the purposes of this introduction, it is sufficient to point out that Sen's view of freedom is much richer than is the norm in a great deal of economic, development, philosophical and political theoretical literature: it encompasses both the requisites for individuals to make their own individual choices and the social, economic and political means for individuals to exert the necessary democratic power within and beyond their own societies. Effectively, Sen is suggesting that citizens themselves, whatever their income level, can budget for themselves, but they cannot do so if, say, 80 per cent of their income has to be spent on health care or education. Within development, Sen is famous for transforming the main indicators with which practitioners and policy makers are concerned about when thinking about development, as he is for his work on famines – for arguing, against the grain, that famines are not ultimately about a shortage of food but a lack of entitlement over food, that is, the power or means to acquire it. He argues convincingly that income maximization or GNP, or any other particular means that enables individuals to live a life they have reason to value, while important, are not the main concern for development.

Development is about generating the capacity, the capability, the power of citizens to determine themselves how best they should live. Some on the left have criticized this kind of approach for feeding into a market-based view – that markets best enable the ability to make choices for development – but Sen has little truck with this criticism for, as he says frequently, in the *longue durée* markets are one central component of enabling this development capability. As Karl Marx argued, despite their deficiencies and failures, as compared to earlier forms of exchange, markets have been revolutionary in enabling more efficient exchange, that is, in empowering individuals to acquire the necessities and luxuries of life. As Sen argues, to be against markets generally speaking would be like being against communication. Yet critics of markets are clearly onto something (however overstated the criticism may sometimes appear): the problem lies not in the nature of markets themselves but in the exploitation and domination to which they can give rise; thus the crucial question becomes whether and how they are regulated. Consequently, more often than not, the first important question in development is how to help poor people enter markets securely, given that many still struggle even to enter them. How to enable them to do so with similar entitlement or power as those already securely enmeshed in existing markets often becomes the key question in development. The seemingly more radical idea of being completely opposed to markets often ends up in practice disabling this process of empowerment and leaving large swathes of poor people in forms of existence and relations of power that are, at best, riddled with traditional forms of domination and, at worst, ripe for extreme misery, as in the causes and consequences of famine. Here, the large amount of empirical research on Indian development, which Sen has undertaken with Drèze, proves very telling (Drèze and Sen 1999 [1989], 1999 [1995], 2002, 2014). Drèze, as Sen himself notes, has been one of his most important and influential collaborators.

In changing the language and the philosophical underpinning for how best to conceive of development, Sen successfully confronts a number of competing alternatives to development that have had more or less impact on actual development over the decades, at least since 'development economics' began as a separate subject in economics. In various forms, and with various different effects, development has always been about outside experts dictating to local people living in poverty. They have dictated either 'directly', or at least via their support for non-governmental organizations (NGOs), or more indirectly via the state in question. The role of the state – or, more exactly, silence regarding the role of the state – has always been pivotal in these arguments. Welfare economics has not kept politics and the state as central to its concerns as it might have done, in line with a more general tendency in economics: the prevalence of the view of economics as a universal science whose 'scientific' findings could be applied, irrespective of contextual conditions of authority and power (or 'externalities'). As the poor cousin within the extended discipline of economics, development economics then more or less assumed that models of development could be determined without reference to the practices and institutions of the developing context in question. Once the core of the problem of development was correctly identified, then the universal solution could be applied anywhere and everywhere (Hirschman 1981).

One of the two main models against which Sen develops his view is the Harrod–Domar model of development, which stresses the importance of savings and investment as key determinants of growth. It is a classical Keynesian model of economic growth, originally devised with advanced industrial countries in mind and quickly adapted by development economists in the planning exercises for developing countries that became common in the 1950s and beyond. It explains an economy's growth rate in terms of the level of saving and the productivity of capital investment (or the capital-output ratio). It suggests that once the capital gap, that is, the shortfall as regards capital brought about either by low levels of savings or low capital productivity, has been found, development programmes can come in to help fill that gap. (As Albert Hirschman [1981] notes, this is based on the 'mutual benefit assumption' – varying in acceptability over the years – that 'core industrial economies' could contribute to the development of the 'periphery' via large injections of financial aid.) This is what you might call 'capital fundamentalism', something that was central to the Bank's thinking for some time.

As Sen (1983c) notes, as well as many others, the shortcomings of this approach, with its assumed capital–output ratio, are most obvious in a case like Ghana between 1960 and 1980, which despite managing a 5 per cent savings rate (as a percentage of GDP), rather than being a stationary economy, it in fact slipped back (its economy shrunk) by 1 per cent per annum. Having said this, in typically subtle terms, in this 1983 article, Sen in fact qualifies Hirschman's more forthright critique of development economics by suggesting that some of the figures from 1960–1980 do not contradict the traditional wisdom of development economics in general and the Harrod–Domar model in particular. He agrees the latter is oversimplified but is not as willing as Hirschman to discard it completely (Hirschman 1981; Sen 1983c: 750).[2] He undertakes similar, nuanced critiques of those development economic theories that focus uniquely on industrialization or the role of disguised unemployment, and contends that, all told, as far as growth is concerned, 'it is not easy to deny the importance of capital accumulation or of industrialization in a poor pre-industrial country' (Sen 1983c: 751).

The second model against which Sen expounds is the idea that, even if it is accepted that markets can fail, states fail more often and more seriously. Thus it follows that the state should play as small a role as possible, maintain law and order and, at most, enable some very large infrastructural interventions. This is what has been called 'market fundamentalism'. This is supported by an ideology of self-help, that is, that left to their own devices, people will make the right choices to develop their own societies. It is therefore best to reduce the power of the state as much as possible. This has a deep and long history in liberal and libertarian thought, but in the 1970s and 1980s it was given extra ballast by Robert Nozick (1974) and the idea of the 'night-watchman state', coupled with the generally accepted ideology that it is good for you to 'pull yourself up by your own bootstraps'.

This view underpinned the infamous structural adjustment programmes imposed by the Bank across large swathes of the planet, most of which failed dismally (Chang 2003). The idea here was that shock therapies would enable 'underdeveloped' societies to wean themselves off bloated public sectors. The Bank supported developing countries financially on condition that they undertake large-scale adjustment of the core structures of their economies. Sen provides a lot of evidence to support the exact opposite conclusion: that, in fact, in low and middle-income countries the best performers are those in which there is a good deal of state intervention and even economic planning. Moreover, success is not dependent on ideology. It was, for example, as true of Soviet centrally planned economies such as Romania and Yugoslavia as it was (and still is) of capitalist South Korea, which has had an economic system in which the market mechanism has been driven hard by an active government in a planned way. In a typical instance of his firm understatement and dry wit, Sen puts his conclusion as follows: 'Trying to interpret the South Korean economic experience as a triumph of unguided market mechanism, as is sometimes done, is not easy to sustain ... If this is a free market, then Walras's auctioneer can surely be seen as going around with a government white paper in one hand and a whip in the other' (Sen 1983c: 752; see also Sen 1981).

Sen criticizes both of these mainstream models for missing three obvious things about development: the first two are more general points and the third is a particular precondition for either of the arguments, or 'fundamentalisms', against which he moves so deftly. First, growth is not the same thing as development, even if it can scarcely be denied that economic growth is one aspect of the process of economic development. Second, his point is not so much that the government is powerful in the high-growth developing countries, but that it is powerful in nearly every developing country. The real issue is that development seems to require the systematic involvement of the state in the economic sphere. As Ha-Joon Chang argues convincingly, although free marketeers (and most of the discipline of economics) would have us believe otherwise, the same has also been true for centuries in what we now call 'developed' countries: not only is the state very powerful but, generally speaking, it has been very interventionist in national and international markets, especially (ironically) in the United Kingdom and the United States (Chang 2003, 2015). The third thing mainstream models in development economics miss, Sen suggests, is that, before people can save or make the right choices to develop their own societies, individuals first need the ability to make choices. It is out of this that he develops his capability approach as an achievements-based (or realizations-based) approach.

Sen's first move is to show that development is not the same as growth. Economic growth is no more than a means to some other set of objectives, insufficient recognition of which has plagued development economics: 'the real limitations of traditional development economics arose not from the choice of means to the end of economic growth, but in the insufficient recognition that economic growth was more than a means to some other objectives'. He does not suggest that growth does not matter. It may matter a great deal, but this is because of some associated benefits 'that are realized in the process of economic growth' (Sen 1983c: 753). He shows that the same level of achievement in life expectancy, literacy, health, higher education and so on can be seen in countries with widely varying income per capita. For example, in 1982, China and Sri Lanka, with less than a seventh of GNP per head in Brazil or Mexico, had similar life-expectancy figures to the two richer countries. Moreover, South Korea at that point, with its 'much eulogized' growth record, had not yet overtaken China or Sri Lanka in the field of longevity, despite being then more than five times richer in terms of per capita GNP. Sen argues that the empirical record shows very well that rather than assume that fast growth will have the effect over time of raising the level of health and the expectation of life, it makes much more sense to reach directly for these objectives through public policy and social change. China and Sri Lanka did exactly this, despite in other ways being quite different – one a planned economy, the other much more market oriented. Sen argues that these examples, and many others, such as the very high literacy rates and low infant and maternal mortality rates in Cuba, higher and lower respectively than the United States, show that dramatic improvement in quality of life, viewed in terms of capability enhancement, is possible, even under conditions of structural poverty and poor economic growth – though, of course, a growing economy is a great help.

The second and third important moves by Sen have been his concentration, not on national product, aggregate income and total supply of particular goods but on the 'entitlements' of people and the 'capabilities' that these entitlements generate. The fact that traditional development economics has tended to do the exact opposite is, for Sen, how it has been most deficient. This shift of emphasis or identification of the real goal of development enables a rich set of objectives that transforms development into a discipline concerned with what people can or cannot do, such as live long, escape avoidable morbidity, be well nourished, be able to read, write and communicate, take part in literary and scientific pursuits and so on. In other words, he shifts development away from concentration on the growth of inanimate objects of convenience to focus on the quality and richness of human lives. Development, he argues, quoting Marx, is all about 'replacing the domination of circumstances and chance over individuals by the domination of individuals over chance and circumstances' (Marx and Engels 1976; Sen 1983c: 754). Entitlement refers to the set of alternative commodity bundles that a person can command in a society using the totality of rights and opportunities that he or she faces. It is important to note that Sen sees an individual's overall entitlement as being comprised of both the limit set by a person's ownership ('endowment') and his exchange possibilities ('exchange entitlement'). So 'exchange entitlement' is only a part of the entitlement picture and is incomplete without an account of ownership or endowment; and 'exchange entitlement' includes not only trade and market exchange but also the use of production possibilities (or what he calls 'exchange with nature') (for more on this, see *PF*).

On the basis of this entitlement, a person can acquire some capabilities, i.e. the ability to do this or be that (e.g. be well nourished), and fail to acquire some other capabilities. Thus, as he puts it, the 'process of economic development can be seen as a process of expanding the capabilities of people' (Sen 1983c: 755). It is as a result of this, and a series of more philosophical moves, that Sen thinks that 'capabilities' provide the right basis for judging the advantages of a person in many problems of evaluation – a role that cannot be taken over either by utility or by an index of commodities (*CWM*: 29–38, 353–69). The various component parts of development, as well as other areas of the evaluation of human life, in politics, ethics, and so on, where we are concerned with a full account of a person's well-being, standard of living, quality of life and freedom requires, Sen argues, the concept of capabilities. We have to be concerned with what a person can do, he argues, and this is not the same thing as how much pleasure or desire fulfilment he gets from these activities (otherwise known as 'utility'), nor what commodity bundles he can command ('entitlements'). In other words, not only is it imperative to get beyond utility and its associated theorization in mainstream welfare economics (and development economics) but also entitlements over commodity bundles viewed on their own. The mental metrics of utility gets us very little way down the path of determining what people can do, and entitlements are crucial as part of the means to capabilities (*CWM*; *CC*; Sen 1983c).

As Sen argues in *PF*, it does not follow from this that entitlement is not centrally important. It is vital for better analysis and understanding of starvation, hunger and famines (rather than the traditional variables of food supply and population size). This is the case because for most of humanity, about the only commodity a person has to sell is labour power, so that the person's entitlements depend crucially on his ability to find a job, the wage rate for that job and the prices of commodities he wishes to buy. When analysing various famines – including the infamous Bengal famine of 1943 – he mounts the innovative argument, generally accepted now but controversial when first aired, that the cause of most famines is not the supply of goods – food, in particular – but the entitlements (or powers) that people have over the good in question. These entitlements, he argues, can be influenced by a number of factors, such as employment, prices, government intervention, its lack, war and so on. There are in fact quite a few examples of famines occurring without any reduction of overall food availability. For example, the Bengal famine was not the result of food shortage but rather the consequence of a sharp increase in basic food prices caused by the hyperinflationary effects of the British colonial masters as they continued to export food from Bengal, ignoring (or not hearing) reports about the reality on the ground, all driven by the 'war effort' against Japan (*PF*: chs 6, 7, 9). Local rural labourers lost their entitlements to basic foods and starved.

Although, of course, it is difficult to anticipate famine in conditions of good or moderate food supply, they can hit suddenly and widely because of the failures of entitlement, that is, as a consequence of a variety of possible factors that put basic foods out of reach – beyond the existing means – of the working poor. Sen's most famous point in this regard is to show why this kind of entitlement failure tends not to occur in functioning democracies with an open media. This is the case because the media within these kinds of regimes act as a mechanism of information feedback and accountability as regards representatives. In a democracy, as opposed to an authoritarian regime, representatives cannot simply ignore the starving poor, even if their numbers are small enough in themselves not to hurt their chances at the polls, and this is because the media publicize the plight of those caught up in the famine and appeal to the sympathy and empathy of other voters, who all then ensure that the existing political masters, even if these representatives are only thinking about how to ensure they get re-elected, must respond quickly to the beginning (or possibility) of a famine. Sen's classic example is the contrast between post-independence, democratic India and non-democratic China. In the case of the former, on a number of occasions potentially large famines have been prevented through extensive and decisive government intervention driven by quick, dramatic and public reports reaching government and the population as a whole. Any democratic government wishing to stay in power must act quickly and decisively to avert disaster. By contrast, in China between 1958 and 1961, the famine was caused by a series of policy failures associated with the Great Leap Forward, and the government in power in this highly censured, authoritarian political environment was not forced to re-examine its policies, nor required to face harrowing newspaper reports and troublesome opposition parties. This led to deaths on a massive scale: an estimated total of 30 million. What drives this point home even more forcefully is the fact that, in a normal year, when things are running smoothly, China did then (and still does) much better than India as regards provision for the poorest and most deprived in their respective countries. In a normal year, at least relative to China, India has been a total failure in dealing with endemic malnutrition and morbidity. I return to this in chapter 5, as I do the point that this may be why Sen lays so much at the door of the media and public reason in his view of democracy.

Sen also takes issue with another set of arguments, which, although far from capital fundamentalist or market fundamentalist, ironically still provide theoretical support for development practitioners from afar knowing what is best for the poor anywhere and everywhere. Ever since 'development economics' became a subject of discussion after the end of the Second World War, critics struggled against the domination of income maximization and the single objective of economic development. As they pointed out, GNP growth might occur along with growing unemployment, increasing income inequality, poor provision of social services and deteriorating indicators of health and nutrition. Initially, some suggested replacing income maximization with other single indicators, such as employment growth, but this was quickly seen as a very narrow and unsatisfactory measure of success (Robinson and Johnston 1971). There were a number of other alternatives, too: weighting income to give more significance to the incomes of the poor (Chenery et al. 1979); devising a measure of the physical quality of life, which included infant mortality, life expectancy and adult literacy (Morris 1979); assessing the provision of basic needs, either by looking at the actual bundle of basic needs goods and services provided (ILO 1976), or by measuring the 'full life', indicated for example by life expectancy and a measure of educational achievement (Streeten et al. 1981; Stewart 1985). These all pointed to the need to improve on GNP in two ways: one was to give priority to the poorest sections of society over the richer; the other to look beyond income to the quality of life, for, as Sen was arguing so convincingly, income is just a means (albeit often an effective one) for improving life conditions, and the translation of income to quality of life is by no means an automatic one.

As will be discussed at length in this book's second chapter, Sen produces a number of important examples of how different conditions and differing individuals' powers, capacities and dispositions affect the translation of goods, like income, into quality of life. Sen's approach is distinguishable from even these critical approaches as regards two major insights related to this point. First, if conditions and capacities are as variable and plural as he suggests, it is vital for the individuals themselves to be involved in the determination of policies for development. This then avoids the paternalism evident in the attempts to 'dethrone GNP' outlined above (Robinson and Johnston 1971; Stewart and Deneulin 2002) and that found in the first two mainstream versions of development: 'capital fundamentalism' and 'market fundamentalism'. Second, unlike nearly all of these alternatives, with the possible exception of the physical quality-of-life approach and the second basic-needs approach, Sen moves away from using inputs to that of outcomes, achievements or realizations. Moreover, unlike these other non-mainstream approaches, Sen has advanced a much more nuanced and philosophically substantiated critique of the utilitarianism that underpins welfare economics and its failure to recognize agency or to acknowledge that individual needs, capacities and context must enter into an assessment of well-being, not just utility or happiness.

Relatedly, Sen engages critically with the predominant twentieth-century political philosophy of John Rawls. While he agrees with Rawls in certain respects, he departs from him as regards many others. Sen agrees with Rawls on giving priority to free choice – hence his emphasis on capabilities, that is, what people may choose to be or do, rather than on functionings, what people actually are or do – but rejects Rawls's focus on primary goods for reasons similar to those he gives for his rejection of the views of mainstream and non-mainstream development economists. As with these other alternatives, primary goods are deemed to be the same for everyone – primary goods, for Rawls, are 'things that every rational man is presumed to want', including 'rights, liberties and opportunities, income and wealth, and the social bases of social respect' (Rawls 1973: 60–5) – and thus do not allow for varying rates of conversion from goods to individual quality of life, depending on the circumstances of the individual or group in question. The whole point of Sen's capability approach is to shift focus from goods themselves to what goods do for the lives of humans. (This presumably must also include the negative effects goods may have on people's lives, though Sen rarely discusses these.) And, given that different humans have different needs and different capacities and priorities in how they are able to convert goods to enhance well-being and the quality of life, Sen argues that a focus on means alone (or inputs alone) will not enable a comprehensive view of how any set of policies or actions are affecting the lives of individuals. For that, we need to focus on outcomes, Sen argues, in the sense of a set of concepts and ideas for assessing well-being and quality of life directly, rather than via a single or even a set of inputs (or means). This, he and many others argue, is one of the great advantages of his capability approach.

As I have argued elsewhere, Rawls and Martha Nussbaum, a philosopher whose work was also very influential on Sen's ideas, even if their respective 'capability approaches' differ quite markedly, as discussed below, are guilty of the same kind of paternalism as that evident within development economics (Hamilton 2003a). The primary goods and central capabilities proposed by Rawls and Nussbaum are conceived as being components that each human being must have if she wishes to live a good life, whatever her conception of the good life may be (Rawls 1973, 1993; Nussbaum 2000). Despite an express desire to avoid paternalism, alongside their avowed liberalism, these approaches enable two kinds of tyranny. First, the tyranny of theory, that is, that at a theoretical level it is possible to determine these matters free of context and practice. Second, they enable the tyranny of the powerful, supposedly well-meaning outsider: the development practitioner or the powerful 'liberal' state intervening in the affairs of a weaker state – often by means of brutal invasion – in the interests of the lives of its citizens, that is, the lives of individuals far away.

Sen, by contrast, refrains from judgement on these matters. Although he provides a framework for evaluating well-being and quality of life – his version of capabilities and functionings – he is steadfast in ensuring that the actual substance of this process of judgement will and must be determined in practice. It thus ought not to be specified at the level of theory. Drawing strongly on his work in social choice theory, he proposes what he calls an 'evaluative exercise' to be performed by individuals and society in order to form judgements regarding functionings and capabilities which embody a system of weighting. Sen puts it as follows:

> For a particular person, who is making his or her judgements, the selection of weights will require reflection, rather than any interpersonal agreement (or consensus). However, in arriving at an 'agreed' range of social evaluation (for example, in social studies of poverty), there has to be some kind of a reasoned 'consensus' on weights, or at least a range of weights. This is a social choice exercise, and it requires public discussion and a democratic understanding and acceptance. (*DF*: 78–9)

As will be discussed at greater length in chapter 2, where the component parts of Sen's concern for capabilities are dissected, this exemplifies agency in two distinct, but related ways. First, the individual agent must be involved in the determination of their well-being and quality of life for two reasons that link back to Sen's commitment to the role of social choice in any evaluative exercise: individuals themselves are best placed to provide the information necessary for an objective analysis of their own well-being and the associated conditions under which they live; and individual judgements about how they would like to live are central to a freedom-based account of well-being and quality of life. In this context, Sen makes a series of distinctions as regards the kinds of agency we are talking about, but for now it is sufficient to point to these two important components of an evaluative process and also to stress that Sen lays much emphasis on the importance of subjective knowledge and judgement for any objective analysis. Needless to say, this, even on its own, delivers Sen from the curse of paternalism that characterizes not only most of development economics, but also a large swathe of liberal political theory.

The second way in which Sen's version of what has become known as the 'capabilities approach' foregrounds agency is that he spends some time arguing convincingly that agency is – in and of itself – a constitutive part of a life worth living. In other words, even beyond its instrumental importance in the evaluation of well-being and the quality of life, humans tend to value agency as it gives them the necessary sense of power and achievement that they have reason to value. We are agents by nature, Sen seems to suggest, and so any assessment, set of policies or forms of behaviour that enable that agency will be more highly valued. Critics who are only interested in more simplistic accounts of equality of opportunity or outcome sometimes therefore accuse Sen of being 'athletic' with his conception of capability. They suggest that all that matters is the provision of the requirements for a person's well-being or quality of life. Sen counters this convincingly by showing that individual involvement in the attainment of outcomes they have reason to value is part and parcel of the process and the outcome itself. It is a constitutive good. If so, provision ought to be made for it.

As will be argued, or at least introduced, especially in the second half of this book, for all Sen's practical contributions and pragmatist bent, his vast, trailblazing work is philosophical, economic or applied. This leads to certain gaps or shortcomings, especially as regards the politics that always lies in between the philosophical and economic analyses and their application. These gaps, I suggest, need to be resolved or filled if Sen's novel ideas are to become effective guides to political action. There is hardly any evidence in this massive corpus of cutting-edge work of a realist's eye for the deep and pressing political questions of the place or time in question. He lays to one side – as economist and philosopher – the trenchant questions of power, how it is propagated and who wields it. Given his view of democratic politics as a form of dialogue or discussion, he assumes that the best argument will always win; and that the resolution of theoretical and technical problems will enable this process. This is even true of his view of development in an international world that, if nothing else, is marked by massive disparities in power relations: '[I]n line with the importance I attach to the role of public discussion as a vehicle of social change and economic progress (as the text will make clear), this work is presented mainly for open deliberation and critical scrutiny' (*DF*: xiv).

This generic problem is even more obvious when Sen discusses justice and democracy directly in the sense that he retains a central role for individual agents in determining how best to overcome instances of injustice or how best to generate, maintain and safeguard democracy. As is argued in chapters 4 and 5, this leaves us with a rather idealistic view of justice and democracy, where discussion, critical scrutiny, impartiality and public reason hold sway over more realist views of the centrality of institutions, power and representation, even in the democratic politics of relatively just or at least rich societies, not to speak of the politics and power relations more common in developing polities and economies.

Even in democracies, planners who are told that their job is to enhance people's capabilities to do or be valuable things may well be at a loss, especially if this injunction is not accompanied by a means of understanding, and thus acting within, the power relations in the place and time in question. Moreover, a great deal of governmental activity is technocratic in nature and does not involve the kind of democratic dynamics that Sen has in mind. These technocrats might well ask at least some of the following questions. Whose capabilities should be given priority? Which priorities are valuable? Are there priorities within the category of valuable capabilities? Sen's answer would probably be something like 'arrive at a democratic understanding by means of democratic discussions, critical scrutiny and public reason'. However, these sorts of discussions are hard to come by in modern, diverse democracies. And, of course, many countries 'lack even the trappings of democracy'. And, where there is democracy, opinions and discussions tend to be filtered through and influenced by political parties, social norms and a complex of different power relations determined by classes, genders, ethnicities and so on. Moreover, as has been argued in many quarters, consensus is the exception rather than the rule in democratic politics as we know it (although Sen insists his social theoretic model does not require it, but this claim lacks force, as will be argued in chapter 5).

Actual existing democracies do not present a neat solution to the difficult problem of defining priorities. If anything, the history of democracies points to the exact opposite of what Sen supposes: they pursue growth objectives at the cost of other objectives, at the cost of the poor, the environment and security. Sen is no doubt right that issues need to be solved within the society concerned and not by outsiders, and this marks him out importantly from a lot of other thinkers, but this clashes directly with a later idea that he puts to significant use in discussing justice: the role of the distant impartial spectator. Moreover, his concept of democracy assumes, against a great deal of historical evidence to the contrary as well as some of his own empirical work on India (Drèze and Sen 2014), that democratic procedures will – by dint of being democratic – move towards the pursuit of capabilities of the poor. Broader empirical evidence seems also to suggest otherwise (Shapiro 2011: 1260). 'The problem is that Sen's concept of democracy seems an idealistic one where political power, political economy, and struggle are absent' (Stewart and Deneulin 2002: 64).

There are at least three main lines of criticism that are discussed in the second half of this book and summarized and extended in the main conclusion. First, there is the concern that a lot of economists have regarding how difficult it is to use Sen's capabilities-based alternative as a tool of effective measurement of poverty, well-being, quality of life and so on. Relatedly, some of the alleged 'fuzziness' of his work has fed into the ways in which the Millennium Development Goals and Sustainable Development Goals have been articulated to their detriment, that is, as ideals in the sky, not practicably achievable targets. Second, we have the problem of the lack of institutional analysis that pervades his work, both in terms of providing a means of thinking about development in general and power and preference formation in particular. These are not things for which it is possible to find easily apparent answers in his corpus. Given this lack of power and institutional analysis – a lack of politics or what some have called a lack of political economy – it is not clear what follows from his normative insistence on prioritizing choice and behaviour above institutional design. What of institutional critique? Third, as discussed at length at the end of the book, it is not clear that Sen's emphasis on realistic and empirically grounded work enables a realist political theory. If this is the case, what follows from his lack of realism on the practicability of his strikingly original alternative contributions?

1

Choice

The idea of choice in human life, and especially in economics and politics, lies at the heart of much that has animated the inspiring work of Amartya Sen. This is as true of his earliest published work on social choice, through his work on welfare economics, inequality, famine, freedom and development, via his revolutionary work on what he now likes to call his 'concern for capabilities', and on to his work on justice. Lest we forget, in 1998 he was awarded the Nobel Prize in Economics for his 'contributions to welfare economics', and, more exactly, for contributions that range from 'axiomatic theory of social choice, over definitions of welfare and poverty indexes, to empirical studies of famine. Sen has clarified the conditions which permit aggregation of individual values into collective decisions, and the conditions which permit rules for collective decision making that are consistent with a sphere of rights for the individual' (Nobel 1998).

Given Sen's predilections and the fact that mainstream welfare economics is infamous for a myriad of philosophical assumptions, a little philosophy will be necessary in this chapter. This is especially important for understanding why and how Sen tackles some of the main assumptions around choice, preference and measurement as inherited from utilitarianism by welfare economists in the first half of the twentieth century. The Nobel award describes these as 'contributions' to welfare economics; truth be told, as will become apparent, they cut to the quick of so much of welfare economics that they end up coming close to undermining it completely, rather than simply contributing to it.

Social choice

All the time in economics and politics, we evaluate or pass judgement on social systems, arrangements and outcomes. We characterize polities, societies and economies as democratic or undemocratic, just or unjust, corrupt or not, good or bad, as we do decisions taken by those in authority and by our fellow citizens. Our judgements here are normally a mix of ethical views, aesthetic and consumer tastes, strategic goals and sheer desires for certain goods or outcomes. At core, they are views about possible desirable social outcomes based on individual preferences, or so social choice theory maintains.

Social choice theory is the study of how decisions are made collectively. It examines the idea that, for a given society, the preferences of individuals can be directly aggregated to reflect a 'social preference'. In other words, social choice theory is concerned with how it is possible to get from a set of individual preferences to a social outcome in a consistent and rational manner that respects individual preferences. Social choice theory is thus primarily concerned with the connection or relation between individual preferences and social outcomes. More exactly, it is concerned with how to aggregate individual preferences into a collective choice outcome.

Social choice theory is not a single theory but a very broad discipline concerned with a cluster of concerns and questions. Sen sums some of them up well by listing a series of problems that are illustrative of its subject matter.

> When would *majority rule* yield unambiguous and consistent decisions? How can we judge how well a *society as a whole* is doing in the light of the disparate interests of its different members? How do we measure *aggregative poverty* in view of the varying predicaments and miseries of the diverse people that make up the society? How can we accommodate *rights and liberties* of persons while giving adequate recognition to their preferences? How do we appraise social valuations of public goods such as the *natural environment, or epidemiological security*? (Sen 1999: 350; italics in original)

In sum, social choice theory is concerned to determine a rational and consistent route from individual preferences to social (or group) outcomes. Or, put the other way around, it is concerned with how best to relate social judgements and group decisions to the views and interests of the individuals who make up the society or the group.

The broad field of social choice theory – at least as a systematic discipline – had its beginnings in the mathematical work of some pioneering thinkers in the eighteenth century, in particular, Jean-Charles de Borda (1781) and the Marquis de Condorcet (1785) and, in the nineteenth century, others such as Charles Dodgson (also known as Lewis Carroll) (1874, 1884). Their main concern was democratic decision making, with particular focus on majority decisions. Their ambition was to develop a framework for rational and democratic decisions for a group, paying adequate attention to the preferences and interests of all of its members. However, their logical or theoretical investigations typically yielded rather pessimistic results. Majority rule, for example, can be thoroughly inconsistent, with A defeating B by a majority, B defeating C by a majority, and C also, in turn, defeating A by a majority. This incongruity at the theoretical level, although we may not find it so disturbing in practice, has led to a great deal of head-scratching and logical reasoning for some time.

While Condorcet investigated a *particular* voting method (majority rule), social choice theory was given its modern form and revival through Kenneth Arrow's famous work on a *general* approach to the study of preference aggregation. Arrow considered a class of possible aggregation methods, which he called *social welfare functions*, and asked which of them satisfied a seemingly mild set of conditions of reasonableness, discussed on p. 27 below. What became known as his 'impossibility theorem' showed that even this set of mild conditions could not be simultaneously satisfied by any social choice procedure within a very wide family (Arrow 1951). This led to a great deal of pessimism both about democracy and welfare assessments because, in order to avoid inconsistencies, both seemed to depend upon dictatorship, which in politics would mean an extreme sacrifice of participatory decisions (one of the underlying presuppositions of social choice theory itself) and in economics would mean a gross inability to be sensitive to the heterogeneous interests of a diverse population. The elegance of Arrow's theorem and this seemingly dark outcome produced veritable libraries of responses, qualifications, modulations and further impossibility results. Sen's interventions in this world were breathtakingly important and simple. He resisted the pessimism by uncovering, and gently criticizing, some of the main presuppositions of the original theorem.

The most important underpinning or presupposition in Arrow's approach was the eschewal of interpersonal comparisons of preferences, understood in terms of utility. Arrow held the view that 'the interpersonal comparison of utility has no meaning and ... that there is no meaning relevant to welfare comparisons in the measurability of individual utility' (1951: 9). One of the things Sen produced was an elegant way of viewing the unnecessary nature of this condition, partly by showing that it was a consequence not of reasonable conditions for social choice but the result of contemporary economic theoretical dogma, which Arrow had simply followed, or more specifically the result of an odd reaction to utilitarian-inspired welfare economics.

More exactly, traditional welfare economics had been developed by utilitarian economists, such as Francis Edgeworth (1881), Alfred Marshall (1890) and Arthur Pigou (1920), who had not been inspired by the vote-oriented work of Borda (1781) and Condorcet (1785), but by their contemporary Jeremy Bentham (1970 [1781]). Bentham pioneered the use of utilitarian calculus to obtain judgements about the social interest by means of aggregating the personal interests of the different individuals in the form of their respective utilities. There is a central problem with utilitarianism's unique focus on utility and the total utility of the community, at the expense of entertaining any analysis of the distribution of that total across the individuals concerned, about which more on pp. 30, 47. However, for our purposes here, it is sufficient to note that via the concept of utility and total utility, utilitarianism assumed it uncontroversial to be involved in interpersonal comparisons of people's interests. It followed that utilitarian welfare economics was deeply concerned with a class of information – in the form of comparison of utility gains and losses of different persons – for which it would soon be heavily criticized. Although utilitarianism has been very influential in shaping welfare economics, in the 1930s it was to come under fire, particularly for the supposed lack of scientific basis for interpersonal comparisons of utility. Economists came to be persuaded by the arguments of Lionel Robbins and others (deeply influenced by 'logical positivist' philosophy) that, as Robbins put it, '[e]very mind is inscrutable to every other mind and no common denominator of feelings is possible' (Robbins 1938: 636). 'Thus, the epistemic foundations of utilitarian welfare economics were seen as incurably defective' (Sen 1999: 182).

As a result of this, there followed attempts to do welfare economics on the basis of different persons' respective ordering of social states *without* any interpersonal comparisons of utility gains and losses. This further reduced the informational base upon which social choice could draw: an already limited Benthamite calculus was made to shrink even further to the kind of information with which Borda and Condorcet were concerned. This was the case because the use of different persons' utility rankings without any interpersonal comparison is analytically quite similar to the use of voting information in making social choice. Given this informational restriction, what became known as 'new welfare economics' from the 1940s onwards used only one basic criterion for social improvement, that is, 'Pareto comparison', or the 'Pareto principle'. 'This criterion only asserts that an alternative situation would be definitely better if the change would increase the utility of everyone' (Sen 1999: 183). Given that the earlier utilitarian tradition was out of favour due to the rise of scepticism about the possibility of interpersonal comparisons of utility, the Pareto principle took centre stage. Much of welfare economics in fact used a slightly stronger version of the principle than the one used by Arrow, namely, the economy is in a Pareto optimal state when no further changes in it can make one person or preference criterion better off without at the same time making another worse off (Walras 1899; Pareto 1906). And economists, it was assumed, could only be in a position to declare an improvement when no such interpersonal comparisons of gains and losses are involved.

At this point, as a consequence of important contributions by Abram Bergson (1938) and Paul Samuelson (1947), it had become amply clear that economists needed to use value judgements if they wanted to engage in policy prescription or evaluation of social states, 'but the set of value judgements that welfare economics focused on in the 1930s and 1940s was remarkably small' (Pattanaik 2014: 2). This led directly to Arrow's pioneering formulation of social choice theory, which accepted that preferences involved value judgements while retaining the stubborn assumption that interpersonal comparison of preferences is not possible. What Arrow called a *social welfare function*, or a possible preference aggregation rule, was the core idea of social choice theory, a relation between social preferences (or decisions) to the set of individual preferences. Arrow (1951) went on to consider a very mild set of conditions, including: (1) Pareto efficiency; (2) non-dictatorship; (3) independence (demanding that social choice over any set of alternatives must depend on preferences *only* over those alternatives); and (4) unrestricted domain (requiring that the social preference must be a complete ordering, with full transitivity, and that this must work for every conceivable set of individual preferences).[1] Arrow's impossibility theorem demonstrated that it is impossible to satisfy these conditions simultaneously. Or, put differently, we cannot move from individual choice to collective decisions without violating one or more of a set of five desirable democratic axioms.

Arrow's findings were taken to be as true of judgements regarding social welfare as of voting procedures. In the context of elections, these are reformulated as a set of four axioms: (1) 'decisiveness', or whatever voters' rankings turn out to be, there should always be a winner and there shouldn't be more than one winner; (2) 'consensus', or the idea that if all voters rank candidate X above candidate Y and X is on the ballot, then Y ought not to be elected; (3) 'non-dictatorship', or the axiom that no voter should have the power to get her way; and (4) 'independence of irrelevant candidates', or the idea that the voting outcome is not affected by a candidate who, whether or not he was on the ballot, would not win (Maskin 2014: 46). In other words, it was shown to be difficult, if not impossible, to move from actual individual preferences regarding individual and social welfare to a collective welfare function and from individual preferences in voting procedures to collective decisions that do not violate some basic set of normative criteria. Social choice theory is full of impossibility theorems, that is, results that cannot satisfy a certain set of conditions.

Some, like William Riker, interpreted Arrow's impossibility theorem to provide a mathematical proof for the impossibility of populist democracy (Riker 1982). Others, most famously Sen, took it to show that ordinal preferences are insufficient for making satisfactory social choices.[2] Moreover, Sen, alongside some other commentators, also suggested that some of Arrow's conditions were not as innocuous as supposed and thus needed relaxing, most famously his adherence to Pareto efficiency, as discussed further on pp. 29, 35 ff. These together were part and parcel of Sen's broader argument: that when a social planner seeks to rank different social alternatives in an order of social welfare, it may be justifiable to use additional information over and above ordinal preferences, such as interpersonally comparable welfare measurements (CWM).

The examples of voting-based procedures in social choice theory – and the highly constrained information they require – are unsuitable models for many other problems of social choice, especially the search for some kind of aggregative index of social welfare. This is the case for two important reasons. First, voting requires active participation, and if someone decides not to exercise his voting right, his preference would find no direct representation in social decisions. By contrast, in making reasonable social welfare judgements, 'the interests of the less assertive cannot be simply ignored'. Second, even with active voting, we will be short of vital information needed for welfare-economic evaluation; through voting, each person can rank different alternatives, but there is no direct way of getting interpersonal comparisons of different persons' well-being from voting data. Sen's challenge is to show how we can systematically and practicably use 'something as complex as interpersonal comparisons involving many persons' (*CS*; *OEI*; Sen 1999: 188).

A great deal of what follows in Sen's work, particularly his 'concern for capabilities', is effectively about creating the conceptual means to meet this demanding challenge, thereby rethinking the conceptual bases and forms of information needed to make economics better at evaluating and improving the lives of people. He is, though, at pains to stress that this is possible even with partial information; as he says, he is 'in favor of partial comparabilities based on evaluation of capabilities'. He is thus a strong supporter of subsequent literature in social choice theory and welfare economics that defends analytically 'broader' systems than that found in the Arrovian model, making them less 'uptight' and less 'impossible' (*CS*; *OEI*; *IR*; Sen 1999: 193).

Sen's major contributions to social choice theory have been manifold. The most important are his subtle internal critiques of Arrow's impossibility theorem (*CS*), especially its principled aversion to interpersonal comparisons, and his subsequent formal proof and non-formal discussions of the 'impossibility of a Paretian liberal', that is, his further critique of the weak Pareto principle, showing that it conflicts with a 'liberal' principle (Sen 1970). He has also pointed out – convincingly – that the various 'impossibility theorems' that the social choice literature throws up are not as negative as many assume, especially the 'everyday' interpretation of Arrow's theory: that it supposedly followed from his theory that democracy was doomed. We should rather view them more optimistically – Sen's optimism is apparent in all his social, economic and political thinking – as means of determining what is possible. One of the characteristics of this way of thinking through problems and outcomes in economics and politics, Sen argues, is that it provides a set of logical results whose impossibility suggests we need to change one axiom or condition marginally to avoid the impossibility. In other words, social choice theory proceeds by setting parameters to what is impossible and possible, the difference between these two states often being much less than this language would normally suggest. Impossibility and possibility do not lie at the extremes of a continuum. Nor are they divided by some insurmountable gulf. Rather, they are often just one logical or axiomatic step away from one another (Sen 1999; Maskin and Sen 2014).

More broadly, Sen's most significant advance within social choice theory has been to criticize two of its central components: its unique focus on utility as an informational base and an associated, highly constrained view of rationality. Partly thanks to Sen's critiques, these have now been overcome, or at least the parameters of social choice theory have been modified to account for them, but they were both assumed as central axioms in early social choice theory and a great deal of the associated welfare economics that Sen confronted.

The informational basis in question is, of course, as already mentioned, utility, the idea that the evaluation of a social arrangement (or action) is best undertaken by means of reference to the expression of a mental characteristic that represents whether the arrangement (or action) would increase pleasure and decrease pain (Bentham 1970 [1781]) or – at one small step from this – whether desires are or are not fulfilled (Hare 1982). Utility is determined, it is supposed, by the expression of a preference (or a preference ordering). Why? How else can we determine whether an economic or political choice would constitute an increase in utility? Choice reflects utility via preference. The choice itself is assumed to be represented by the preference (or preference ordering). In line with a general hangover of utilitarianism, at least initially, it was assumed that what an individual prefers is a direct and unambiguous representation of the mental process of choice that has taken place. The correspondence of choice and preference is taken to be empirically obvious, especially in the classic framework of demand theory (Hicks 1939; Wold 1963). This relationship then becomes definitional in the approach of 'revealed preference'. As Sen notes, '[p]reference here is simply defined as the binary relation underlying consistent choice' (*CWM*: 1). And, if this were correct, there would be little or no need for interpretation, which was what much of this economic view of welfare and measurement was after. If I choose X over Y, then that choice behaviour is taken to 'reveal' my preference for X over Y. And it follows that I would consistently choose X over Y. This is based on two related assumptions: that choices are consistent; and *de gustibus non est disputandum* (in matters of taste there can be no disputes). The combined implication of these two assumptions is that everyone's personal preferences are merely subjective opinions that cannot be right or wrong and that in a repeat scenario (or given a similar choice) the outcome will remain the same (known formally as 'cyclicity').

This is a central tenet of utilitarianism and welfarism, as it is of early twentieth-century social choice theory. As I have shown, the latter takes the form it does as a result of a general scepticism around the idea of interpersonal comparisons of utility, most trenchantly articulated in Robbins (1938), welfare economics' related death knells and Arrow's subsequent revival of it via the interest generated by his impossibility theorem, which embraced the prevailing scepticism around interpersonal comparison. The significance of utilitarianism, via welfarism, in modern economics (and many related forms of understanding politics) is easily understood if we recall that utilitarianism is made up of three distinct elements: (1) consequentialism, or judging all actions or policies entirely in terms consequent of states of affairs; (2) welfarism, or 'judging states of affairs entirely in terms of personal utility information relating to the respective states'; and (3) sum-ranking, 'judging personal utility information entirely in terms of their sum-total' (*CWM*: 28; Sen 1979; Sen and Williams 1982). The focus of Sen's illuminating work in social choice theory (and many other areas) has grown out of four main criticisms of utilitarianism that focus on the second and third of these elements: welfarism's unique reliance on utility; its related tendency to define utility entirely in terms of choice; the associated persistence of the Pareto principle therein; and a broader critique of the underpinning of sum-ranking, the idea that humans are self-interested utility maximizers, the 'rational fools' that thereby underpin much of the contemporary behavioural assumptions of welfare economics.

Taking the first two together, Sen argues that they are based in welfare economics 'weak axiom' of revealed preference, whose two main assumptions – consistency and transitivity of choice – come up against very real problems. Consistency is simply the idea that if X is revealed preferred to Y, then Y should not be revealed preferred to X (Sen 1973, republished in *CWM*: 54–73, at 57). This seemingly simple, innocuous demand is contravened all the time, not least of all by the fact that over time tastes change. In other words, although the original welfarist (and demand theory) view does not balk at short-term variety of choice ('fish tomorrow and steak today is not inconsistent'), it has trouble accounting for longer-term changes of taste, a very unrealistic restriction. Transitivity – also for some a condition of consistency – is the condition that states: 'if X is regarded as at least as good as Y, and Y at least as good as Z, then X should be regarded as at least as good as Z'; in the case of preference, the same structure holds – if X is preferred to Y and Y preferred to Z, then it should also be the case that X is preferred to Z (Sen 1973, republished in *CWM*: 54–73, at 58).

At the core of the problem here is 'revealed preference', that is, the fundamental assumption that people do reveal their underlying preferences through their actual choices. Sen argues convincingly that the animating force behind this assumption was a misplaced obsession to found economic analysis on market behaviour, that is, a version of the positivist insistence on observable facts, here propped up by the supposedly obvious idea that it is possible to observe revealed preference patterns by observing behaviour without any need either to access the minds of humans or to carry out any inter-personal comparisons of utility. This drive to a science based on behaviour, which revealed preference via choice, was expressed best by Samuelson and Hicks, even if they did not fully subscribe to the idea of revealed preference (Samuelson 1938a, 1938b, 1947, 1948; Hicks 1956). The goal was to found a theory of demand solely on consistent behaviour. For, as Hicks put it, 'the econometric theory of demand does study human beings, but only as entities having certain patterns of market behaviour; it makes no claim, no pretence, to be able to see inside their heads' (Hicks 1956, quoted in *CWM*: 56; recall the Robbins quote above). The nub of Sen's critique of this view is that the idea that it is possible to use revealed preference to explain 'behaviour without reference to anything other than behaviour' is sheer rhetoric. If there is anything in the idea of revealed preference, it 'lies in the skilful use of the assumption that behaviour reveals preference' (*CWM*: 72).

That is, though, only the start of his critique. He goes on to make a series of moves that both undermine the supposedly obvious link between choice, preference, utility and welfare and question the very idea of the rational utility maximizer. In a series of essays and talks from the early 1970s, he argues that in many instances choice (or revealed preference) is not a good indicator of preference; or, in other words, it does not reveal preference. He uses a prisoner's dilemma example, which is understandable – given the time and context – but unfortunate: it fails to make the case from the perspective of a real-world example, which is, of course, part of the point of his critique. He uses this version of the dilemma. Two prisoners are known to be guilty of a serious crime, but there is not enough evidence to convict them, but enough to convict them of a minor offence. They are separated and given the option of confessing if they wish to, where for the good behaviour shown in squealing they would get 10 years each in prison if each confesses to the major crime, 20 years in prison for the one that does not confess and zero years for the one that does in a situation in which one confesses and the other does not, and two years' conviction for the minor crime if neither confesses. In this version, it is relatively easy to show that, no matter what the other does, it is better for him to confess. So both do confess, guided by rational self-interest, and each goes to prison for 10 years. Given that if neither had confessed, each would have been in prison for only two years, rational choice would seem to cost each person eight additional years in prison. In much of the game-theory literature, this kind of case has been used to substantiate the failure of individualistic decision making and as a justification for a collective contract. Sen is less interested in that and more interested in the very common situation, which this hypothetical case points to anyhow, in which moral rules of behaviour play out without the possibility of a contract, that is, a situation that generates similar kinds of collectively rational outcomes as if there were a contract without the existence of a formal contract. His primary interest is in showing the implications of this for the theory of revealed preference.

Suppose, he suggests, that each prisoner in this dilemma acts not on the basis of the rational calculations outlined in the case but proceeds to follow the 'dictum of not letting the other person down irrespective of the consequences for himself', a not unreasonable position to take (*CWM*: 64). Then neither person will confess and they will get just two years each. Now, consider the job of the observer trying to guess the preferences that have been revealed by the choice of non-confession. Despite the inherent uncertainties of the situation, were the theory of revealed preference true, it must be presumed that each prisoner prefers at least one of the possible outcomes resulting from his non-confession – the consequence of his non-confession given the other prisoner's non-confession (two years), or the consequence of his non-confession given the other prisoner's confession (20 years). But, in fact, neither happens to be true. The prisoner does not prefer to go to prison for 20 years rather than 10; nor does he prefer a sentence of two years to being free. The choice he makes has therefore not revealed his preference in the manner postulated by revealed preference theory. It is important to note that this problem for revealed preference does not require any relaxing of the requirement that each individual makes these decisions based solely on consideration of their own welfare. It in fact occurs exactly because this – as in revealed preference theory – is not assumed. Each is assumed to be self-interested; the choice of non-confession follows not from calculations based on this welfare function, but from following a moral code of behaviour suspending the rational calculus. As Sen says, '[t]he preference is no different in this case from that in the earlier, but behaviour is. And it is this difference that is inimical to the revealed preference approach to the study of human behaviour' (*CWM*: 65).

Of course, if each prisoner was motivated by the other extreme – each other's welfare (the opposite of the self-interested utility maximizer) – neither would confess and they would get two years each. Thus, the result of each trying to maximize the welfare of the other will lead to a better situation for each in terms of their own welfare, too. They do not actually have to have this kind of concern, but if they behave as if they do, they will end up being better off in terms of their real preference. The point of this is neatly evident: 'This is where the revealed preference theory goes off the rails altogether. The behaviour pattern that will make each better off in terms of their real preferences is not at all the behaviour pattern that will reveal those real preferences. Choices that reveal individual preferences may be quite inefficient for achieving welfare of the group' (*CWM*: 66).

This is not just an exercise in hypothetical logic: most of the important results in economic analysis at the time – and still in many areas today – were dependent on the relationship between behaviour and welfare through the intermediary of preference. In general equilibrium theory, for example, in establishing the correspondence of equilibria with Pareto optimality, 'preference' plays a dual role, linking choice and preference on the one hand and preference and welfare on the other. Individual decisions or choices or, more generally, the behaviour of individuals, is assumed to be determined by (or, less strongly, revealed by) their respective preference orderings; and preferences serve as the basis of Pareto optimality judgements, that is, it is assumed that a preferred position equates to a higher level of individual welfare within the broader framework of whether the market can lead to a position which yields maximal social welfare in some sense (optimality of equilibrium) (Hicks 1939; Samuelson 1947; Debreu 1959; Arrow and Hahn 1971). As Sen puts it well, '[t]ogether this amounts to assuming that individual choices are guided exclusively by the requirements of maximizing the respective individual welfares' (*CWM*: 5). In sum, at least in economic theory if not in most of mainstream economics, this amounts to the reduction of rationality to the regularity of consistent pursuit of self-interest.

Sen, again, puts it very well:

> The thrust of the revealed preference approach has been to undermine thinking as a method of self-knowledge and talking as a method of knowing about others. In this, I think, we have been prone, on the

one hand, to overstate the difficulties of introspection and communication, and on the other, to underestimate the problems of studying
preferences revealed by observed behavior. (*CWM*: 72)

Sen takes these criticisms even further in his justly famous article,
'Rational Fools: A Critique of the Behavioural Foundations of Economic Theory' (Sen 1977, reprinted in *CWM*: 84–106). He reiterates
the role played by revealed preference in most economic analysis
and argues that what underpins and overlays this – the self-seeking
egoist (the utility maximizer) and Pareto optimality – excludes a
whole series of human motivations, the exclusion of which leaves
'economic man' looking like a 'rational fool'. He starts with Edgeworth and his model based on egoistic behaviour and shows that
there is a remarkable correspondence between exchange equilibria
in competitive markets and what in modern economic terms is called
'the core' of the economy. Central to this idea of equilibria at 'the
core' is a set of conditions of unimprovability, determined mostly
by Pareto optimality, or the idea that an outcome is said to be at 'the
core' of the economy if it is the case that no one could be made
better off without making somebody else worse off, coupled with
the idea that no one is worse off than he would be without competitive trade. In terms of social welfare, being at 'the core' is not a big
deal from the perspective of the person who starts off ill-endowed
and who may stay poor and deprived even following these transac-
tions and forms of competition.

This history and context is important, as are the various attempts
to answer the deeper question – 'in what sense and to what extent
would egoistic behaviour achieve general good?' – but, as Sen points
out, there is also another non-empirical and simpler reason why the
conception of man in economic models may be that of the self-seeking
egoist: it allows us to define a person's interests in such a way that
no matter what he does he can be seen to be furthering his own
interests in every isolated act of choice. As with revealed preference
theory, the rationale of this approach is that the only way of understanding a person's real preference is to examine his actual choices,
'and there is no choice-independent way of understanding someone's
attitude towards alternatives' (*CWM*: 89). Sen then dispenses with
the simple, archly pared-down view of rationality as consistency of
choice and introduces two concepts – sympathy and commitment
– that he shows are central for understanding all human behaviour,
including economic behaviour. He identifies various ways in which
they are central to economic behaviour and how, in particular,

commitment upsets the apple cart as regards Pareto optimality. Commitment, he argues, involves 'counterpreferential choice, destroying the crucial assumption that a chosen alternative must be better than (or at least as good as) the others for the person choosing it', thus constituting an externality but one that requires the model to be completely reformulated (*CWM*: 93).

Moreover, commitment 'drives a wedge between personal choice and personal welfare, and much of traditional economic theory relies on the identity of the two' (*CWM*: 94). *En passant*, Sen makes two important moves. First, he shows how the main underpinnings of much of traditional economics produce a 'social moron' in a strait-jacket of social choice. The economic theory of utility gives a person one preference ordering and this is somehow supposed to cover three complex and not obviously similar things: reflect his interests; represent his welfare; and reveal his idea of what should be done. As Sen famously puts it, '[a] person thus described may be "rational" in the limited sense of revealing no inconsistencies in his choice behaviour, but if he has no use for these distinctions between different concepts, he must be a bit of a fool. The purely economic man is indeed close to being a social moron' (*CWM*: 99). One possible way out of this is Harsanyi's response within the framework of utility, where he makes a distinction between 'ethical' preferences and 'subjective' preferences, where the former expresses what an individual prefers (or would prefer) on the basis of impartial, impersonal social considerations and the latter what is actually preferred, that is, the individual's conception of his own welfare (Harsanyi 1955: 315). Sen makes the very important riposte to this idea as follows: '[b]ut what if he departs from his personal welfare maximization (including any sympathy), not through an impartial concern for all, but through a sense of commitment to some particular group, say to the neighbourhood or to the social class to which he belongs?' This move by Harsanyi, according to Sen, does not get us very far, which is why the introduction of commitment is so central and telling in this article. I've quoted this passage in full as this is also worth recalling for later in this book, in chapter 4 on justice, where seemingly, in the face of this early critique of Harsanyi's binary utility versus impartiality, Sen defends impartiality at the expense of further political analysis of class and group commitment. As he says at the end of the essay, '[g]roups intermediate between oneself and all, such as class and community, provide the focus of many actions involving commitment' (*CWM*: 106).

Sen's second move is to propose a ranking of preference to express moral judgements, a moral meta-ranking. Whether or not this moves us along much is a moot point, as what is more interesting is what this expansion of the structure of preferences enables and requires. The structure demands more information than is yielded by the observation of people's actual choices. It requires and enables a role for introspection and communication. As Sen puts it, 'once we give up the assumption that observing choices is the only source of data on welfare, a whole new world opens up, liberating us from the informational shackles of the traditional approach' (*CWM*: 102). Whether we conceive of rationality simply in terms of consistency of choice or, relatedly, the justification of each act in terms of self-interest, in doing so we leave out a whole spectrum of human behaviour and motivation for action (and choice): commitment. (There are many others too, of course, such as *akrasia*, or weakness of will, or moral principle cashed out in a variety of forms, e.g. liberty, equality, and so on, but for Sen's purposes here 'commitment' suffices.) More broadly conceived, rationality, or 'the power of being able to exercise one's reason' is not necessary for commitment, but nor is it excluded by commitment; 'in fact, in so far as consequences on others have to be more clearly understood and assessed in terms of one's values and instincts, the scope for reasoning may well expand' (*CWM*: 105).

In sum, this important paper – one that stands out even in the company of Sen's many excellent contributions – defends the need to accommodate commitment as part of behaviour, introduces greater scope for reasoning in economics in general, and suggests that preferences as rankings have to be replaced by a richer structure involving meta-rankings and related concepts (*CWM*: 105). As will repeatedly become apparent in this book, despite these important internal criticisms, choice remains central to the work of Amartya Sen across his manifold contributions to economics, philosophy and politics.

Deprivation

As mentioned in the main introduction to this book, the deprivations associated with poverty, inequality and famine are also conceived by Sen in terms of deprivations across a range of powers to choose a life an individual has reason to value. Sen is justly famous for the positive theoretical moves encapsulated by what has become known as his 'capability approach' and what he prefers to call his 'concern for capabilities', but it is important to see how this is developed out of his more empirical work on famines, poverty and inequality, especially (but not only) in the context of India.

The tendency in much of the welfare economic literature that Sen criticizes, as well as in the political theoretical literature, is to view inequality as a species of inequality across a domain: inequality of income, inequality of wealth, inequality of opportunity, and so on. And in the political philosophical literature that Sen simultaneously admires and criticizes, especially the work of John Rawls, there is an assumption that his empirical work leads him to critique: the idea that universal means – what Rawls calls 'primary goods' – will be sufficient in all contexts as means for individuals to enact their power to choose the diverse 'doings and beings' their lives entail. While these different components of inequality are all important for Sen, and while he can see the point of ideas such as 'primary goods', he is most fascinated in measuring, and determining the consequences of, inequality, poverty and famine on the lives of individuals as compared to one another and in terms of their powers or entitlements over goods, that is, under what conditions they are able to choose and how their preferences are formed.

Sen counters the general received opinion that the cause of famines was the decline of food availability by reference to a series of famines, particularly the Great Bengal famine of 1943, the Ethiopian famine of 1972–4 and the Bangladesh famine of 1974. He argues that the primary cause of famine is a failure of exchange entitlements, that is, the inability of a person to exchange his primary entitlement, normally labour, for food, when his employment becomes erratic or is eliminated. Famines are due to the inability of a person to exchange his entitlements rather than to food unavailability. He marshals empirical evidence from a wide range of cases to show that the link between starvation and food supply is ultimately about ownership relations, which are one kind of entitlement relations. To understand famine specifically and poverty more generally, '[i]t is necessary to understand the entitlement relations within which the problem of starvation is to be analysed' (*PF*: 1).

In a market economy, Sen argues, people can exchange what they own for another set of commodities by means of trading or production or a combination of the two. Sen calls the set of alternative bundles of commodities that a person can acquire in exchange for what she owns the 'exchange entitlement' of what she owns. Various influences determine a person's exchange entitlement, including:

(1) whether she can find employment, for how long and at what wage rate; (2) what she can earn by selling her non-labour assets and the cost of the things she wishes to buy; (3) what she can produce with her own labour power and resources she can buy and manage; (4) the costs of purchasing resources and the value of the products she can sell; and (5) the social security benefits she is entitled to and the taxes and so on that she must pay. A person's ability to avoid hunger will depend on her ownership and exchange entitlements. Although a general decline in food may cause her to be exposed to hunger through a rise in food prices, her immediate reason for starvation will be the decline in her exchange entitlement. Moreover, her exchange entitlement may worsen for reasons other than a general decline in food supply. For example, given a stable food supply, other groups becoming richer and buying more food can lead to a rise in food prices, causing a worsening of her exchange entitlement. Or some other change may affect her employment possibilities, leading also to worse exchange entitlement; similarly, her wages can fall behind prices; or the price of necessary resources for the production she engages in can go up relatively. These are all as relevant as the overall volume of food supply (*PF*: 4).

What a person owns and his exchange entitlements will depend on his position in the economic class structure, as well as the modes of production in the economy. 'But even with the same ownership position, the exchange entitlements will be different depending on what economic prospects are open to him, and that will depend on the modes of production and his position in terms of production relations' (*PF*: 4–5). Unsurprisingly, Sen references Karl Marx here, and he goes on to emphasize, using the example of the famines under analysis, that '[i]n understanding general poverty, or regular starvation, or outbursts of famines, it is necessary to look at both ownership patterns and exchange entitlements, and at the forces that lie behind them' (*PF*: 6).

The reference to Marx is important as it underpins an approach that at this stage is articulated, as in Smith and Marx, in terms of necessities and needs, and that later, as we will see in chapter 2, Sen rearticulates in terms of capabilities. Part of the inspiration for this move is the insight that Sen lays out clearly in *PF*: that poverty is a matter of deprivation, but that what matters here is only in part captured by the contemporary shift in focus from absolute to relative deprivation as the basis of an approach to poverty. While identifying the importance of relative deprivation (and thus inequality more generally) in understanding poverty, Sen provides an account of supplementing it with a view of 'absolute dispossession' (*PF*: 22). Absolute dispossession or deprivation not only allows a means of providing an objective measure of poverty but also keeps issues of starvation and hunger at the centre of the concept of poverty.

There is normally nothing illegal about the process leading to starvation. In the Bengal famine of 1943, for example, the people that died in front of well-stocked food shops protected by the state were 'denied food because of a lack of legal entitlement, and not because their entitlements were violated' (*PF*: 49). Their entitlements had simply collapsed. The same was true in 1845–51 in Ireland, 'when the potato famine killed about one-fifth of the total Irish population and led to the emigration of a comparable number' (*PF*: 39). One wonders, though, what is wrong with a system that allows these kinds of things to occur legally, and it is easy to see why the Irish supposed lack of reverence for British laws is well justified. For, of course, the common denominator in these two cases – as in quite a few others – is that we are dealing with the British Empire administering their subjects from afar and without as much concern for their needs and preferences as democratic governments supposedly show. The imperial masters, in other words, acted callously and unintelligently, but not illegally, at least in terms of their own laws. As was discussed in the introduction and will resurface in chapter 5, Sen lays a great deal of explanatory focus on the seemingly settled fact that democracies with a free press and functioning representative institutions have *never* presided over famines, and that is exactly because they are democracies with free presses and accountable rulers. While this may be one important factor, it is unlikely to be the full picture, especially if democracy is understood in the way proposed by Sen.

As regards the grinding poverty involved in long-term deprivation, Sen's interests and advances have not been simply in poverty but in inequalities among the poor, and especially in the poorest of the poor. Standard measures of poverty identify a 'poverty line' – an income level below which people are said to be poor. The number of those below the poverty line is then counted and the poverty index is defined as the proportion of a given population which is below the poverty line. Sen has criticized this approach repeatedly for being too dependent on seeing deprivation in terms of low income as such, or uniquely. The same is true of the 'income gap' approach, the idea that measures poverty in terms of the income that would be required to bring all the poor up to the poverty line. Even if we combined these two approaches as a composite measure of poverty, we would still be left with an inadequate measure, argues Sen. The reason for this is that neither pays any interest to the distribution of income among the poor. Two people could both be below the poverty line, one richer than the other; and a transfer of income from the poorer to the richer may not bring either above the poverty line and yet make the poorer person a lot worse off. None of this would be captured by the two standard views. Sen therefore argues for and proposes a means of measuring the inequality existing even among those below the poverty line. Only then does utter destitution have a voice, Sen suggests, though it is not clear at this point what exactly he means by this (but all shall be revealed anon). Sen develops an axiomatic derivation of a poverty measure which encompasses the two preceding indices and is also sensitive to the distribution of income among the poor (*CWM*: 373–87). This gives the greatest weight to the poorest of the poor.

This measure has subsequently been further refined and has become known as the Sen–Shorrocks–Thon index. It combines measures of the proportion of poor people, the depth of their poverty and the distribution of welfare among the poor. This measure allows one to disaggregate poverty into three components and to ask: Are there more poor? Are the poor poorer? Is there higher inequality among the poor? This 'Sen measure' of poverty has been used in many empirical studies. In *Inequality Reexamined* (*IR*), Sen provides an extensive list of references to such work dealing with Bangladesh, India, Iran, Malaysia, the United States and Brazil (*IR*: 105). There are now many more than this. He remains sceptical of measures of poverty based on low income, even if the income space is hard to avoid, given the relatively greater availability of income statistics. Given the recent work of Thomas Piketty on inequality measurement based upon previously unutilized measures of wealth, such as the public availability of tax returns and what these tell us about the growth of inherited and other forms of capital, it is not inconceivable that, as countries become better equipped to source data beyond income statistics, Sen's insistence on information beyond income may come into its own (Piketty 2014 [2013]). Equally, of course, unless governments work out better means of collecting tax at both ends of the spectrum – that is, formalizing informal economies and controlling tax avoidance and evasion by the wealthy – these tax-dependent measures will only provide a partial measure, as evinced by the recent scandals around the 'Panama Papers' and the 'Paradise Papers'. Also, of course, simply moving from income to wealth replaces one means with another. Sen, by contrast, defends a broader view: that poverty should be examined in the space of capabilities. His other associated key contributions are his distinction between identification and aggregation and the need to consider poverty depth and inequality among the poor in aggregation (Sen 1983d).

In any case, three important things follow from Sen's alternative to the standard measures. First, it removes from governments the temptation to concentrate on the best-off of the poor – this being the easiest way to reduce the head-count ratio. Second, the Sen measure of poverty (and the like) lays the foundation for showing that poverty understood as persistent deprivations can be strikingly high in 'affluent' countries; that is, that poverty is not just a matter for 'poor' countries and thus also that poverty levels can thus be compared across countries and within countries. Sen highlights evidence that men in New York's Harlem region have less chance of surviving past the age of 40 than Bangladeshi men have (*IR*: 114). Third, relatedly, it would thus be a mistake to suppose that Sen's work on poverty, famine and inequality is mainly or only in terms of individuals' entitlements, power and deprivation; rather, his measure enables and inspires measurement and aggregation of these matters in the light of groups, classes and so on. The deprivations that are associated with the inability to exercise entitlements, the lack of power to convert incomes into overcoming deprivation, are often common to individuals within specific contexts and as members of identifiable groups and classes. Women, for example, often require, for biological, social and cultural reasons, higher income than men to overcome persistent deprivations (or, more positively, and in the language we will soon encounter, to secure the same capability). Other factors too – such as age, location and epidemiological atmosphere – also strongly affect a person's power to convert money into the elements of a worthwhile life (*IR*: 113).

The role of group and class analysis proves central to what Sen says about inequality, too. In fact, we could go so far as to suggest that Sen provides an excellent framework for thinking through a very topical matter today: intersectional inequality. The reason for this is because, with Marx, he rejects seeing people only as workers. He is simultaneously fascinated by the rich diversity of people and determined to find an objective measure for inequality. In other words, in answering the question as regards what follows from this diversity for inequality, he is singly interested in determining which of these diversities is the most important in the content of inequality. He starts where many have begun, with traditional Marxist class analysis and even – unusually for economists of his stripe – connects a positive reading of the labour theory of value to this under the guidance of Maurice Dobb (*OEI; IR*: 118–19).

However, ultimately, he parts ways with labour values and is more deeply moved by appeal derived from inequalities of needs. This is most apparent in his earlier *On Economic Inequality* (*OEI*) but resurfaces strongly later in his more famous *Inequality Reexamined*. In both works, he is clear that there are two main ways of viewing inequality, at least if one is concerned with a departure from a notion of appropriate distribution: those based on desert and those based on needs (*OEI*: 77–106). Although this is qualified via his concern for capabilities introduced later, and discussed more fully in chapter 2, there is little doubt that he favours need over desert as a basis for 'distributional' judgements as such, to which the concept of 'inequality belongs' (*OEI*: 104). He argues that none of the following four conceptions of desert seem more appropriate: those based on incentive, merit, the value of labour, or neo-classical marginal productivity. Sen makes a great deal of these arguments based on desert as he takes issue with the fact that arguments in favour of inequality are often based on incentive grounds, that is, on the notion that inequality is necessary because, without it, individuals will not be incentivized to work as efficiently as possible. His main concern here is that we are better placed to be sensitive to inequalities in terms of needs as these vary depending on conditions, family size and so on (see also Marx 1996 [1875]: 215).

Given that needs vary interpersonally, as does the transformation of resources into need fulfilment, even equality of incomes, or more generally of primary goods (Rawls 1973, 1993) or resources (Dworkin 1981: 200), can fail to yield equal satisfaction of needs. In other words, in pursuing the demands of equality in the 'space of well-being, or need fulfilment', as Sen puts it, 'we have to go beyond the income-based categories and also the so-called Marxian classes (indeed, as Marx himself has argued)' (*IR*: 121). So he has little truck with the idea that inequalities of all kinds can be correlated with class, even if in certain circumstances they do correlate quite well: 'race and colour may have a good statistical correlation with class in the United States or the United Kingdom. But the deprivation associated with being black is not *just* a matter of its class correlates' (*IR*: 121).

The diversity of humans in general and in terms of various forms of deprivation and inequality is exemplified by this reference to deprivation associated with race. Gender, too, is central to Sen's concerns. Deprivations in line with gender become more and more important in his work for three main related reasons. First, the effects of poverty on the lives of people, Sen's prime concern, are most often experienced most severely by women – poverty, you might say, is etched into the bodies of women more than men. Second, he uses examples of how women tend to experience poverty and inequality in specific kinds of ways to reinforce his point about the importance and diversity of group classification. Third, gender sensitivity plays an important role in helping us see better how systematic disparities and deprivations are often not – and thus ought not to be – reducible to differences in incomes and resources. While income inequality is still a central and burning issue for women across the globe, there exist many other deprivations associated with the role and place of women in many societies, for example, the division of labour within the household, the extent of care or education received, the liberties that different family members are permitted to enjoy, and so on.

In his discussion of 'gender and inequality' in *Inequality Reexamined*, for instance, Sen suggests that inequality inside the household is one of 'resource-use and of the transformation of the used resources into capability to function, and neither class of information is well captured by any devised notion of "income distribution" within the family' (*IR*: 123). He goes on to show that in many parts of the world, for example, among rural families in Asia and North Africa, in the face of what could be expected on the basis of biological potentials, given symmetric care, there exists a mortality differential against women (where the crude female ratio varies between 0.93 and 0.96, as compared to 1.05 in Europe and North America) (Sen 1990a). The higher mortality and morbidity rate of women vis-à-vis men in these areas reflect serious 'attainment inequality' and 'shortfall inequality', elementary and important aspects of gender inequality whose assessment need not be 'derivative on any constructed concept of income inequality within the family' (*IR*: 124). In other words, the gender inequalities can be measured and explained without the necessity to refer to income inequality. Thus, in departing from the traditional perspective of income distribution towards a more direct accounting of gender inequality reflected in functioning differences (and the corresponding disparities in the elementary capabilities to avoid escapable morbidity and mortality), Sen shows how gender inequality and deprivation cut across a variety of income levels.[3] This is reinforced, he suggests, if we look towards more complex inequalities in freedoms – for example, even though anti-female bias in nutrition, morbidity or mortality is much less present in sub-Saharan Africa, there are often big gender differences in being able to read and write, in being able to avoid bodily mutilation, in being free to pursue independent careers, or being in positions of leadership. Moreover – and I would suggest very importantly to avoid a certain kind of 'developmental gaze' – Sen also goes on to show here and elsewhere that, once we move away from just the means – income, primary goods or resources – to admittedly more complex measurement of 'those things that intrinsically matter', we can understand how, even in the rich countries of Europe and North America, gender inequality is still very prevalent (*PF*; Sen 1985; Sen 1990b; *IR*: 125).

Much of the second chapter of this book is about what exactly Sen means here by 'capability' and 'function' or 'functioning'. For our purposes now, Sen is most concerned to show that these kinds of disparities, along with many others in complex, diverse and interdependent societies, generate situations in which the deprivations and inequalities about which we are most concerned are not ultimately about income or primary goods or resources, but about the power or means to transform income (or primary goods or resources) into functioning or living without deprivations. Although he is very clear that poverty and inequality are distinct concepts and neither subsumes one under the other, he is also careful to say that they relate closely to one another. This is brought out best by this focus on moving the assessment of poverty and inequality away from low income or relatively low income to what he initially calls 'income inadequacy'. This idea is that we should view poverty as being ultimately about the deprivation associated not just with low income but income that is inadequate to generate the possibility to live a life at 'minimally acceptable levels' (*IR*: 109). These are not ever fully specified for the reasons discussed in chapter 2, but nevertheless this allows us to see two important things about poverty and inequality. First, the choices we make about how we measure poverty and inequality affect how we conceive of them and vice versa; or, in other words, concepts matter, even at these seemingly basic levels of social analysis. Second, the pre-existing accounts of how to measure poverty and inequality fall short in a number of ways.

Sen argues that the relevant concept of poverty has to be inadequacy rather than lowness. The approaches discussed above that use a 'poverty line' are concerned with the latter, and they are partly attractive as they can be determined independently of personal characteristics and contextual conditions. The problem is that, in ignoring personal characteristics and conditions in the determination of the measure, they 'cannot do justice to our real concerns underlying poverty, viz. capability failure because of inadequate economic means' (*IR*: 111).

Similarly, in the case of inequality, the standard measures of inequality, what Sen calls 'welfare-based inequality evaluation', are concerned with income inequality. Even Atkinson's (1970a, 1970b, 1983) famous measure is concerned with lowness of income – more exactly, the social loss involved in unequal income distribution in terms of shortfalls of equivalent incomes. He arrives at his measure of inequality by determining the percentage reduction in total income that could be sustained without reducing social welfare, by distributing the new reduced total exactly equally (*IR*: 96). This involves judgements of the following kind: a 22 per cent smaller total income, if equally distributed, would be just as good for the society as the present (higher) income distributed as (unequally as) it in fact is, and thus this (22 per cent) is the measure of inequality (*IR*: 96). As Sen points out, this is in fact not so much a measure of inequality but a measure of its badness; and it is only useful in a fairly limited format in which individual diversities are left out of account. As Sen puts it, the 'format makes no room for substantial interpersonal variations in the conversion of individual incomes into personal well-beings' (*IR*: 101). Second, therefore, unlike many of the competing earlier accounts of poverty and inequality, Sen escapes the grip of welfarism both in terms of the category for measurement – utility – and the end goal. For Sen, the end goal is not some notion of welfare, understood as desire satisfaction, but a more complex notion: well-being. Resources and incomes are important for well-being but so are the disparate means to transform resources and incomes into well-being and freedom (as we shall see in the chapters that follow). The objective analysis of well-being requires subjective input as to living conditions, personal characteristics and specific needs and deprivations, but, in arguing that an objective account of well-being can be given – even if only at the level of groups in societies – Sen is thereby proposing alternative objective accounts of poverty and inequality that do not need to fall back on the poverty of analysis provided by utilities or incomes or resources or goods alone.

Before we can say clearly what Sen means by well-being and the associated idea of standard of living, we need to grasp what he means by capabilities and functionings.

Conclusion

The welfarism that Sen debunks emerges out of the general triumph of utilitarianism and the justification it provides for a mechanistic view of the polity and the economy, which ends up in the idea that markets can manage themselves, responding organically to preferences via the price mechanism, and the view that individual political preferences are not only sovereign but can successfully be aggregated to generate coherent decision outcomes. In other words, with a few caveats thrown in, the legacy of utilitarianism provides justification for purely preference-based economics and politics (Bentham 1970 [1781], 1970 [c.1782]; Becker and Stigler 1977; Menger 1981 [1871]; Arrow 1951; Sen 1970, 1973, 1977; Sen and Williams 1982).

In the real world of politics, this triumph of utilitarianism within economics has had unfortunate consequences. Utilitarianism's subject-relative approach to morality, which treats pleasure or desire satisfaction as the sole element in human good, has provided constant support for the reduction of economics and politics to the aggregation of individual preferences (or avowed wants). This involves an understanding of human agency as equivalent to utility maximization. In other words, utilitarianism offers justification for the evaluation of individual actions or social achievement in terms of their consequences on individual or social utility, as determined by individual preference alone. The concept of preference has therefore come to be prioritized because of its alleged epistemological importance in calculating individual welfare and the moral imperative to respect the judgement of individuals (as expressed in their preferences).

While these matters of consequentialist reasoning, epistemology and the sovereignty of individual judgement are arguably vital in any form of individual or social evaluation, the utilitarian framework for understanding and safeguarding them is counterproductive. In its quest for a universal 'calculus', it has excluded most of the real world that it purports to understand. Utilitarianism's prioritization of subjective preferences excludes any systematic understanding of how preferences have, in fact, been formed and any evaluation of how they are and ought to be transformed within, for example, existing state institutions, legal practices, welfare provision, production and consumption practices and so on (Hamilton 2003a: 7–8). As Sen puts it, 'Most actual public judgements make extensive use of non-utility information, varying from relative incomes and ownerships to the description of who is doing what to whom' (*CWM*: 18) – not to mention the outright schizophrenia of many of our public judgements, such as the desire to defend freedom of speech and the desire for a quiet life.

Sen, at this stage, has not parted ways entirely with the welfarism at the heart of one of utilitarianism's main legacies – mainstream economics – but, as I have shown in this chapter, he begins his efflorescent career with a set of searching critiques into its main foundations: 'scepticism regarding interpersonal comparison'; 'Pareto optimality'; 'revealed preference'; 'utility'; 'rationality'; 'poverty'; 'inequality'; and 'welfare'. Moreover, a constant concern of his is the informational basis for measurement in economics in general and the assessment of living standards in particular – income, primary goods and resources. Sen casts damning doubt on all three. In doing so, he helps set the agenda for a series of searing criticisms of the two main foundations of modern economics, undermining the idea that individuals are always the best judges of their own preferences or wants, given the fact that, as we now know, individual preferences are consistently prone to adaptation to context and condition and not always driven by self-interest; that what is produced and consumed should be determined by the private consumption and work preferences of individuals. In short, the central assumptions in welfare economics – that all individuals have 'given and complete preference functions' and that all seek to maximize their utility – have been on shaky ground for some time (Elster 1983; Hamilton 2003a; Hodgson 2013; Gough 2017). As will become clear in chapter 2, Sen does eventually leave the language of preferences behind, even if he rightly argues that individual preferences must always remain morally and informationally important. However, as will become clear in the rest of the book, Sen never completely discards some of the main tenets of social choice theory.

2

Capability

Amartya Sen spent much of the 1960s and 1970s criticizing the most important assumptions in economics. His main concerns were methodological and substantive. Utilitarianism and the welfarism it gave rise to in economics was inadequate in two ways, he argued. First, it constrained what he called the 'informational base' for economic analysis, especially if the category of need was taken to be central therein. Second, it was crudely unable either to provide safeguards for egalitarian outcomes or principles that a polity might want to enshrine irrespective of utility calculation. Sen was trained as an economist and has held posts in economics departments in the United Kingdom, the United States and India, but it was while he held a prize fellowship at Trinity College, Cambridge, that he began to investigate some of the main philosophical responses to utilitarianism. This prize fellowship was a wonderful opportunity that gave him years of freedom to do anything he liked, 'no questions asked', and which he used to branch out from economics and development into philosophical analysis. This period, and the subsequent magnificent march of his career in the United Kingdom, as a fellow of Trinity, a professor at the London School of Economics and at Oxford, interspersed with visiting stints at various US universities, enabled him to become a major figure within the nascent revival in analytical political philosophy (Meeks 2018; that this can be described as a revival is disputed in Geuss 2008).

Sen was particularly influenced by the work of John Rawls and sought to assess whether the alternative structure provided by Rawls's *Theory of Justice* (Rawls 1973) could be the basis of a defensible and workable alternative to the inadequacies of utilitarianism and welfarism. He was especially interested in the nature and role of what Rawls terms 'primary goods', that is, the universal means necessary for individual choice as to which kind of life to lead (individual conceptions of the good life) or, in Rawls's words, 'those goods that anyone would want regardless of whatever else they wanted' (Rawls 1973: 60–5). Given the moral theoretical basis upon which much of this discussion was based, there is a great deal of moral meta-theory that comes into play here. For the purposes of clarity and brevity, I leave that to one side in this chapter. I begin with Sen's famous Tanner lecture of 1979, 'Equality of What?' (EW), where he first introduces his idea of 'basic capability equality' as an alternative to both utility and primary goods. I start here as this is the first formulation of what has become known as his 'capability approach', which, as I have already noted, is a phrase he himself disowns, preferring the less doctrinaire-sounding 'concern for capabilities'. What are capabilities? How do they relate to functionings? How do they relate to well-being and the standard of living? How do we arrive at knowledge about them? Are they measurable? What is so good about them? What is not?

The 'capability approach', as it has become known, has taken on a life of its own beyond Sen's work, particularly inspired by the work of the philosopher Martha Nussbaum (1988, 1993, 2000; and Nussbaum and Sen 1989) and many others currently actively involved in various professional academic research bodies, such as the highly successful Human Development and Capability Association (HDCA), founded in 2004 with Sen as its first president, which meets annually, and the more recently founded Cambridge Capability Conferences (CCCs). Partly due to these developments and partly due to its social, economic, political and philosophical novelty and implications, the capability approach is now much discussed by political theorists, philosophers and a range of social scientists. Given that this is a book about Amartya Sen's ideas, not the capability approach *tout court*, I will desist from delineating how others have developed his path-breaking initiatives. Readers who are interested in a discussion of the capability approach from the perspective of the social sciences would do well to start with Comim, Qizilbash and Alkire (2008) and Deneulin and Shahani (2009); for discussions in the light of welfare economics, see Kuklys (2005), Schokkaert (2009) and Basu and López-Calva (2011); for the approach related to global public health, see Venkatapuram (2011); and for its application to environmental policies, see Schlosberg (2012), Holland (2014) and Gough

(2017). For a comprehensive introduction to the human development approach, see Fukuda-Parr (2003) and Fukuda-Parr and Kumar (2009); and for the most recent comprehensive study of the capability approach, see Robeyns (2017).

Sen's work on the idea of capability has also produced other very significant developments in the arena of policy formation. For example, along with development economist Sudhir Anand and economic theorist James Foster, Sen has helped to make the capabilities approach predominant as a paradigm for policy debate in human development, inspiring the creation of the UN's HDI. This is now a popular measure of human development, capturing capabilities in health, education, income and so on. In addition, the approach has also been used in the context of high-income countries (Anand, Pattanaik and Puppe 2009; Anand, Santos and Smith 2009; Anand et al. 2009).

Capabilities

The notion of capability is, as Sen himself admits, a rather unfortunate choice of term (CW: 30). It is clunky, reminiscent of 'Capability Brown', the byname for Lancelot Brown, the eighteenth-century English landscape architect. However unfortunate a term, it is apt, and Capability Brown helps us see why. The reason this very influential gardener was given the nickname 'Capability' was that he would tell his clients that their property had 'capability' for improvement, and by this he meant 'potential' (*Encyclopedia Britannica* 2018). I suggest that the easiest way to access what Amartya Sen means by the term 'capability' is 'potential'.[1] In other words, 'capability' is more capacious than just 'ability', as that is too redolent of individual powers and capacities alone. 'Capability' points towards the more general human potential to enact agency dependent upon whether the right conditions prevail: societal and economic relations and means to enable basic and more developed human functioning. Individual abilities – and the diversity thereof – are vital components of this, but as Capability Brown probably had in mind when describing the natural potential of a garden, the helping hand of a good architect to shape the environment in which the plants may develop to their full potential was necessary for them to do so. This is evinced by the *Oxford English Dictionary*. Although it suggests that, in its most general sense, we can use 'capability' in English as a synonym for 'ability', we tend to do so in specific circumstances: for example, 'he had an intuitive capability to bring out the best in people', or 'this job is beyond my capabilities' or 'the United States' nuclear weapons capability is without peer'. At play in all these various formulations are the powers, forces, resources and means to do or be something.

As I have noted, Sen first introduces the notion in a discussion of equality and inequality, suggesting that, when thinking about equality, we are always thinking about 'equality of what?' As the following bears out, and as suggested in the main introduction to this book, the broader practical context is Sen's proposals regarding how best to think about famines, poverty, inequality and development. The idea that we should propose equality without reference to anything, he suggests, makes little or no sense. Yet the existing main contenders for answering this important question are inadequate, Sen argues, even if we try and put them together into some all-encompassing scheme. So, rather than talking about equality (or inequality) of incomes, resources or other kinds of goods, or supposing that a mental metric of pleasure or desire satisfaction is sufficient, Sen proposes that when talking about well-being and advantage, we are best placed to think about them in terms of 'a person's ability to do valuable acts or reach valuable states of being'. In other words, 'capability' was chosen to represent the alternative combinations of things a person is able to do or be – the 'various "functionings" he or she can achieve' (CW: 30).

Sen's illuminating work on capabilities and functionings has grown out of criticisms of utilitarianism and welfarism in which value is seen only in individual utility, defined in terms of some mental characteristic, such as pleasure, happiness or desire (IR: 6). Sen maintains that these approaches are guilty of both 'physical-condition neglect' and 'valuation neglect' (CC: 20–1). They are guilty of 'physical-condition neglect' because, by only considering mental states, no account is taken of the freedom the person had in reaching these states, and her objective condition is not considered separate from any reference to how she feels about it. They are guilty of 'valuation neglect' because they leave no room for the possible evaluation of states and conditions: by taking wants as given and the informational basis for an assessment of the 'wellness' of someone's life, they create 'premature fixity' (CC: 30).

These are central issues for Sen. The very poor person whose conditions of existence would give him a very low objective well-being might score quite well on a utilitarian scale that only tests his own analysis of his situation in terms of his happiness or pleasure (the welfarist approach). He may do so because: (1) he has a naturally sunny outlook on life; or (2) he has become accustomed to penury and hardship – he has formed adaptive preferences; or (3) he has both.

One of the reasons that utility measurement cannot get out of the starting blocks is the diversity of ways in which persons respond to the conditions of their lives: some are never satisfied, grumbling as they are showered in champagne and caviar, while others retain a sunny disposition, however bleak their lives may be in objective terms. Sen puts it as follows.

> A thoroughly deprived person, leading a very reduced life, might not appear to be badly off in terms of the mental metric of desire and its fulfilment, if the handicap is accepted with non-grumbling resignation. In situations of long-standing deprivation, the victims do not go on grieving and lamenting all the time, and very often make great efforts to take pleasure in small mercies and cut down personal desires to modest – 'realistic' – proportions. (*IR*: 55)

This exemplifies the circumstantial contingency of desires and supports the point that internal criteria alone are bad indicators of what most people would think of as good criteria for an analysis of well-being (*CC*: 35).

Utilitarian equality can only really make sense if one claims for utilitarianism an exclusive ability to avoid unfair discrimination between 'one person's and another person's equally urgent human needs' (Harsanyi 1977). As Sen points out, needs are reduced to utility here or, more exactly, the moral importance of the former is based exclusively on the latter (*EW*: 199). Sen disputes this here and elsewhere. His most important insight, among quite a few others, is that as regards distributional questions, which are at the heart of the matter for Sen, utilitarianism in general provides little comfort: '[e]ven the minutest gain in total utility sum would be taken to outweigh distributional inequalities of the most blatant kind' (*EW*: 202). Sen produces a more technical knock-down for total utility equality, but this need not detain us. The more general point is the relevance of non-utility information to moral judgements. The utilitarian and welfarist routes to thinking about equality are only interested in one of the end products of the distribution of goods, that is, the mental states these goods may (or may not) produce – utility, normally via 'revealed preference' – without any reference to how these are produced or what effects the variety of conditions and human characteristics may have on pleasure, happiness or desire fulfilment. These utility-based approaches are not very accommodating of freedoms and rights that may be valued for non-utilitarian reasons.

Sen also takes issue with some of the reactions against the utilitarian approach that are much more accommodating of freedoms and rights, for example those developed by Rawls (1973, 1993) and Dworkin (1981, 2000). The former opts for a set of 'primary goods', and the latter 'equality of resources', which provide the means to a life of free choice as regards the 'good life'.[2] The belief is that the individual should be free to choose whichever 'good life' she wishes, and the state should ensure that this choice can be made. They assume that means can be valued outside any valuation of the ends. Sen argues that this is impossible and an unrealistic simplification of what occurs. Rawlsian primary goods or Dworkian resources are guilty of artificially severing means from ends. In contrast, Sen begins with valued 'doings and beings', the valued ends themselves (*IR*: 79ff).

Sen submits that Rawls's emphasis on primary goods fails to take proper account of the diversity of human beings. If people were quite similar, a universal index of primary goods may turn out to be a good way of judging advantage, but, of course, if that were the case utilitarianism would not fare too badly either. 'But, in fact, people seem to have very different needs varying with health, longevity, climatic conditions, location, work conditions, temperament, and even body size (affecting food and clothing requirements)... Judging advantage purely in terms of primary goods leads to a partially blind morality' (EW: 215–16). Sen argues that Rawls takes primary goods as the embodiment of advantage, rather than taking advantage to be a relationship between persons and goods. This is a central concern when he goes on to argue in a variety of places that Rawls and Dworkin are guilty of artificially separating means from ends. In other words, were we to resist this tendency and still strive for universalism (or at least objectivity) we may be able to uncover a more appropriate index of advantage, that is, a means of determining the extent of existing inequalities and where to focus on overcoming them.

Sen argues that what is missing in all these contending frameworks is some notion of '"basic capabilities": a person being able to do certain basic things'. These include the ability to meet one's nutritional requirements, the wherewithal to be clothed and sheltered, the ability to move about, the power to participate in the social life of the community, and so on (EW: 218). The notion of urgency related to this is not captured either by utility or primary goods, or any combination of the two, Sen contends. Primary goods are too concerned with good things rather than with what these good things do to human beings. Utility is concerned with what these things do to human beings, but its metric means it focuses only on mental reaction. The case for reducing the handicap of the disabled person or the disadvantage of the epidemiologically challenged person, and so on and so forth, must rest on something else. Sen thinks it is 'the interpretation of needs in the form of basic capabilities' (EW: 218; cf. Hamilton 2003a). This type of equality Sen calls the 'basic capability approach'.

Sen is therefore interested in 'shifting attention from goods to what goods do to human beings' (EW: 219). In other words, given the diversity of human beings and the conditions under which they live, he thinks it unhelpful and even disingenuous to assume that one can get to capabilities via universally applicable primary goods, that is, by divorcing means from ends. There is ample evidence, he argues, that the conversion of goods to capabilities varies from person to person substantially. The equality of goods therefore does not ensure the equality of capabilities.

The basic notion in Sen's alternative, in his 'capability approach', is a person's functionings, 'which represent parts of the state of a person – in particular the various things that he or she manages to do or be in leading a life' (CW: 31). These are constitutive of the person's being and an assessment of well-being must take the form of an evaluation of these elements (*IR*: 39). The capability of a person 'reflects the alternative combinations of functionings the person can achieve, and from which he or she can choose one collection' (CW: 31). The capability to function comprises the various combinations of functionings – the set of vectors of functionings – that reflect the person's freedom to lead one type of life or another; that is, it reflects the person's ability (that includes her living conditions) to choose from possible lives. The actual functionings of a person therefore make up part of the capability set but are not equal to it.

The capability set is the 'primary informational base' because there are four conceptual categories in the capability set which are all valuable for the quality of life but are not functionings per se (CW: 38). They are: well-being achievement; well-being freedom; agency achievement; and agency freedom (WAF: 202; *OEE*: 60ff). Unlike some approaches that see the person as being able to have an adequate well-being achievement without having had much freedom of choice, Sen maintains that there is more to an assessment of well-being, and especially the broader quality of life, than the achievement of well-being. (This does not negate the importance of an external point of view that can clarify whether a person has basically everything she requires for her well-being, even though she might not have been involved herself in decisions over what her well-being entails, about which more below.) He places much importance on the ability to achieve well-being and the freedom to choose between different lives that lead to well-being.

Furthermore, it is often the case that we have goals and aspirations that are important for our sense of agency but have little or nothing to do with our well-being. An example is the doctor who would earn a larger salary and live a life that would increase her well-being if she stayed in England but is devoted to the cause of helping Africa's fight against malaria, and so she spends her life living in Africa to face up to the realities of the illness. People often do things that they feel are important to their lives that others, and they themselves, know are contrary to their personal well-being.[3] An evaluation of a person's well-being, according to Sen, does require an evaluation of her functionings (well-being achievement), but a life worth living must incorporate more than well-being; it must also take into account agent-centred evaluation – self-evaluation – and the freedom to achieve valued functionings, as discussed below.

The criticism levelled at Sen by socialist political philosopher G. A. Cohen's and Sen's replies within the same collection indicate the important role that freedom plays within Sen's version of the capability approach (Cohen 1993; CW). Cohen maintains that Sen is confused in his use of the idea of capability and ambiguous in his discussion of freedom. Cohen argues that there is a distinction that the capability approach fails to recognize because Sen is trying to do too much with capability. What he wants to show is that 'midfare', something midway between goods and utilities, is a more restricted and better domain in which to work. He maintains, furthermore, that the confusion within Sen's notion of capability arises because of Sen's attempt to incorporate freedom under capability, and that this is misguided (Cohen 1993: 20–3). Sen accepts the distinction within the capability approach but points out that Cohen's midfare is Sen's functionings (that is, a list of valuable 'doings and beings') and that the freedom to achieve these functionings does add something to a person's achieved well-being.

Cohen's midfare, therefore, leaves out a fundamental aspect of what Sen sees as being in the true interest of the individual: her freedom. Sen holds that, 'In the space of functionings any point ... reflects a combination of the person's doings and beings, relevant to the exercise. The capability is a set of functioning[s], representing the various alternative combinations of beings and doings any one (combination) of which the person can choose' (CW: 38). In other words, *choice* is important not simply because an increase in choice might provide better alternatives but that acting freely and being able to choose, having well-being freedom, might itself be 'directly conducive to well-being' (CW: 39). Sen's argument is that 'doing X' is distinct from 'choosing to do X and doing it', and the latter is, and ought to be, more highly valued (*IR*: 52). The centrality of choice and freedom of choice is obvious. Freedom is not being seen in the 'negative' way in which it is often represented, as principles of rights and non-interference, about which more in chapter 3, but rather the 'issue is the positive ability to choose', which is constitutive of the 'good life': 'the "good life" is partly a life of genuine choice, and not one in which the person is forced into a particular life – however rich it might be in other respects' (CC: 69–70; cf. *IR*: 52 and SL: 36).

This is far removed from Cohen's midfare, and that is in fact the focal point of Cohen's worries. He thinks that Sen is too 'athletic' with his conception of freedom and capability. This, I submit, is because Cohen is more concerned with a static notion of well-being that assigns no positive value to freedom as regards the ability to choose and act. As Cohen puts it, '[n]o serious inequality obtains when everyone has everything she needs, even if she did not have to lift a finger to get it' (Cohen 1993: 28). By contrast, Sen's model, in incorporating well-being freedom into well-being assessments, does want to make room for action (and agency) but it does not necessarily require actual action in the form of choice. He wants, rather, to accommodate counterfactual opportunities, which help to assess whether the person in question would or would not have made certain choices given different conditions and knowledge, understanding of which is important in an analysis of the relative freedom of the choice actually made (WAF; cf. *CC*). The example Sen gives of the use of the question 'What would you choose given the choice over X and Y' is the distinction between fasting and starving. They are so distinct exactly because one (fasting) involves a choice and the other (starving) does not, despite the fact that their well-being achievements might be the same. The nature of the actual options is also important: a set of three choices that the person values as 'bad', 'worse' and 'terrible' is not the same as a set whose options are valued as 'good', 'great', 'superb' (SL: 36).

It is vitally important at this juncture to point out that Sen is very careful to do two things with this new idea of capabilities. First, it is not intended as a replacement for arguments – and thus prescriptions – around the notion of universal human goods. Capabilities are not universal goods to be imposed everywhere, even if that were possible, without reference to individual preferences as regards both the conditions of their existence and the lives they wish to live. This is partly to do with his original idea that although – or one might say because – the notion of basic capabilities is a very general one, any application of it must be rather culture dependent (EW: 219). On the other hand, it is also to do with an acute awareness on Sen's part that even analysis of the objective conditions of existence in any particular place will depend upon the subjective preferences of those living in the conditions in question. And, of course, any analysis of how best to proceed – as his work on famines brings out only too forcefully – will be riddled with error and poor judgement if it does so without reference to the preferences of actual humans on the ground. Second, he therefore adheres with remarkable consistency to what he calls an 'incomplete' theory, despite the insistence of many of his collaborators and acolytes that he says something more fulsome about the substantive content of human capabilities (Nussbaum 1988, 1993, 2000).

It is also important to note that Sen's accommodation of counterfactual reasoning does not fall into the problem of indeterminacy of 'optimal conditions' and 'full knowledge' because the counterfactual is created within the sphere of knowledge of the evaluator and evaluated – an interactive process that itself leads to more knowledge acquisition. The importance of this sort of interactive process that has no specific end goal is particularly crucial in the light of a theory of true interests that seeks to stress the method of ascertaining true interests rather than paternalistically laying them down. Posing the counterfactual, therefore and furthermore, helps keep the fasting person from being forced to eat and makes it clear that the starving person wants to eat (somewhat irrelevant in the latter case; just asking the person would suffice) (Hamilton 1999, 2003a).

Similarly, the explanation and evaluation of a person's agency achievement is made more comprehensive with knowledge of the agency freedom, the choices involved (their nature) and their feasibility. It could be argued, however, that though it seems obvious that achieving the goals that are central to your life is constitutive of a 'good life', having more freedom to choose is less clearly connected to the 'good life'. There is an intuitive sense in which too much choice can be counterproductive for both (1) well-being and (2) obtaining personal goals. The overabundance of possibility can be confusing and debilitating. Yet it is a mistake to think of choice only in terms of supplying something which is an addition rather than a subtraction. The choice to rid my life of too many confusing choices is a subtracting choice, but still a beneficial one. It is ultimately choice, therefore, that is valued and productive (Hamilton 1999: 526). The question of the need for control over every choice is, however, not so clear-cut. For example, having little control over public policy that has rid my area of malaria does not decrease my choices, it increases them. Something outside of my control has led to an increase in my freedom and control (*IR*: 68; 'control' and 'freedom' are discussed in detail in chapter 3). Although, of course, if public debate is organized such that all (or most) voices that are affected by the policy are at least heard, the detrimental effects of some malaria-control policies would become public knowledge and lead to the more uniform distribution or restructuring of the policies themselves. (This relates to what counts as 'the public' and 'the political' and is discussed later in this chapter, in chapter 5 and in the book's conclusion.) The fact that I am born into a malaria-free area and obviously benefit without having had control over the policy is another, less problematic, point.

Objectivity

The important novelty of Sen's approach lies in his elaboration of functionings and capabilities, and the fact that the substantive and conceptual novelty is not found solely in one or the other; it comprises certain valued functionings, the capability to achieve these and the freedom to pursue personal goals. I therefore now shift focus to explicate the dynamism of the approach: that it requires reflection and self-evaluation; and how and why preferences have to be taken into account if illusions are to be overcome. It is here that Sen's theses on positional-objectivity, valuation and incompleteness play their part. He must provide an argument concerning the procedure of escape from illusion and clarify the scope of his claims about the centrality of certain functionings and freedoms in a person's life. Assessment of choice and counterfactual opportunity prima facie demand a lot of objectivity since choice and the evaluation thereof is impossible outside of beliefs. Hence, just as Davidson's (1986) work has shown that want-regarding theories do not sit on an epistemological pedestal within processes of interpretation, it is also necessary to scrutinize the valuation involved at and within different stages of Sen's work, and especially as regards external evaluation of the extent of freedom and well-being.

What then is self-evaluation and what is the role of reflection in uncovering preferences that are only apparent or illusory? Self-evaluation is a reflective exercise undertaken by each agent that tells us each person's assessment of her own quality of life vis-à-vis that of others; not to be confused with utility because it is 'quintessentially an evaluative exercise' (SL: 31, 32). It does not occur in a vacuum; it takes place within the framework of contemporary standards and beliefs, as does 'standard-evaluation', which evaluates issues like well-being and the standard of living objectively as outcomes (SL: 30). If contemporary standards are widely shared, these two forms of evaluation can converge, but both need to be held under the microscope of critical scrutiny that aims to determine 'why these opinions are held and these values cherished' (SL: 32). Hence self-evaluation is not a purely subjective exercise and can be critically evaluated, using evidence and analysis from external positions, and 'standard-evaluation' requires agent-centred reference. In other words, apparent wants and interests are used and tested in the light of additional information and different positions. This is not paternalistic because, though interpretation might depart from direct reference to utility, a move which many utilitarians would deem the definition of paternalism, the outcome of self-evaluation is not rejected. Sen's point is that reference is made to the subject herself, but the reference must only be made after, not before, the process of self-evaluation has occurred. The difficulty, however, is that self-evaluation is under-determined compared to standard-evaluation and the result can be a remoulding of agent-centred standards to that of the larger community. How does or can the individual distinguish between different wants and interests, labelling some illusory and some true?

This is best clarified in the light of Sen's position as regards objectivity. He argues that objectivity should not be seen only in the form of invariance with respect to individual observers and their positions, a 'view from nowhere', but also as a view 'from a delineated somewhere' (PO: 127; cf. Nagel 1986). He uses the following analogy: the statement 'the sun and moon are the same size' is an objective one if others who stand in the same position on the earth verify it and there is no other information available (of the sort, say, we now have for measuring their sizes). The idea that observational claims are claims about appearance and not about reality is overcome by Sen when he argues that observational claims are themselves part of the world that makes up reality (PO: 130; cf. Putnam 1987). His point is that it is possible to check the claim by noting what other people observe in the same position. Yet there is also another sense of objectivity: 'trans-positional objectivity'. Sen argues that beliefs are, and should be, tested 'trans-positionally', beyond positional objectivity, and verified if there is still convergence thereafter, though there is no assumption that this will occur. Hence, with this binary sense of objectivity, a statement can be objective and false. For example, a community that has no knowledge of optics could be shown to be mistaken about the belief that the sun and the moon are the same size; this will not make the belief a subjective one, but it will show that the community's objective belief is mistaken. It will lose its positional objectivity over time and no longer be a legitimate belief. This final step is left unstated by Sen but I take it to be assumed.

The question that needs to be asked of this analogy is whether it will work in the sphere of beliefs, interests, wants and choices. Sen thinks it will and he carries the analogy on into an analysis of 'objective illusion'. For a belief to be shown to be objective and illusory, it has to be shown to have had general agreement, coherence, within a certain observational and deliberative context, from a certain position, and it must be diagnosed as erroneous with the use of extra information and critical scrutiny. As Sen puts it, 'illusion relates to beliefs that are formed on the basis of a limited class of positional observations. And these beliefs – false as they may be – could nevertheless have been derived objectively in the absence of access to other positional scrutiny' (PO: 133). He gives two convincing examples of 'objective illusion': the difference, in Indian states with different levels of health awareness, between the self-perception of morbidity and the observed life expectancy; and the gender bias in self-assessment of morbidity related to observed mortality. They show that beliefs are often erroneous, though objective, because of a general lack of exposure to information – a lack of 'trans-positional' scrutiny. Criticism, Sen argues, must be internal, but it is not ultimately significant whether some of the ideas might have originated from without or not. He shows convincingly that many arguments that defend a form of cultural relativism use overly restrictive parameters: they assume that communities are unrealistically cut off from 'foreign' influence and are free internally from dissenters and criticism (Sen 2005, 2006a; Nussbaum and Sen 1989: 533–4).

In both examples, the moon and mortality, however, there is a relatively secure truth touchstone; the laws of optics and the ability to measure the life expectancy of people are not very problematic, or at least not hugely disputed in the world today. By contrast, competing belief systems are distant poles apart, at least concerning some issues. It seems that for Sen the truth of something emerges after sufficient trans-positional scrutiny and some form of agreement on what is ultimately valued. Is this asking too much, and if this is the assumption, is it not begging the question of the reality of political interaction?

Incompleteness

To answer this question, I will look at how objectivity relates to the valuation of functionings, capabilities and the 'good life' in Sen's system, and why he maintains that the theory must remain an incomplete theory (and not an evaluative blueprint), despite taking particular motivations and outcomes into account. The point of the 'positional objectivity' thesis, allowing as it does for the possibility of 'objective illusion', only holds force within a conception of human nature that delineates a set of capabilities which include valued functionings: being adequately nourished, adequately housed, adequately clothed and so on, allowing the individual, for instance, to do certain things like take part in the entertainment of the community and appear in public without shame (*IR*: 115–16; Smith 1976 [1776], V, II, 2, iv). It tries to encompass all of these and yet leaves the substantive process open; it emphasizes incompleteness.

Sen defends what he calls 'assertive incompleteness' at two levels: (1) at the level of the theory; and (2) at the level of practical political decision making. The former he stresses to overcome the Rawlsian, neo-Kantian position (a foundational argument) which holds that the process can be completed at the level of theory (of justice as fairness) and that this theoretical resolution prefigures any practical solution, that is, the belief that a theory can incorporate the answers to the means to a just society *in abstracto* from actual political reality (exemplified in Rawls's hypothetical 'original position'), about which more in chapter 4. Sen argues that the issues cannot be fully solved at this level by theory alone, but he does not want to discard the foundationalist position, rather simply overcome it by depicting its incompleteness. Similarly, at the level of political decision making, he takes issue with the typical extension of the Kantian argument that holds that if theory fails, there is the transcendental rationality of practical discourse, exemplified by the Habermasian position: a universal 'ideal speech situation' which assumes agreement. At this point, Sen argued that, like Rawls, Habermas's arguments rest on a metaphysical assumption that falls short of the reality of politics.[4]

(For how, in his later work, Sen changes tack and incorporates a Habermasian stress on deliberation in politics, see chapter 5 below; and for the consequences of this move for the realism of his approach as a whole, see this book's concluding chapter.) Complete agreement is unusual, and it is asking too much of human rationality to begin with this assumption. Incompleteness, therefore, relates to the structure of the theory, that it assertively tries not to foreclose on things and create fixity, and to the level of practical discourse, that though humans tend to try to come to reasoned agreement, the assumption that they will is too strong an assumption.

So when Nussbaum argues that 'Sen needs to be more radical ... by introducing an objective normative account of human functioning ...', Sen is at pains to stress that, though this could be done to eliminate the incompleteness of his approach, he is intent on maintaining a 'deliberate incompleteness' (Nussbaum 1988: 176; CW: 47). *Prima facie*, it might seem that Sen's emphasis on incompleteness makes him commit the very error for which he criticizes writers such as Rawls, Dworkin and Scanlon, of working from means to ends rather than ends to means. This could be seen to be supported by the following: 'There are substantive differences between different ethical theories at different levels, from the meta-ethical (involving such issues as objectivity) to the motivational, and it is not obvious that for substantive political and social philosophy it is sensible to insist that all these general issues be resolved before an agreement is reached on the choice of an evaluative space' (PO: 49).

That, however, would be to misinterpret the above sentence in the light of Sen's methodological position and within his theory more generally. He does not require the type of agreement that the Rawlsian and especially the Habermasian approach must assume; the agreement he is concerned with here is agreement on the evaluative space, not on all the ethical and structural questions that emerge in actual political debate. Those substantive issues cannot be decided by theory and, when they are not decided in discourse, the exercise must be resolved via a social choice exercise.

Agreement on the evaluative space, arguably, does actually go some way down the Aristotelian path because it is clear that the 'objects of value' that constitute the 'evaluative space' are valued functionings, capabilities to function and the different freedoms (PO: 32–3). The nature of what sort of 'doings and beings' Sen values has already been noted, but it is helpful here to look at what the evaluative space excludes. For reasons already outlined, it rejects emphasis on the psychological, on mental states, exemplified by the utility-based approaches that rely on professed wants and value only happiness, or on only desire fulfilment. It also rejects other – non-utilitarian – approaches that can be broadly defined as resource-based, which focus either on commodities for their sake alone or that take primary goods as such (Rawls) or resources as such (Dworkin) to be the objects of value. As Sen notes, '[t]he possessing of commodities ... has derivative and varying relevance' in assessment of things such as the living standard, well-being and quality of life (SL: 25). Instead, the evaluative space Sen advances takes the state of being happy as one among many objects of value, desire as evidence – though frequently distorted and imperfect – of what the person values, and primary goods and resources as instrumentally valuable and only in so far as they promote valued capabilities (CC: 32; PO: 48).

The evaluative space, therefore, clarifies certain interests that are valued in the theory. Decision on what these are – valuation – is intrinsically important and therefore unavoidable. This is the case because, although some functionings are so elementary – like being adequately nourished – that they will be strongly valued by all, there are others that are more complex and possibly less obvious that still require evaluation. It is here that the central feature of Sen's views on objectivity and incompleteness plays its most important role and, as already noted, is the central active feature of Sen's approach: the use of external and internal valuation. When substantive issues cannot be decided through evaluative deliberation, Sen emphasizes the role of social choice. By this, for the reasons discussed in the first chapter, he does not mean traditional social choice theorizing that has revealed difficulties with combining individual preference orderings into aggregative social welfare judgements (Arrow's impossibility theorem) and then retreated into a purely procedural view of social decisions (*à la* James Buchanan [Buchanan 1954; Buchanan and Tullock 1962]). Rather, he argues for the need to incorporate consequences into procedural concerns and, more importantly, for the role of practical reason in public discourse: 'many of the more exacting problems of the contemporary world ... actually call for value formation through public discussion' (Sen 1995: 18, reprinted in *RF*: ch. 8). Social choice, therefore, must be seen in light of the fact that public discussion has, and should have, an educative role. Theories of social choice have tended to assume that people's preferences are given, but it is a fact of life in democratic politics that on a lot of issues people do not have clear preferences. It is through practical discourse that true interests are not simply collated but refined, changed and decided upon.

It is obvious that the pre-deliberative opinion of the majority is not given epistemological priority in Sen's approach and true interests are rather seen to emerge from interaction with an 'expert' sector. Is this a helpful and workable view of democracy? Is this not itself a kind of majority opinion, not in the sense of numerical majority but in the sense of holding the 'majority' of knowledge or understanding? As is discussed in chapter 5 of this book, and again in its main conclusion, these questions about the nature of power in the political realm are not analysed much in the work of Amartya Sen, leaving us with a view of democracy that lacks realism. It is clear that the evaluation of the capabilities and so on (the 'good life') as described here must be an intersubjective process out of which communal knowledge of true interests arises, not an instance of Plato's 'philosopher kings' or Lenin's 'dictatorship of the proletariat'. However, an alternative institutional matrix for this is not envisaged. What is clear in Sen's work is that, in a democracy, information must be kept pervasive and constructive, and it must move beyond national borders to break the yoke of different 'objective illusions'. The latter is often taken to be the definition of cultural imperialism, but it is what goes on and will continue to go on between cultures. The counterfactual questioning of whether people would change 'if they knew otherwise' is what is continually carried out in social, economic, ethical and political contexts. Indeed, the very idea of 'development' would lose its defining feature if this was negated. It is only in this manner that contingent opinion from our present 'delineated' point of view can move closer to an objective trans-positional knowledge of what might be called 'true interests' (Hamilton 1999).

This process is relatively easy when what is being talked about are the basic notions of survival, shelter, dignity and so on, but an issue like the western emphasis on autonomy is more problematic. An obvious example is the position of women in parts of the Arab world, Africa and Asia, among others, where power relations create an 'objective illusion' among the majority of women as regards their position as second-class citizens; that is, they themselves often regard their position as 'natural'. Entrenched gender bias and inequality here can only be rent from its state of 'objective illusion' by influence from without that works with elements of internal criticism and remains sensitive to local custom and practice (Sellar 1994; Nussbaum 2000). The moral squeamishness this often creates in the West either occurs prior to reflective analysis on the issue or comes from the more libertarian quarters of liberalism, the most ethnocentric of western thought. The evaluator, who may be in a privileged position 'trans-positionally' speaking, often feels compelled to persuade those under 'objective illusion' to reflect on the importance of freedom and change. There are certain true interests that from certain positions are not accepted, yet they are taken to be true because they are accepted by those who are privileged as regards 'trans-positional' knowledge. 'Truth' here is not some atemporal end-state but, rather, what is attained with an increase in knowledge or change in position or condition that necessitates input from others and critical scrutiny. What this shows, and if we are to learn at all from history, is that what we take to be in our true interests necessarily will include certain 'objective illusions' from which we might, or might not, escape in the future. (The question is who are 'we' here? For more on this, see chapters 4 and 5 below.) It is important, therefore, to refrain from completeness and foreclosure that could stifle the possibility of new forms of human flourishing, but rather we should see theory as working like a filter, undermining illusory interests and supporting the capability of individuals to lead lives they have reason to lead.

In an excellent interview in *Feminist Economics*, Sen himself best puts his insistence on incompleteness:

> The problem is not with listing important capabilities, but with insisting on one predetermined canonical list of capabilities, chosen by theorists without any general social discussion or public reasoning. To have such a fixed list, emanating entirely from pure theory, is to deny the possibility of fruitful public participation on what should be included and why. I have, of course, discussed various lists of capabilities that would seem to demand attention.... What I am against is the fixing of a cemented list of capabilities, which is absolutely complete (nothing could be added to it) and totally fixed (it could not respond to public reasoning and to the formation of social values). I am a great believer in theory. The theory of evaluation and assessment does, I believe, have the exacting task of pointing to the relevance of what we are free to do and free to be (the capabilities in general), as opposed to the material goods we have and the commodities we can command. But pure theory cannot 'freeze' a list of capabilities for all societies for all time to come, irrespective of what the citizens come to understand and value. That would be not only a denial of the reach of democracy, but also a misunderstanding of what pure theory can do, completely divorced from the particular social reality that any particular society faces. (Sen 2004a: 77–8)

Public reason and its role in democracy, as conceived by Sen, lies at the heart of this book's final two chapters and the book's main conclusion, which mount critiques of Sen's accounts of justice, democracy and public reasoning. For now, it is important and sufficient to note Sen's determination to keep his concern for capabilities an instance of an 'incomplete' theorization and how he links this directly to freedom, the subject of the next chapter.

Conclusion

In this chapter, I have entered more explicitly into the dynamics of what Sen now calls his 'concern for capabilities'. The concern constitutes both a novel conceptual and substantive view of how it could be determined in the context of what it is that individuals have reason to value. Even if his choice of terminology can sometimes feel a little clunky, Sen's focus on a space of public evaluation that he encapsulates via two main notions – functionings and capabilities – constitutes a novel and rich alternative to a series of ideas in economics and political philosophy that have predominated for more than a century: utility (via utilitarianism in general and welfarism in economics), primary goods (Rawls) and resources (Dworkin). Sen's conceptual innovations, especially combined with a subtle view of objectivity and objective illusion and an assertive incompleteness as regards the role of theory in practice, provide an important way around a number of problems with the two main competing philosophical positions in the modern era: utilitarianism and Kantianism.

In particular, Sen moves attention in economics and politics away from goods and means seemingly separated from humans and refocuses it on what goods do for humans, that is, how they enable (or disable) humans to lead the lives they would choose to lead. This provides economics and politics with a more substantive and less truncated view of how to determine what to do in any particular context and in response to a set of existing policies or a set of proposed policies. In particular, Sen provides a conceptual reorientation and a means of evaluating those things that really matter to humans: well-being, agency, quality of life and standard of living. And yet he manages to resist the temptation to lay down a series of substantive goods that always everywhere will, as it were, fill the evaluative spaces. He remains assertively incomplete in his theorizing, particularly as regards laying down a list of valuable functionings and capabilities. This is a great strength, but it does lead him to leave a lot to what he calls the social choice processes of evaluation that would have to be carried out in each and every context, especially given the seemingly idealistic – or, at least, optimistic – view he has of human rationality in democratically determining social choice outcomes. This conceptual advance on utility, primary goods and resources situates freedom at the centre of any capabilities-oriented assessment of that which is valuable. What, then, does Sen mean by freedom?

3

Freedom

There are a number of ways in which freedom is central to the work of Amartya Sen. Right across his many contributions to economics, philosophy and politics, he is driven to defend a nuanced and practical view of freedom. In this chapter, I suggest that, as he himself explicitly articulates in *The Idea of Justice* (*IJ*), the freedom he propounds and defends is best described as 'effective freedom', related to the fact that 'a capability is the power to do something' (*IJ*: 19). It follows that I shall argue that for Sen freedom is 'effective power'. As he puts it, '[t]he question whether a person can bring about the objects of her reasoned choice is crucial to the idea of freedom that is being pursued here ... [It is achieved by means of] direct control ... or "indirect power"... the issue of effective power' (*IJ*: 301–2).

Moreover, as will become clear in this chapter, this view of freedom does not contradict Sen's repeated assertion that '[f]reedom is an irreducibly plural concept' (*RF*: 585; *DF*; *IJ*: 227–30, 301–5). It is this 'plural' view of freedom as effective power that underpins and follows from his concern for capabilities, his alternative and rich account of development, and his thoughts on justice and democracy. Also, though, and of much greater significance than has so far been suggested, this idea of freedom as effective power is closely linked to much of Sen's earlier work on preference and choice. As I shall argue, this is the case because freedom, for Sen, is ultimately about the kind of economic, social and political environment that enables a person's preferences to be effective. In other words, freedom too remains grounded in his first love – social choice – however modified and humanized via a sensibility to the demands of development and capabilities opportunity.

So I begin by looking at the three main ways in which freedom has been understood in the philosophical, political and economic literature. I then move on to how Sen links preference to freedom, particularly via rationality. I then show how, in time, this ends in a clear account of freedom as effective power and how this differs from most mainstream views of freedom. I end with a short account of his analysis of 'indirect power', adding a few slight concerns, which may (or may not) form the basis of criticisms of Sen on freedom. I conclude that, although Sen explicitly positions himself in the 'positive' freedom camp, his thoughts on freedom constitute the basis for a fourth, more comprehensive, account of freedom as power.

Literature

Like most thinkers and writers in English, Sen uses the terms 'liberty' and 'freedom' interchangeably. Pitkin (1988) and Williams (2001) are exceptions to this rule, but the distinctions they draw are so fine that nothing much hangs on them, at least not for an understanding of Sen's view, so I will follow the general trend and use the terms interchangeably.

There have been three main ways of thinking about freedom since the late eighteenth century: negative freedom, positive freedom and republican freedom. These are now terms of art in political theory and philosophy, but a little time spent on them may be helpful in situating Sen's alternative vision.

Defenders of negative freedom argue that to be free is to act unimpeded, to do what one wants or chooses without external obstacle or impediment. Jeremy Bentham and later, most famously, Isaiah Berlin maintained that it is for this reason that it is best to think of freedom as a 'negative' concept: its presence is said to be marked by the absence of something – in particular, an impediment or obstacle that inhibits the agent from doing what she or he wants or chooses (Bentham 1970 [1781]; Berlin 1996 [1969]). This way of thinking has its source in Thomas Hobbes's diligently naturalist and negative concept of freedom, where freedom just means non-obstruction of action, as the water in a canal (or 'Channel') is free when unimpeded (Hobbes 1996 [1651]: 146). This view takes various forms in John Locke, Friedrich Hayek, Robert Nozick and others, but all retain an emphasis on its negative characteristic, and especially among Sen's important philosophical and economic contemporaries, such as John Rawls, Milton Friedman, Nozick and Hillel Steiner, it retains this basic 'negative' structure. As Rawls puts it, 'this or that person (or persons) is free (or not free) from this or that constraint (or set of constraints) to do (or not to do) so and so' (Rawls 1973: 176). In these kinds of liberal and libertarian contractarian thinkers, freedom and unfreedom are understood relative to potential impediments or obstacles created by the actions of others and dependent upon whether these 'others' had a right to act as they did (Nozick 1974: 262; cf. Hamilton 2014a). Any action that imposes an impediment is therefore an instance of coercion, the epitome of unfreedom on this view.

The second important view of freedom is what Berlin calls 'positive' freedom. By contrast to 'negative' freedom – where to be free involves the mere absence of (external) impediments – 'positive' freedom is linked to concepts such as 'self-determination', 'self-realization' or 'autonomy', that is, the conditions or prerequisites for determining, controlling or autonomously deciding how to lead one's life. In Berlin's formulation, this is then linked to authoritarian forms of political power based on a spurious argument: if the values and conditions in question are, more or less, the same for all, and knowledge of them is acquirable by all simply by dint of my knowing what is good for you, I have a warrant to coerce you to be free in this 'positive' sense. However, to get to this extreme point of view, one needs to add the existence of a social agency (a state, say) who is 'the real me' and thus all of whose actions are really mine so that none of its actions against me can even in principle count as coercion. So Berlin has misdiagnosed the basis of the threat of totalitarianism: the culprit is some thesis about the relation between the individual and social agency and not the positive conception of freedom (Geuss 1995, 2001; Hamilton 2014a).[1] This is important, for as we will see Sen, if anything, is closest to the 'positive' view of freedom; and he is relentlessly opposed to allowing room for authoritarian or totalitarian political power, helped by his adherence to social choice and the primacy of preferences and his associated resolute insistence on human diversity.

The third important, countervailing view of freedom is the republican (or neo-Roman) view of freedom, which just over two centuries ago more or less disappeared from the mainstream, effectively being replaced by what we now call 'negative' freedom. It was a view of political freedom which took the condition of slavery to be the antithesis of freedom, that is, a person is unfree in so far as they live in *potestate domini*, in the power of a master. Of late, this third view of freedom has been made famous again, principally in the works of Quentin Skinner and Philip Pettit. In short, to be free, in this sense, is to be an active citizen within a free state, that is, to be an active citizen in the sense that one is not in the power of someone who can interfere on an arbitrary basis – 'without having to be guided by their [the citizen's] readily avowable interests' (Pettit 2001: 18). In other words, citizenship status, and all that goes with it, ensures that the 'rulers', supposedly especially under democratic conditions, cannot arbitrarily interfere in the lives of citizens; the rulers rule by law, not by means of arbitrary diktat or interference.

This republican view of freedom is contrasted with 'negative' freedom as, unlike the latter, 'even if people make choices without interference – even if none of the options available are put beyond their reach – they will be unfree in the making of those choices, according to the republican view, if they have to act in the presence of someone who *could* interfere on an *arbitrary* basis' (Pettit 2001: 18; my emphasis; see also Pettit 1997; Skinner 1997, 2002). Republican freedom requires, therefore, not just the absence of interference but also the absence of a power of arbitrary interference by others: the absence of what Pettit calls domination (cf. Weber 1978; Lovett 2010; Hamilton 2014a). Pettit goes on to suggest that Sen's theory of freedom coincides with a republican approach as it similarly emphasizes the connection between freedom and non-dependency, between freedom and being independent of the will of another.

In what follows, I will contest this interpretation, arguing that the closest his view of freedom as 'effective power' comes to any of the three main alternatives in the literature is 'positive freedom', as Sen himself explicitly suggests in his early forays into the topic of freedom. As early as his famous 1970 work on social choice theory (*CS*) and then in 'Liberty, Unanimity and Rights' (Sen 1976) and 'Rights and Agency' (Sen 1982a), he argues that the 'constraint' view or 'negative' conception of liberty is fundamentally flawed. Then, in 'Liberty as Control: An Appraisal' (Sen 1982b) and in 'Liberty and Social Choice' (Sen 1983a), we see a critique of the 'control' view of freedom and the outlines of a full defence of the 'power' view of freedom. The 'control' view of freedom is the idea that a person is free relative to the degree of control he or she has over decisions in specified spheres, a view he first ascribes to the libertarian thinker Robert Nozick, especially in his famous *Anarchy, State and Utopia* (Nozick 1974), and then later correctly diagnoses in the republican thought of Pettit (Sen 1982b: 207; *IJ*). Sen thinks this view, too, is fundamentally flawed, about which more below. (Thus, although Sen's account of freedom as effective power is first fully formulated in his 1984 Dewey Lectures [WAF: 208–12], and is then succinctly summarized and tweaked in *DF* and *IJ*, it would be wrong to assume that his view on liberty is in some sense a direct outgrowth of his capability approach or is somehow secondary to it, something the chapter ordering of this book might suggest.)

If we combine Sen's later arguments around the idea of freedom as 'effective power', usually by means of 'indirect power', we can see his work helping to open up the possibility of a distinct account, a view of freedom as power. In other words, given modern conditions, our preferences and choices will often, if not normally, be dependent on the will of another (or at least interdependent with the wills of others), as Sen himself suggests, and thus cannot be construed as an account of republican freedom. His view of freedom as effective power is in fact closer to a view of freedom as power, what might be called a fourth conception of power. To see this, we first need to clarify the clear link he makes between choice, rationality and freedom.

Rationality

Sen draws from both 'positive' and 'negative' freedom, although he favours 'positive' freedom as it is more concerned with a power to do something we have reason to value. Even though he argues that 'negative' freedom has a 'basic value of its own' (*CS*; WAF; *RF*: 587), ever so mildly he criticizes Berlin's view of 'positive' freedom as being overly focused on the freedom to achieve in so far as it relates only to influences working within oneself. He prefers to see 'positive' freedom as 'the person's ability to do the things in question taking everything into account (external restraints and internal limitations)' (*RF*: 586; WAF; cf. Hamilton 2014a). 'Negative' freedom under this conception is still important since a violation of it must also be, normally, a violation of 'positive' freedom, but not vice versa. Compare this to Berlin's distinction between negative and positive freedom, where each can be violated without violating the other. So, as Sen notes, this way of seeing 'positive' freedom is not the one preferred by Berlin but is 'closer to the characterization presented by T. H. Green: "We do not mean merely freedom from restraint or compulsion … When we speak of freedom as something to be so highly prized, we mean *a positive power or capacity* of doing or enjoying something worth doing or enjoying"' (Green 1881: 370; italics added by Sen, cited in *RF*: 586–7). This is no surprise. The emphasis in Green on a seemingly objective account of what is 'worth' doing is mirrored in Sen's defence of the value of freedom – freedom is centrally valuable, he claims, as it gives us more opportunity to achieve those things that we value and have reason to value (*DF*; *RF*: 585; *IJ*: 18–19, 227–30, 301–4). Sen therefore mirrors Green as he seems to equate 'the things we value' and the things 'we have reason to value'. Or does he? If so, why?

The short answer to these questions has to do with the fact that Sen views freedom through the lens of social choice theory in general and the priority of reasoned preferences in particular, and this is based on a specific view of rationality. I shall now delve into the dynamics of this, and we shall see the central roles played by preference, reasoned scrutiny and Sen's account of capabilities, clearly evident in his early works and reiterated forcefully and more accessibly in *DF*, *RF* and *IJ*. As I bring these to the fore, and as Sen reiterates in a number of works, I shall show why, unlike liberal and libertarian contractarians, who are most concerned with process, Sen is interested in what he calls the 'process' and 'opportunity' aspects of freedom, partly because these are both important in giving individuals the power to achieve or do the things they choose and partly because, relatedly, he is ultimately concerned with what he calls the 'comprehensive outcome' of an individual's freedoms (*IJ*: 22–3, 215–21, 230). I shall also specify what exactly he means by this distinction and its component parts.

Having reiterated his earlier distinctions with regard to social choice and preferences in general and his criticisms of parts of mainstream economics, in particular the tendency to reduce preferences to what a person would choose to further her interests best,[2] Sen suggests a view of preference that is at once more general and, some might say, more exacting. Sen argues that subtle use of social choice is advantageous for thinking about and assessing freedom because it is concerned with the reasons for preferences. Many thinkers understandably balk at the idea of founding liberty in the crude version of utility so common in economics, that is, based on the assumption that individuals always seek their best interest by maximizing personal well-being or on its counterpart in some areas of moral philosophy, where the term 'preference' is used to indicate the feeling of preference (no matter what lies behind it). The former is too simplistic and the latter too prone to be hijacked by whim and caprice. By contrast, one can, Sen submits, following Kenneth Arrow, view preferences more amply as 'the values of individuals rather than their tastes' (Arrow 1951: 23). These, in Arrow's terms, reflect the entire system of values, including values about values, a person's general standards of equity and socializing desires (Arrow 1951: 18). Sen admits that this framework for representing what a person values may not be 'as apt – and as natural – a use of the word "preference" as some philosophers would like'. It is, he accepts, an 'adaptive' sense that social choice has made common. But, he submits, once the interpretations are 'unambiguously explained', as he puts it, 'there need be no further confusion' (*RF*: 590). As with much of Sen's work, there is a great deal of optimism at play here. Many remain much more sceptical or at least confused.

Indeed, he suggests a further stipulation as regards preferences: 'we can go even further and require reasoned scrutiny as a requirement of a preference ordering to have an important status in the evaluation of freedom' (*RF*: 590). The rationality at play here is what he calls 'the discipline of subjecting one's choices – of actions as well as objectives, value and priorities – to reasoned scrutiny … [R]ationality is seen here … as the need to subject one's choices to the demands of reason' (*RF*: 4). In other words, in the use of preference as the basis of evaluation of the opportunity aspect of freedom, Sen requires that we give a special place to the 'valuational interpretation of preference' and 'the need of compatibility with reasoned scrutiny' (*RF*: 590). While there is little doubt that at least some of our preferences will include values, it is hard to be convinced by the idea that all of them are or ought to be; some may simply be tastes, unscrutinized desires, whim, caprice, and far from complete or coherent preference rankings. What of these and their effects on our other, more scrutinized preferences, even on our preferences regarding our preferences, our second-order preferences? And how would or could they affect our views on freedom? Despite criticizing those thinkers in both the economic and philosophical literature who base their thinking around freedom on too tight or constrained an account of reason or rationality – internal consistency, self-interest, and so on – Sen's focus on 'the demands of reason' is itself a predetermining constraint. Having placed so much emphasis on the role of individual preferences in various measures, does this not *ipso facto* rule out a whole collection of preferences that do not meet the standard of having been through reasoned scrutiny? The answer to that, needless to say, depends on what Sen means by 'reasoned scrutiny'.

'Reasoned scrutiny' returns, ultimately, to Sen's account of capabilities in the context of a basic presupposition within his interpretation of social choice theory: it is possible to 'understand the demands of rational decisions for a society when all members of the society have the freedom to participate, directly or indirectly, in the decisional process, and this involves respect for their voice, influence and rights' (*RF*: 46). Whether he is speaking about 'weights, valuations and social choice' in the context of development (*DF*: 76–9), or the 'plural features of freedom' as part of his discussion of the 'materials of justice' (*IJ*: 312), or his rather optimistic view of 'democracy and public reasoning' (*IJ*: 321–416), he is concerned to stress that the rationality is viewed as a discipline, not as a favoured formula or as an essentialist doctrine. The discipline in question 'includes the use of reasoning to understand and assess goals and values, and it also involves the use of these goals to make systematic choices' (*RF*: 46). He is careful to make clear repeatedly that this does not require the idea that the pursuit of some pre-specified aims must be taken to represent the essence of rationality; and if his constant rebuke of the idea that self-interest is the exclusive navigator of rational behaviour can become a little tiresome, you would be forgiven for giving him a break (as he understandably finds mainstream economic theory's constant emphasis on self-interest extremely bothersome). In fact, he thinks that this emaciated view of rationality subverts the 'self' as a free, reasoning being, mainly because it completely overlooks the 'freedom to reason about what one should pursue' (*RF*: 46). By contrast, Sen is particularly interested in the human capacity for 'self-reasoning'. Citing Nozick (1993) approvingly, Sen suggests that mainstream economics' devotion to self-interest as the basis of rationality 'repudiates the most profound capacity of the human self which distinguishes us, in many different ways, from the rest of the animal kingdom, namely our ability to reason and to undertake reasoned scrutiny' (*RF*: 46). Sen makes it very clear that, on the grounds of rationality as 'reasoned scrutiny', nothing substantive is banished: a person may come to the view that she should actually pursue self-interest, just as she may equally likely come to the view that socially responsive conduct is best (Rawls's 'reasonable' behaviour), but on Sen's account of rationality there is no necessity for either to happen. Moral reasoning may demand something like the latter but, Sen stresses, that is only one kind of reasoning and not the only way of using reason in general (*RF*: 47; Williams 1985).

The need for reasoned scrutiny, Sen argues, applies not only to accommodating moral and political concerns in personal choices and social living but also in incorporating the demands of prudence. All of these involve the experience and understanding of others, but

Sen remains resolutely individualistic when he argues that, ultimately, it is the person – the adult, responsible person – that must learn from others and incorporate the wisdom that may come from elsewhere into her own assessment and scrutiny. In effect, Sen is calling for necessary understanding and sufficient freedom in context for individuals to make the kinds of decisions that are valuable to them.

What is needed is a fuller understanding, in which others could quite possibly help, as to how to make reasoned choices with an incomplete preference or with unresolved conflicts. Seeing rational choice based on reasoned scrutiny has far-reaching implications on decisional complexity precisely because of the extensive reach of reason, which cannot be captured by a priori axioms or by very general admonitions (*RF*: 47–8).

He goes on to note a series of possible problems with this kind of approach to rationality, but he remains convinced that freedom and rationality are interdependent: '[w]e need both rationality and freedom, and they need each other' (*RF*: 52). So, at least as regards his own expression of this relationship between rationality and freedom, reasoned scrutiny is not a predetermining constraint.

Freedom has a dual role in this relationship. Or, to put this as Sen himself does, freedom is valuable for at least two different reasons. He calls them the 'opportunity' and 'process' aspects of freedom. The former is important because 'more freedom gives us more opportunity to achieve those things we value, and have reason to value' (*RF*: 585). Noticeably, in his latest work, he rephrases the end of this definition as follows: 'more freedom gives us more opportunity to pursue our objectives – those things that we value' (*IJ*: 228). This aspect of freedom is concerned with our ability to achieve what we value, rather than with the process through which the achievement comes about. The latter – the process through which things happen – is also an important aspect of freedom. We are also driven by concerns over whether or not we are being forced into some state because of 'constraints imposed by others' (*IJ*: 228). The difference between me freely deciding to stay at home on a Sunday and do nothing (scenario A), as compared to being dragged out and forced to do something (scenario B), as compared again to being commanded not to leave my house that same Sunday (scenario C) is illustrative of the subtle point Sen is making by means of this distinction. It is easy to see that scenario B involves a violation of both the 'opportunity' (opportunities are curtailed) and 'process' aspects of my freedom (I cannot decide for myself what to do). If the basic 'opportunity' aspect of freedom is the only criterion, then there would be no difference between A and C. But Sen wants to go further than simply doffing his cap to versions of both 'negative' and 'republican' views of freedom that are concerned with the 'process' aspect of freedom, respectively viewed in terms of constraint and control.

He suggests that we do not – and ought not – 'judge opportunities ... only by whether or not we end up in the state that we would choose to be in, irrespective of whether or not there are other significant alternatives that we could have chosen if we wanted ...' (*IJ*: 229–30). What about choosing to go for a nice walk that Sunday or changing one's mind, he suggests? He draws, thus, an important distinction between 'the opportunity to choose freely to stay at home rather than the opportunity just to stay at home (and nothing else) ...'. There are therefore differences between scenarios C and A even in terms of opportunities. Sen is proposing a broader definition of the 'opportunity' aspect of freedom than the one he first proposed by drawing parts of the process aspect of freedom into it. He calls this a 'comprehensive outcome' (as opposed to a more simplistic 'culmination outcome'). We thereby, more plausibly, also take into account the way the person reaches the 'culmination situation' (*IJ*: 230). Means matter, as do ends: the 'opportunity' aspect of my freedom is clearly undermined in scenario C by my being ordered to stay at home (I cannot choose anything else). By contrast, in scenario A I retain the opportunity to consider the various alternatives that are feasible and then choose to stay at home. In other words, this more comprehensive view is exactly that – more comprehensive – because it enables us to see how opportunity is, in part, determined by 'the process of choice involved' and the alternatives that could have been chosen within the actual ability to do so (*IJ*: 230).[3] Sen does see this earlier, especially when discussing rationality and freedom. He states unequivocally that the procedure of free decision by someone is an important requirement of freedom (irrespective of how successful the person is in achieving what he would like). For example, under democratic conditions that have been around for some time, competitors in an electoral process may want to win an election fairly rather than just win (*RF*: 585) (though, of course, there is also a lot of evidence to show that, in many contexts, they simply want to win, something Sen conveniently ignores or at least leaves unstated).

In sum, although earlier in his career he discards the 'control' view of freedom (and by extension the republican view of freedom), by recognizing the importance of the 'process' aspect of freedom in assessing a 'comprehensive outcome' view of freedom, he is effectively reintroducing components of the 'control' view of freedom into his account. What explains the subtle readjustment?

The answer to this, of course, is that – in between these periods – Sen has refined his 'concern for capabilities'. Freedom, when understood by means of more specific concepts, such as the capabilities that a person has, must include the opportunity and process aspects in a single comprehensive conception. As has already been discussed, capabilities are a mechanism for judging an individual's advantage. Capability is, at core, about 'real opportunity': 'A person's advantage in terms of opportunities is judged to be lower than that of another if she has less capability – less real opportunity – to achieve those things that she has reason to value' (*IJ*: 231). It is again important to note that at this point Sen is clearer on what he means as regards 'reason to value' than he was in earlier versions, but there are four important components to this. First, the focus here is on the freedom that a person actually has to do this or be that; second, these are things 'that he or she may value doing or being'; third, the things we value most are particularly important for us to be able to achieve; and, fourth, the idea of freedom at work here focuses on the fact that the very idea of freedom 'respects our being free to determine what we want, what we value and ultimately what we decide to choose' (*IJ*: 231–2).

Sen's concept of capability is therefore not only linked closely with the 'opportunity' aspect of freedom but also needs to be seen in terms of 'comprehensive' opportunities, the evaluation of which has to draw in the procedures – or processes – of the choices involved. In other words, having been so critical of 'control' accounts of freedom earlier in his work for their exclusive obsession with procedure, he now seems to be rowing back a little and drawing at least parts of these views into his broader view of freedom. Sen brings out the importance of capabilities as a necessarily incomplete 'informational focus' here, as discussed in chapter 2 and something to which we will return in chapter 4, as well as the fact that it is concerned with a plurality of different features of our lives and concerns. He also warns against the fact that, given that it is all too easy to speak about individual capabilities, that which is really at stake is a combination of functionings that we can 'compare and judge against each other in terms of what we have reason to value' (*IJ*: 233). This too will be discussed at much greater length in chapters 4 and 5, but it is noted here in order to point out the intersubjective nature of both the 'informational focus' – capabilities – of freedom and Sen's very view of freedom. As the informational basis for coming to a 'comprehensive' view of an individual's freedom, the focus is on 'human life' in its entirety, not just some detached objects of convenience, such as incomes, commodities or primary goods; in other words, rather than focusing on the means of living, it focuses on the actual opportunities of living or 'the opportunity to fulfil ends and the substantive freedom to achieve these reasoned ends' (*IJ*: 234). In much more simple terms, Sen is interested in what might be called the formation of the human capability for freedom. Central to this, at least for Sen, is that if we move beyond achievements – simply conceived – to opportunities more comprehensively conceived, we will quickly see that the processes or procedures through which we make choices, and choices about choices, must also be seen to be central. Needless to say, that does not make Sen revert to a view of freedom based on 'control' alone or a view of freedom anything like as confined as Berlin's 'negative' conception.

Of course, the grounds for this subtle rearticulation of his views has its base in the substance of his capability approach as originally articulated, particularly as regards well-being, agency and freedom and the role of choice therein (as also discussed in chapter 2). The basic notion in Sen's capability approach is a person's functionings, 'which represent ... in particular the various things that he or she manages to do or be in leading a life' (CW: 31). An assessment of well-being must take the form of an evaluation of these elements (*IR*: 39). Moreover, the capability of a person 'reflects the alternative combinations of functionings the person can achieve, and from which he or she can choose one collection' (CW: 31). In other words, the capability to function comprises the various combinations of functionings that reflect the person's freedom to lead one type of life or another; that is, it reflects the person's ability (that includes her living conditions) to choose from possible lives. The capability set is the 'primary informational base' because there are four conceptual categories in the capability set which are all valuable for quality of life but are not functionings per se (CW: 38). They are: well-being achievement; well-being freedom; agency achievement; and agency freedom (WAF: 202; *OEE*: 60ff). Unlike some approaches that see the person as being able to have an adequate well-being achievement without having had much freedom of choice, Sen maintains that there is more to an assessment of well-being, and especially the broader quality of life, than the achievement of well-being. (As noted in chapter 2, this does not negate the importance of an external point of view that can clarify whether a person has basically everything she requires for her well-being, even though she might not have been involved herself in decisions over what her well-being entails.)

Sen places much importance on the ability to achieve well-being and the freedom to choose between different lives that lead to well-being. Furthermore, he stresses the fact that often we have goals and aspirations that are important for our sense of agency but have little or nothing to do with our personal well-being, as in the example I used in chapter 2 of the English woman who chooses to live in Africa as she is devoted to the cause of helping Africa's fight against malaria. An evaluation of a person's well-being, according to Sen, does require an evaluation of her functionings (well-being achievement), but a life worth living must incorporate more than well-being; it must *also* take into account agent-centred evaluation – self-evaluation – *and* the freedom to achieve valued functionings. As has already been discussed in chapter 2, this also explains Sen's replies to Cohen's criticisms of the 'athleticism' of his capability approach.

Sen's argument is that 'doing X' is distinct from 'choosing to do X and doing it', and the latter is, and ought to be, more highly valued (*IR*: 52). The centrality of choice and freedom of choice is obvious. Freedom is not being seen in the 'negative' way in which it is often represented, as principles of rights and non-interference, but rather the 'issue is the positive ability to choose', which is constitutive of the 'good life': 'the "good life" is partly a life of genuine choice, and not one in which the person is forced into a particular life – however rich it might be in other respects' (*CC*: 69–70; cf. *IR*: 52; *SL*: 36). Sen incorporates well-being freedom into well-being assessments, and makes room for action, choice and agency, at the level of both well-being achievement and agency achievement. In more accessible terms, the focus of the capability approach as the basis for Sen's view of freedom is thus 'not just on what a person actually ends up doing, but also on what she is in fact able to do, whether or not she chooses to make use of that opportunity' (*IJ*: 235). In other words, having begun this journey ultimately concerned with 'equality', Sen clearly ends by giving greater emphasis to 'freedom', though in his original 'Equality of What?' (EW) essay we already see the clear emphasis on agency, choice and freedom.

In slightly different terms, this is reinforced when Sen argues that an increase in choice per se is part and parcel of both the 'opportunity' aspect and the 'process' aspect of freedom, but he ultimately returns to an abstract account of objective goodness in terms of capability (founded in freedom). I think this is brought out best by two important distinctions he makes as regards choices and his points about the importance of multiple preference rankings, counterfactual reasoning and meta-rankings. Sen positively defends the importance of accommodating counterfactual opportunities, which help to assess whether the person in question would or would not have made certain choices, given different conditions and knowledge, understanding of which is important in an analysis of the relative freedom of the choice actually made (WAF; cf. CC). The two distinctions that point to the objectivity at work here come out in Sen's discussion of the use of the question 'What would you choose given the choice over X and Y?'. The first important distinction he constantly refers to is that between fasting and starving. They are distinct exactly because one (fasting) involves a choice and the other (starving) does not, despite the fact that their well-being achievements might be the same. The second distinction highlights the fact that a simple increase in choice is not the answer. The nature of the actual options is also important; a set of three choices that the person values as 'bad', 'worse' and 'terrible' is not the same as a set whose options are valued as 'good', 'great', or 'superb' (SL: 36). So, obviously, the substance of the choice options matters, and this is partly why he introduces two clauses to the definition as regards the centrality of preference for freedom – things that we value and things that we have reason to value. The importance of counterfactuals in this process of reasoned scrutiny around well-being, agency and freedom is therefore vital as it is helpful to posit alternative, imagined states of affairs as regards well-being and agency in which a person may have had a different set of choices. So, contrary to what Cohen suggests, Sen's view does not necessarily require actual action in the form of choice; counterfactual consideration is sufficient – or, to put it somewhat differently, it is a necessary condition for reasoned scrutiny and thus also rationality. But then Sen assumes we do this as a matter of course.

My reference to 'objective goodness' in the preceding paragraph may have been too hasty. However abstract the substantive content of Sen's account of capabilities – the ability to meet one's nutritional requirements, the wherewithal to be clothed and sheltered, the ability to move about, the power to participate in the social life of the community, and so on (EW: 218) – this dependence on 'objective goodness' is contested directly by Sen. In his discussions of freedom, rationality and social choice, he is at pains to stress that what is at stake here is not a criterion of 'objective goodness' but rather a 'multiplicity of preferences' based on a 'multiplicity of reasons'. In other words, he is determined to remain open, incomplete and pluralist in his account of rationality and freedom. As he puts it,

> Multiple preferences are particularly important to invoke in understanding the role of freedom, since part of the freedom an individual enjoys is to entertain different preference rankings ... [and] to acknowledge the possibility that a person may have multiple lines of reasoning which would lead to different preference rankings would not, in themselves, indicate what kinds of reasons these are, and what their epistemological status might be. The important issue here is multiplicity of reasons, rather than multiplicity of reasons that are parasitic on the idea of 'objective goodness'. (*RF*: 615–16; cf. WAF)

This is in response to Robert Sugden's interpretation and criticism of Sen's earlier attempt to capture the idea of multiplicity of preferences among concerns that focus on 'the freedoms' that an individual enjoys 'to choose lives that they have reason to value' (*IR*: 81) in terms of an individual's range of different preference rankings, 'each of which corresponds with a different but equally valid conception of her good', an idea that poses a problem for 'those who are sceptical about the existence of objective goodness – even if of the pluralist kind' (Sugden 1998: 325).

This criticism clearly lands a blow, and Sen has not helped his own cause by making constant reference to the idea of a person's freedom being closely tied up with the capabilities, choices and lives 'that they have reason to value'. It seems this is intentionally ambiguous as to who is to determine that they have reason to value the choices, capabilities and lives, and the reason for this is the inherently intersubjective – and thus contextual – nature of an analysis of capabilities and freedom. Sen is determined to keep his theoretical structure incomplete, not simply because he is averse to imposing and cajoling others to live certain kinds of lives but also because he is sensitive to the fact that freedom is dependent both on various objective conditions being met and on the views and values of the individuals in question and that all of this 'material' must be assessed in context. This contextual assessment is important as without it 'the assessors' may miss out on information necessary to determine the state of the conditions in context and the freedoms, choices and kinds of lives that the individuals in the context in question would like to lead. It is for this reason that Sen obstinately requires both subjective and objective input into the determination of freedom and capabilities and lays so much emphasis on counterfactual reasoning: both will provide vital information as regards the kinds of lives being led in the context in question and the kinds of lives and freedoms these conditions enable in the minds of the individuals concerned. Human imagination knows no bounds, but intersubjective assessment based on comparison of actually existing conditions in different places and on the counterfactual reasoning this may engender is a *sine qua non* of the desire to provide greater and better freedom as opportunity and process. As Sen puts it, 'the relevance of counterfactual choice also turns out to be quite crucial for understanding the content of freedom' (*RF*: 658).

In context, the freedom to choose the sets of things that will enhance well-being and the life prospects of individuals is a necessary component of determining their content and how best to meet them. In other words, freedom is necessary in the determination and response to actually existing well-being. Moreover, freedom is not just instrumentally helpful in this sense; it is also intrinsically good in that it is part and parcel of human agency. The difference between well-being freedom and agency freedom is brought out very well in Sen's own words.

> Well-being freedom is freedom of a rather particular type. It concentrates on a person's capability to have various functioning vectors and to enjoy the corresponding well-being achievements. This concept of freedom, based on the well-being aspect of a person, has to be clearly distinguished from a broader concept of freedom, related to the agency aspect of a person. A person's 'agency freedom' refers to what the person is free to do and achieve in pursuit of whatever goals or values he or she regards as important. A person's agency aspect cannot be understood without taking note of his or her aims, objectives, allegiances, obligations, and – in a broad sense – the person's conception of the good. Whereas well-being freedom is freedom to achieve something in particular, viz., well-being, the idea of agency freedom is more general, since it is not tied to any one type of aim. Agency freedom is freedom to achieve whatever the person, as a responsible agent, decides he or she should achieve. That open conditionality makes the nature of agency freedom quite different from that of well-being freedom, which concentrates on a particular type of objective and judges opportunities correspondingly. (WAF: 203–4)

He suggests directly after this that the 'agency freedom' he is discussing here has 'claims to be taken as freedom *tout court*' (WAF: 204, fn. 1). This is in contrast to well-being freedom, which clearly does not. It must also follow from this comment that 'agency freedom' must incorporate well-being freedom, as Sen himself notes a little later (WAF: 206). This is corroborated by the fact that he argues at a number of points that the evaluation of a person's well-being does require an evaluation of her functionings (well-being achievement), but a life worth living must incorporate more than well-being. It must also take into account agent-centred evaluation – self-evaluation – and the freedom to achieve valued functionings, as well as the freedom to carry out this agent-centred evaluation. Yet, even though agency freedom is broader than well-being freedom, the former does not subsume the latter. Sen provides an important instance of counterfactual reasoning that illustrates well the relationship and distinctness of the two kinds of freedom. You are eating a sandwich for lunch beside a river, and hundreds of miles away someone is drowning in a river. Imagine he is drowning in front of you and you take it to be an important part of your agency freedom that, if you can, you discard your sandwich and save him. In this instance, your agency freedom has gone up at the expense of your well-being freedom; in line with the choice driven by your agency freedom, you have endangered yourself and replaced your lazy lunch with no sandwich and a stressful dive into an icy cold river. In other words, an increase in agency freedom does not always mean an increase in well-being freedom; sometimes the opposite may be the case. As Sen puts it, 'the ranking of alternative opportunities from the point of view of agency need not be the same as the ranking in terms of well-being, and thus the judgments of agency freedom and well-being freedom can move in contrary directions' (WAF: 207).

Moreover, directly after the above-quoted long passage, Sen goes on to argue that this 'open conditionality' does not imply that a person's view of his agency has no need for discipline, and that anything that appeals to him must come into his accounting of his agency freedom. On the contrary, the careful assessment of aims, objectives, allegiances and so on will normally be 'important and exacting'. However, despite this need for discipline, the agency aspect is, importantly, a matter for oneself to judge – the person is seen as the 'doer and judge' – by contrast with the well-being aspect, where the individual is seen as 'a beneficiary whose interests and advantages have to be considered' (WAF: 204, 208). Sen here is trying to show that we take account of one another not simply as entities with a basic level of well-being but also because this rests on a view that, as adult persons, we account for one another as responsible agents. Yet he is also reiterating that, while these two aspects of freedom are quite distinct from each other, they are not independent of one another: a person's agency may affect her well-being; and being well may help a person's ability to act in pursuit of other objectives.

Power

It now becomes possible to see why and how Sen defends an account of freedom as effective power. As will now be clear from the preceding section, for Sen, what matters in assessments of liberty are often counterfactual considerations of what someone would have chosen had the conditions been different and so on. Sen points out convincingly that, when thinking about freedom in these terms, we cannot rely on the 'control' view; we can only rely on the 'power' view. This is because in being guided by a preference – what someone would have chosen – we acknowledge that the person should have power over the decision, even if he does not happen to have control over it (Sen 1982b: 216). Sen argues that this is described best by reference to the idea of 'indirect liberty', which allows us to make judgements about how best to proceed based on an assessment of what someone would have chosen, that is, the use of counterfactual reasoning. Sen is enough of a realist to see how important this is. As he puts it:

> Society cannot typically be so organized that each person himself or herself commands all the levers of control over his or her personal life. The policeman helps my liberty in stopping mugging – presuming of course that I would choose not to be mugged if I had the choice – rather than giving me the control over whether to be mugged or not. Outcomes are also relevant for liberty, and not just the procedures of control. (Sen 1982b: 216; see also Sen 1983b)

As Sen reiterates in his 1984 Dewey Lectures, what matters is that in modern society many powers are indirectly exercised and, in this context, concentration on the levers of control skews our view of freedom (WAF: 209). Like many others, but in contrast to liberals and libertarians who defend 'constraint'/'negative' and 'control' views of freedom, Sen suggests it is obvious that, under modern conditions, we would best assess liberty in terms of power, that is, 'the power to achieve chosen results: whether the person is free to achieve one outcome or another; whether his or her choices will be respected and the corresponding things will happen'. Even at this relatively early stage, Sen calls this freedom 'effective power, or power (for short)', and notes that it 'is not really concerned with the mechanism and procedures of control'. He suggests that it does not matter for effective power precisely how the choices are 'executed'; indeed, often, the choice may not even be directly addressed. 'Effective power can take note of counterfactual choice: things might be done because of knowledge of what the person would choose if he actually had control over the outcome' (WAF: 208–9).

He returns again here to his mugging example, noted in the quote above, suggesting that under modern conditions this kind of situation is much closer to the norm than anything that defenders of freedom as control suggest. If we want the freedom not to be mugged and to move around the streets at liberty, we are concerned, he suggests, with effective power. Precisely who exercises the control may be less important than the ability to achieve what we would have chosen. If the streets are cleared of muggers because we would have chosen not to be mugged, 'our freedom is being well served, even though we have not been given control over the choice of whether to be mugged or not' (WAF: 210). He might have added – but he did not – that, like the matter of public policing (as opposed to private gun-toting), there are many collective-action situations where it is in fact much more efficient (in terms of achieving what we would have chosen, that is, having effective power) if we do not individually have direct control over the decision and action. His point is very well made, but it is at the very least odd that he does not take the next step, especially given the fact that he goes on to note the socially interdependent nature of a lot of these matters.

As I have argued elsewhere, despite the fact that Sen is a relative outlier in his time, there is nothing crazy about the idea of freedom as power. When I say 'I am free', normally I am not saying, 'I am externally unimpeded', 'I am self-determining' or 'I am directly in control of a procedure'. What I usually mean is 'I am free to do X' which concretely means 'I have the power or ability to do X'. It follows that it is more helpful to conceive of freedom as a combination of my ability to determine what I will do and my power to do it or bring it about, which is exactly what Sen proposes via his account of freedom of choice coupled with his view of capabilities (Hamilton 2014a).

Moreover, freedom as power in this sense chimes with most of the struggles for freedom across the ages: the revolutions that brought about the democracies of ancient Athens (Cartledge 2016); the sharp distinction between freedom and slavery in Antiquity; subsequent slave revolts like the Haitian Revolution and later liberation struggles against colonialism, apartheid and domination; and the everyday attempts to gain more independence and freedom from the church, the community, the law, poverty and so on. Frantz Fanon and Amilcar Cabral both argue, for example, that the human condition is to be free and that freedom resides in the capacity to choose and to act (Cabral 1974; Fanon 2008: 280). And it is no accident that democracy in its various forms emerged in combination with revolution, or at least resistance. In the fifth century BCE, the 1640s, 1776, 1791, 1989 and 2011, 'revolution inspired the creation of democratic ideas and radically enlarged the circle of political participants' (Wolin 1982, 1994: 17).

And, despite Sen's sense of being alone, it turns out, moreover, that thinking about freedom as about both being able to determine what one will do and having the power to do what one decides to do is more common in the western intellectual tradition than is normally supposed. It is a mainstay of much of Antiquity. As Titus Livy put it, 'freedom is to be in one's own power' (Livy 2005: Bk. XXXV, ch. 32, 11). See, too, the associations found in the following diverse array of modern thinkers: Thomas Hobbes, Jean-Jacques Rousseau, Edmund Burke and John Stuart Mill (Hobbes 1996 [1651]; Rousseau 1997 [1762]; Burke 2004 [1790]; Mill 2008 [1859]). It is in the work of Karl Marx that we see an unequivocal identification of freedom with power. He distinguishes three conceptions of liberty, the first two roughly akin to Berlin's 'negative' and 'positive' liberty and a third, 'materialist' conception, in which freedom comprises 'the conjunction of the ability to determine what one will do and the power to do what one decides to do'; and he goes on to argue that anything less than this is a mere shadow of the concept of freedom (Marx and Engels 1976 [1867]; Geuss 2010, 2017; Roberts 2016). This means that for Marx the other two concepts he discusses, and a fortiori the main three conceptions analysed in the modern literature, are poor approximations of this real form of freedom. In other words, all of these thinkers, even those that Berlin lauds as standard-bearers for his 'negative' conception of freedom, are ultimately concerned with whether or not someone is able to exercise his or her power to act, that is, to bring something about, to do something.

As Joshua Cohen notes in his pithy review of *IR*, Sen's view of effective freedom rejects two common views on equality. The first is the idea that people ought to be provided with equal means for pursuing their disparate aims. The second requires the distribution of resources to ensure that everyone gets equally good results, equally good lives. Sen rejects both of these, arguing that people ought to face equally desirable life prospects (cf. *IJ*: 295–8). Given the diversity of abilities and conditions, equally desirable life prospects will require unequal means (Cohen 1995: 275). His approach promises this by being much more sensitive than the existing alternatives to the diversity of abilities and conditions. This is due to the fact that it focuses on the effective freedom of individuals and a different informational base to enable this more comprehensive view of freedom: the capability – or power – to choose to do something (*IJ*: 19).

Despite Pettit's attempts to argue otherwise (2001) and Sen's richly accommodating 'plural' view of freedom, which sees freedom as being made up of several distinct features, 'focusing respectively on capability, lack of dependence and lack of interference' (*IJ*: 309), it is clear that his view is both a more comprehensive and more distinct account of freedom. While he sees that lack of interference (the 'negative' conception) and lack of dependence (the 'republican' conception) may come into play at various points, he distinguishes his account carefully from these other two competitors. It is up for debate whether that makes his account equivalent to a 'positive' conception of freedom. I would suggest, though, that it is an example of a view of freedom as power. In distinguishing himself from the republican view, Sen is very clear that the latter fails to capture a central component of life under modern conditions: the interdependence of our lives provides many examples of persons having the freedom as power to do or achieve things in an indirect fashion, often by the 'favour of others' or as a consequence of being dependent on social policy. These situations are not instances of people having direct control over some action, free from interference and dependence, and yet they are examples of a person really being 'able to do the things that she would choose to do and has reason to choose to do'. For example, individual parents may not be able to set up their own school for their children, and may be dependent on public policy, which may be determined by a number of factors and influences, such as national and local politics, but we would therefore not say they were not free to have their children educated. As Sen puts it, 'yet the establishment of a school in that region can be sensibly seen as increasing the freedom of the children to be educated' (*IJ*: 307). In his characteristically capacious way, he draws in the competing theories, suggesting there is room for more than just one conception of freedom, but the combination of his view of freedom as effective power and his emphasis on interdependence and indirect power mark his account of freedom out as quite distinct from the three other prevailing views.

In sum, the best way to see how the various component parts of the capability approach fit into his view of freedom is to recall a distinction he repeats again and again. I provide one example: 'While the combination of a person's functionings reflects her actual achievements, the capability set represents the freedom to achieve: the alternative functioning combinations from which this person can choose' (*DF*: 75). As I noted at the start of this chapter, this is an argument for freedom as 'effective power', as Sen notes specifically at various points in *IJ* (*IJ*: 19, 205, 271, 301–2). Drawing on Gautama Buddha's analysis of obligations which emerge out of the effectiveness of one's ability and power, among other analyses in different places and times, Sen then links this view of freedom in general, and agency freedom in particular, to a central means of understanding our obligations. In other words, due to this view of freedom as power, he can link it directly to questions of justice in terms of opportunity and advantage, with an emphasis on consequential reasoning, as well as the demands of duty that emanate from the ability and power to carry out choices, with an emphasis on deontological demands. Fleshing out these and other moves is the concern of chapter 4.

Conclusion

In this chapter, I have contextualized Sen's account of freedom within the three main competing, dominant accounts of freedom: negative, positive and republican freedom. I have, again, emphasized the central role played by choice. In fact, in relation to how he constructs his view of freedom, what we see is an account of effective choice, or the power to make and scrutinize the whole range of choices that make up a human's life. That humans have these choices and the power to bring them about and to provide and assess the reasons for having them are central to his view of freedom as effective power. In sum, I suggested that, while Sen positions himself closest to a positive view of freedom, when viewed over the last half-century or so, we see the development of, at the very least, the basis of a fourth conception of freedom, what I have called 'freedom as power' (Hamilton 2014a). The resultant position is important as he spends some time rejecting the tendency in Pettit, for example, to incorporate Sen's advances in analysing freedom within a republican account of freedom as non-domination, particularly the idea that non-freedom is always defined by being under the control of another agent. Sen argues astutely that, given the complexity and interdependence of human life within and between modern polities and economies, it is more helpful to conceive of freedom as power, even if that power may only be indirectly under the control of the agent in question or may not even be under their control at all. This is an important insight for the realities of modern democracies that, as we will see in chapter 5, Sen does not seem to fully realize.

In other words, in this chapter I have provided a positive assessment of Sen's view of freedom as effective power. There are, though, two possible lines of critique of Sen's account of freedom. I can merely point to them in the context of this introductory book. You can judge for yourself whether they may or may not merit further work.

The first line of criticism is that Sen does not think very hard about how freedom will play out in the world of politics where power and representation are central. Sen avoids the most important political question around the relationship between power, politics and the formation of agents' capabilities for freedom: the capacities (the powers) to determine what is deemed feasible. This is both the power to set the political agenda and to determine what is deemed a preference at all. This second point is taken up below, but it is – in general terms and despite Sen's insightful moves as regards the formation and effects of preferences – a weakness with Sen's emphasis on choice as central to freedom. Taking the former, for now I can only assert that, without a concomitant framework for dealing with how existing power relations secrete around themselves justifying practices, institutions and forms of rationality, it becomes difficult to see how Sen's contextually bound 'concern for capabilities' can provide critical tools for assessing these power relations. More specifically, which forms of political and economic representation would have to be under constant scrutiny for individual agents to retain the freedom as power that Sen defends? *Sans* an institutional analysis of power relations, it is difficult to see how Sen's account of freedom as effective power can address this question (cf. Hamilton 2014a, 2014b). The answer as to why his account of freedom – at least as it stands – cannot address this question may lie in the fact that he retains an essentially liberal view of freedom in the sense that it is, at base, what I have called a 'private' view of freedom, that is, a view that aligns with a long history of freedom that is interested in delineating a private sphere of effective choice free from the coercive force of the state and its associated institutions (Hamilton 2014a: ch. 1). As he puts it himself, freedom is 'the power that the person has over decisions in certain personal spheres, e.g. in the conduct of his or her personal life' (Sen 1983a: 207).

A second line of criticism runs as follows. Although Sen places a great deal of emphasis on the normal preferences, and the normal reasons individuals might have for holding them, he also places a lot of emphasis on discipline, the preferences individuals might have about their preferences, meta-rankings of preferences and the role of what he calls 'preference revision'. At one point, he approvingly cites Tibor Scitovsky's famous study, *The Joyless Economy* (Scitovsky 1976), reminding his readers of the important distinction made there between a person's actual desires and what would be her 'scrutinized' desires. This, he suggests, points to the volitional possibility of changing one's preferences, which he suggests is particularly important in the analysis of 'cultural freedom' and 'the role of cultivation in being able to enjoy music and the fine arts'. To support the point, he refers to John Stuart Mill's famous championing of 'higher' over 'lower' pleasures and argues that the 'scrutiny and cultivation of preferences – and the freedom to be able to do that (whether or not one actually does) – can be quite relevant to the assessment of a person's overall opportunities' (*RF*: 618).

Is this the kind of thing Sen has in mind when he refers to 'reasoned scrutiny' and, by extension, 'things we have reason to value'? If so, does he not assume, as does Mill, that we can come to agreement about these 'higher' pleasures, that is, that reason will take us all in the same – the right, rational – direction? Is this not too much of an assumption, given the plurality of human life he points to over and over again? Furthermore, citing Mill to support this position may not turn out as felicitous as Sen assumes. Many have argued convincingly that what Mill is doing here is introducing an aesthetic distinction under the guise of a supposed agreement around a set of pleasures. But can he assume there is this agreement?

Also, in suggesting confidently that it was better to be Socrates dissatisfied than a pig satisfied: how did Mill know? Can he simply assume that, unlike the higher pleasures of the human, the pig is satisfied with the 'lower' pleasures of contented eating and wallowing? In the original quote, he provides the answer, the last part of which has inspired and worried philosophers ever since, including Sen: 'It is better to be a human dissatisfied than a pig satisfied; better to be Socrates dissatisfied than a fool satisfied. And if the fool, or the pig, is of a different opinion, it is only because they only know their own side of the question' (cited, with further discussion, in Geuss 2017: 13). 'Mill asserts very firmly that if one is dealing with a disagreement of this kind about the relative merits of two states, one should disqualify the opinion of a judge who has direct experience of only one of the states in question, in favour of the judgement of someone who has direct experience of both' (Geuss 2017: 15). This brings us neatly to the question of justice in Sen: as we shall see, like Mill, but via Smith, he also wants to find a means of deciding between what kinds of judgements are best for justice. The answer, in his case, is rational judgements based on the views of an impartial spectator.

4

Justice

Today, most political theorists and philosophers view justice as the central concept or concern in politics. More exactly, it has come to be assumed that a particular form of justice – distributive justice – is the central question. Amartya Sen is no different.

Moreover, Sen takes freedom to lie at the heart of justice. In line with his concern for capabilities and his view of freedom, he suggests that justice is to a great extent about enabling people to develop and fulfil their own capabilities. In other words, as with many of his other substantial and novel contributions in economics, politics and philosophy, he resists the idea that there is a fixed list of human goods, purposes or virtues. He proposes, rather, an open-ended account of justice that makes room for individuals' own sense of their priorities and purposes both at the level of the structure of a theory of justice and as regards the materials of justice.

As regards the former – how best to approach the problem of justice – he takes issue with one of his teachers and colleagues he admires most: John Rawls. He posits that Rawls's theory of justice is an example of a transcendental theory of justice concerned ultimately with the institutions of an ideally just society, and what he submits in contrast is a comparative theory of justice that, first and foremost, is set up to deal with existing instances of injustice. In his own words, what he proposes is a theory of justice 'in a very broad sense'. Its aim, he says right at the outset, 'is to clarify how we can proceed to address questions of enhancing justice and removing injustice, rather than to offer resolutions of questions about the nature of perfect justice' (*IJ*: ix). He thinks that much can be drawn from social choice theory to achieve this end and that his distinct account of justice is more practicable than the approach adopted by Rawls and company. It is more practical and helpful as it does not require agreement on what he calls the 'transcendental' institutional questions of perfect justice and some associated meta-ethical concerns, in order to tackle particular instances of injustice in the world: obstacles to capability development; instances of deprivation; and so on.

Moreover, as has also been argued by, among others, Michael Sandel (1982, 2009), Charles Taylor (1985), Michael Walzer (1983) and Bernard Williams (1985), a plural approach to justice is necessary to capture 'valuational plurality' or the fact that '[r]easonable arguments in competing directions can emanate from people with diverse experiences and traditions' and they can even come from 'within a given society, or for that matter, even from the very same person'. And yet it is important not to stop there. Sen suggests that reasoned argument and scrutiny is vital in dealing with these conflicting claims, not necessarily to resolve them once and for all but to provide a means of imparting impartial scrutiny and critical examination to avoid lazy resolutions such as 'disengaged toleration' or unexamined relativism. Though he is resolutely clear that the result of this application of reason may not resolve conflict over competing priorities and so on, he argues that this does not compromise the importance of impartial scrutinizing reason: '[t]he plurality with which we will then end up will be the result of reasoning, not of abstention from it' (*IJ*: x).

As regards the latter, the materials of justice, he resists appeals to externally identified 'interests' that might trump an agent's purposes and priorities or, in other words, her wants (her preferences and preferences about preferences) (*IJ*: 376–9), while at the same time reiterating the inadequacy of preference-satisfaction as a moral yardstick. As has already been discussed at length, the yardstick is the means for more and more people to have the freedom and wherewithal to achieve their best potential, best captured, he proposes, by means of the freedom as power to achieve valued capabilities. The theory of justice he proposes is all about identifying obstacles to this eminently humane vision and by means of its component parts pointing the way to their removal.

In what follows, I briefly introduce various approaches to justice, ending with Rawls's theory. I then go on to show how Sen's view differs from Rawls's (and other accounts) of justice, especially as regards the extent to which it can in fact deal with instances of injustice. Thereafter, I analyse what it means to posit a comparative view of justice and the role that impartiality plays in Sen's idea of justice. I end with a couple of important criticisms of Sen's view of justice, particularly as regards the nature and role of impartiality within his alternative vision of how best to overcome injustice.

Distribution

There are at least four distinct notions of justice that concern moral and political philosophers, social justice activists and ordinary citizens. First, 'just' designates that which accords with existing legal codes. Second, 'just' accords with what we – which 'we'? – think ought to be the enforced legal code. Third, 'justice' is used to refer to 'all the human excellences together', as Aristotle (1980: 1129b–30a) argued – what he called 'universal justice'. 'Just' here in this third notion refers in a rather indeterminate way to that which is 'socially excellent, desirable, and so on' (Geuss 2014: 157). It is important not to confuse this third sense with the second sense as there might well be things we think are socially desirable that we also think cannot be formulated in a legal code. Take, for example, gratitude: it is precisely an important part of the value of gratitude that it is exhibited and linked to those from whom I might receive benefits without it being legally required or associated with sanction (Geuss 2014: 157; cf. Robeyns 2017: 148). Fourth, there is a conception of justice that focuses on questions of distribution. Although there has been theoretical disagreement about what should be distributed – goods, welfare, opportunity, possibilities of agency, rights and so on – and about whether the principles of distribution should be some version of equality (goods distributed equally to each) or proportionality (goods distributed according to a person's perceived merit or contribution), over the last half-century there has been considerable consensus around the idea that the theoretical study of politics is (or at least ought to be) about the realization of the ideal of distributive justice. At the end of this chapter I assess whether this recent myopic view of justice is a good or bad thing. The important thing to note for now is that it is out of this tradition that Sen's views on justice emerge; and also, as we shall see, the extent of his critique of the fountainhead of this tradition – the work of John Rawls – does not necessarily mean he escapes some of the problems associated with it.

More exactly, there are two main versions of this last view of justice – the view that reduces justice to questions of distributive justice – and they are both avowedly liberal: 'justice as mutual advantage' and 'egalitarian justice' (Robeyns 2017: 149). Their liberalism is based in a strict recognition of the diversity of views of the good life, which a just society should respect by concentrating on the means to enable individuals unimpeded choice as regards the leading of their diverse conceptions of the good (or good life). In essence, this constitutes a view of state power: for these (and similar) thinkers, the question is not so much who should rule but rather the extent of state power, that is, from which spheres of life should state power be excluded (Geuss 2001). It is partly as a result of this that the two main representatives of these liberal theories of distributive justice – Rawls and Dworkin – posit a highly constrained view of justice. The core of Rawls's view is the fair distribution of benefits of social cooperation, that is, that the rules of justice he proposes (or that would emerge as part of a specified kind of contract) would ultimately be more beneficial to everyone than if they were to pursue their own advantage by themselves (Rawls 1973). The premise of Dworkin's view is the idea that people should be treated with equal respect and concern (Dworkin 2000). The basic main claim of both theories is that each person should be treated as being of equal moral worth (Robeyns 2017: 150). This chimes well with Sen's critique of utilitarianism, which shows convincingly how utilitarianism does not hold to this strict dictum. But then this basic claim is true of a wide range of theories of distributive justice, as is the fact that they are all concerned with the equality of something (as Sen famously argued so succinctly in EW). The main difference between them arises around the idea of what kind of equality of opportunity they defend – entitlement (Nozick 1974), primary goods (Rawls 1973), resources (Dworkin 2000) and so on (for other, related kinds of equality, see Barry 1995; Van Parijs 1995). Very few in this tradition defend the idea of equality of outcome in material terms, given that people have different needs, circumstances and capacities to make use of opportunities. Even from very early on in his career, Sen was most concerned with liberal egalitarian theories of justice, in particular the version proposed by John Rawls.

First fully articulated in his famous *A Theory of Justice*, but refined many times over since, Rawls argues that the health and stability of a modern democracy depends on the justice of its 'basic structure', and thus that the 'basic structure' of society is the primary subject of a theory of justice (Rawls 1973: 7; 1993: 257–89). The foundation for this institutionally ideal approach is a set of 'principles of justice' that will emerge with unanimous agreement in the 'original position', where all, it is supposed, do not know their status, power or wealth in the society about which they are deliberating. The two principles are as follows: (1) lexical priority for all having a right to a 'scheme of equal basic liberties' compatible with a 'similar scheme of liberties for all'; and (2) social and economic inequalities are to satisfy two conditions: first, fair equality of opportunity vis-à-vis offices and positions; and, second, any social and economic inequalities must 'be to the greatest benefit of the least advantaged members of society' (Rawls 1993: 291). Rawls puts liberty on an absolute pedestal, and while Sen thinks there is something excessive in this, he follows the general claim that lies behind it that liberty cannot be reduced to only a facility that complements other facilities (such as economic opulence); Sen agrees that 'there is something very special about the place of personal liberty in human lives' (*IJ*: 59). Liberties enter again under the second part of Rawls's second principle – known as the 'Difference Principle' – but this time only as a facility that comple- ments other facilities, such as income and wealth. This principle is concerned with distributive equity and overall efficiency, and within this analysis of equity in the distribution of resources Rawls invokes his index of 'primary goods', which includes such things as 'rights, liberties and opportunities, income and wealth, and the social bases of self-respect' (Rawls 1973: 60–5; see also 1982: 162 and 1988: 256–7).

There are three broad problems with this approach to justice. First, it is hard to see how the lexical priority of liberty and the inequalities Rawls seems keen to retain will allow for the greatest benefit of the least advantaged, especially given Rawls's seemingly laissez-faire allowance for inequality as necessary to generate incen- tive structures in market economies (Cohen 2008). (Given that this has generated libraries of published debate, I will leave it to one side here.) Second, as argued by Sen, this is a 'transcendental' account of justice, concerned with institutions alone; that is, it is concerned primarily with providing an institutional answer to the idea of an ideally just polity as opposed to tackling the various injustices that bedevil modern life by means of a focus on outcomes or realizations – a form of consequentialism that does not eschew liberty or pro- cesses but focuses on which decisions, judgements and forms of public reason enable better outcomes in terms of Sen's capability approach (*IJ*). Third, it is devoted to one particular social ideal: the ideal of justice.

Injustice

I return to the third problem in this book's main conclusion. I focus on the second point for most of the rest of this chapter.

Before I elaborate, it is important to point out a performative move Sen makes in *The Idea of Justice*, which is not completely novel to his work in general but which he foregrounds and returns to throughout this book. I am, of course, talking about his extensive reference to ideas from non-western societies, particularly from Indian intellectual history but also from elsewhere, in his defence of his view of justice. He makes the important, if not novel, point that the contemporary – and largely western – pursuit of political philosophy in general and of demands of justice in particular has been limited and parochial (*IJ*: xiv; Mills 2015; Hamilton 2015, 2018). However, unlike some others who make this claim, especially those within what has become known as subaltern studies and post-colonial thought, he stresses that it does not follow from his use of diverse traditions that this constitutes some kind of 'radical dissonance' between 'western' and 'eastern' (or 'other') thinking on these subjects. As he has argued with great force in a number of works, there are many differences of reasoning within the West, and it is simply 'fanciful' to think of a united West confronting 'quintessentially eastern' priorities (Sen 2005, 2006a). He suggests, by contrast, that similar ideas of justice, fairness, responsibility, duty, goodness and rightness have been pursued in many different parts of the world and at different times, and 'the global presence of such reasoning is overlooked or marginalized in the dominant traditions of contemporary western discourse' (*IJ*: xiv). For example, some of Gautama Buddha's reasoning, as well as that produced by writers in the Lokayata school and so on, are closely aligned, rather than adversarial, to many of the critical, leading works of the European Enlightenment. This general emphasis and desire to foreground less studied thought is exemplary of one of his overall points: it is an act itself against a particular kind of epistemic global injustice, that is, it attempts to overcome a kind of injustice without having to depend on a fully worked-out account of ideal justice.

Moreover, of course, as already noted in passing, the Enlightenment authors did not speak with one voice. Sen contrasts the social contract tradition, exemplified in the works of Thomas Hobbes, John Locke, Jean-Jacques Rousseau and Immanuel Kant, whom he suggests were concerned with identifying perfectly just social arrangements, with another strand, exemplified by Adam Smith, the Marquis de Condorcet, Mary Wollstonecraft, Jeremy Bentham, Karl Marx and John Stuart Mill. This latter tradition, he argues, took a variety of approaches but shared a common interest in making comparisons between different ways in which people's lives may be led, influenced by institutions but also behaviour, social interactions and so on (*IJ*: xv–xvi). However, as Robertson (2015), among others, has shown, if anything the overriding concern of the so-called Enlightenment is thoroughgoing scepticism, and it is much more diverse than has normally been supposed. In particular, many of the most celebrated Enlightenment figures not only directed their scepticism at religious and other traditional ideas, but also at the reach of reason itself, in particular the practical effectiveness of reasoned discussion, something Sen spends a great deal of time celebrating and, moreover, is keen to identify as a common concern even of the two Enlightenment blocs he posits as different traditions (*IJ*: xvii–xviii). If Sen had been a little more receptive to this idea, that is, a little more sceptical of the reach of reason, he might not have found it so easy to identify two opposing blocs (both concerned primarily with justice) and found himself siding so easily with one bloc, and thus might have avoided some of the problems identified below.

Sen states without hesitation that the work of Kenneth Arrow in particular, and social choice in general, belongs to the second tradition or strand he follows in discussing justice, and he suggests that social choice, 'suitably adjusted', 'can make a substantial contribution to addressing questions about the enhancement of justice and the removal of injustice in the world' (*IJ*: xvi). So what exactly, according to Sen, is wrong with the contractarian tradition and how can social choice help provide a more practicable view of justice focused on avoiding or overcoming injustice in the real world?

The culprit is clearly not reason because Sen thinks not only that reason is common to all these traditions but also that some kind of reasoning, however 'coarse', 'defective' or 'primitive', is common to a whole variety of bigotries, such as racist, sexist, classist and caste-based prejudices. He is clear at the outset that his account of justice does not depend on 'the omnipresence of reason in everyone's thinking right now'. 'The claim that people would agree on a particular proposition if they were to reason in an open and impartial way does not, of course, assume that people are already so engaged, or even that they are eager to be so.' What matters, he proposes, is the examination of what reasoning would demand for the pursuit of justice – allowing for full pluralism as regards reasonable positions

– and that this is particularly important for a world that contains much 'unreason' (*IJ*: xviii–xix). What is this reasoning? Whose is it? What is it about?

The short answer is that, at least as regards the backbone of his view of justice, he is much less distant from Rawls than he supposes. In fact, he repeatedly celebrates at least one strand of Rawls's theory of justice: the nature of objectivity in practical reason (*IJ*: 4–5, 31–51, 62, 112 and *passim*). At least twice, he quotes approvingly in full this argument made by Rawls: 'The first essential is that a conception of objectivity must establish a public framework of thought sufficient for the concept of judgement to apply and for conclusions to be reached on the basis of reasons and evidence after discussion and due reflection' (Rawls 1993: 110; cited in *IJ*: 42, 62). As Sen notes the first time he quotes this, Rawls goes on: 'To say that a political conviction is objective is to say that there are reasons, specified by a reasonable and mutually recognizable political conception (satisfying those essentials), sufficient to convince all reasonable persons that it is reasonable' (Rawls 1993: 119, cited in *IJ*: 42, 112). Sen notes the clearly normative elements being drawn in by the centrally important idea of 'reasonable persons' used here – and in many other areas – of Rawls's work, but he does not seem to be too concerned about it, suggesting that simply by dint of the fact that we are all capable of being open-minded about welcoming information and reflecting on arguments coming from various quarters, we are all capable of being 'reasonable persons'. Given the greater weight that Sen accords to actual interests and positions, this matter is more important for Sen to tackle than Rawls, especially the fact that this assumption begs the question. What really matters is not whether or not we are capable of reasonableness, but whether in fact – dependent on conditions and positions – we are motivated to act reasonably. Given the structure of Rawls's theory of justice, he can – or at least does – simply assume so: 'Everyone is presumed to act justly and to do his part in upholding just institutions' (Rawls 1973: 8). Sen cannot since he is determined to focus on actual instances of injustice and compare actual responses to them; or, as he puts it, 'this book is an attempt to investigate realization-based comparisons that focus on the advancement or retreat of justice … [which involves] exploring ways and means of basing comparative assessments of social alternatives on the values and priorities of the people involved' (*IJ*: 8, 17).

Unlike Rawls's theory of justice, which for Sen exemplifies the 'transcendental institutional' account, Sen suggests we should be asking a different kind of question. Asking the question 'What would be perfectly just institutions?', which he argues characterizes 'transcendental institutional' accounts or, more generally, contractarian views, is much less helpful in the goal of overcoming injustices than questions such as 'How would justice be advanced?'. This, he argues, has the dual effect of: (1) taking the comparative rather than the transcendental route; and (2) focusing on actual realizations in the societies involved, rather than only on institutions and rules. In discussing this second point, he draws a distinction between arrangement-focused views of justice and realization-focused understandings of justice and suggests that we may be misguided in thinking that we need to be so confined to getting the basic institutions and general rules right. We can be bolder, he suggests, and look at what emerges in the society, including the kind of lives that people can lead, given various influences, including those produced by institutions, rules, actual behaviour and so on (*IJ*: 10).

Sen argues that Rawls's account of the ideally just society is too demanding in two related senses: in terms of the way it tends to think about the problem of justice, as only resolvable once we have worked out the ideally just society, and in terms of the details of the account, which assumes there is only one right answer to the question of which principles would ground an ideally just society. The latter problem he calls the 'feasibility' problem and the former the 'redundancy' problem (*IJ*: 8–11). As regards feasibility, Sen argues that Rawls's assumption that there will be unanimous choice of a unique set of 'two principles of justice' in a hypothetical situation of primordial equality (what Rawls calls the 'original position') assumes that there is basically only one kind of impartial argument, satisfying the demands of fairness, shorn of vested interests. Given what we know about the plurality of values, different positions and impartiality, Sen argues that this is unfeasible: there 'may be no reasoned agreement at all, even under strict conditions of impartiality and open-minded scrutiny ... on the nature of the "just society"'; there can even be 'serious difference between competing principles of justice that survive critical scrutiny and can have claims to impartiality'. We simply do not know whether the plurality of reasons for justice would allow one unique set of principles (*IJ*: 9–11). Thus the feasibility of finding an agreed transcendental solution is too much to ask, he submits. The subsequent step-by-step approach – constitutional, legislative and so on – that Rawls develops from this base would get stuck at the very base. As regards redundancy, he argues that 'an exercise of practical reason that involves an actual choice demands a framework for comparison of justice for choosing among the feasible alternatives and not an identification of a possibly unavailable perfect situation that could be transcended' (*IJ*: 9). If this is the case, then Rawls's complex system of institutional construction based upon a conception of an ideally just society becomes redundant in the face of the more practical everyday concerns and demands of determining instances of injustice and how best to overcome them.

Sen spends some time and energy elaborating further on the differences between his and Rawls's account of justice (especially at *IJ*: 52–74). I am going to skip the details of this and focus instead on his own positive account of justice. It is important to note, though, that some have convincingly argued that Sen's account of justice is not as different to Rawls's as he himself suggests, and, more trenchantly, others have argued that he fails to achieve his two main goals: to defend his synthetic view of freedom; and to establish his view as superior to the one developed by Rawls (Shapiro 2011).

Sen's view of how best to tackle the question of justice is driven by four main concerns.

1 He emphasizes a deep and irrevocable pluralism as regards questions of justice. He is convinced by the idea that reasoned scrutiny may end up providing us with a number of objective, impartial positions as regards justice in general but particularly as regards how to deal with a particular injustice. In this regard, as he notes, he is convinced by Bernard Williams's argument that, '[d]isagreement does not necessarily have to be overcome … [indeed it] may remain an important and constitutive feature of our relations to others, and also be seen as something to be expected in the light of the best explanations we have of how disagreement arises' (Williams 1985: 133). The logical (and pithy) conclusion to this view is defended by Stuart Hampshire in his *Justice is Conflict* (Hampshire 2000). Interestingly, despite his emphasis on deep and irrevocable pluralism (an attempt to line himself up with Williams's position), as we shall see, the rest of his approach is at odds with this kind of position.

2 As with much of his other concerns in economics and philosophy, he is driven to think about relative advantage, particularly as regards the least advantaged in actual societies and how best to improve their lives. This humane view of the world drives him towards a synthetic view of justice whose prime focus is on instances of injustice in the real world.

3 He is concerned to show the 'inescapable relevance of actual behaviour' for thinking about justice and how this drives us to assess

institutions and public behaviour patterns in terms of the social consequences and realizations they yield (*IJ*: 67). He goes even further and suggests that 'we have good reasons for recognizing that the pursuit of justice is partly a matter of the gradual formation of behaviour patterns' and not a question of an immediate jump into 'redesigning' everyone's actual behaviour in line with the institutions and rules of a perfectly just society.

4 In order to carry out the kind of challenges posed by (1)–(3) above, we cannot but be involved in comparisons between beliefs, values, behaviour patterns, choices and institutions.

Comparison

Some have suggested that Sen's emphasis on comparison as central to thinking practically about justice, or, more accurately, assessing actual injustices and proposing means of overcoming them, can just as easily be achieved via a comparison between ideal theories of the kind Rawls proposes – 'institutional transcendental' theories in Sen's terms – and the real world in the here and now. In fact, some go even further and suggest that exactly this kind of comparison is the very point of the kind of ideal theory proposed by Rawls (Shapiro 2011). Sen thinks otherwise. He does so for four main reasons: pluralism; incompleteness; diversity of interpretation and partial resolution; and the role of public reasoning.

What lies behind this conviction, and the associated further critique of Rawls, is the idea that real comparison is not only brought out best by emphasis on social choice but also that the kind of comparison that social choice enables can work under conditions of incompleteness and yet still provide guidance in important problems of social injustice, 'including the urgency of removing manifest cases of injustice' (*IJ*: 70). A little later, while discussing the 'behavioural restriction' associated with 'transcendental institutionalism' and contractarian thinking, he puts his interest in practical injustices well.

> And yet if we are trying to wrestle with injustices in the world in which we live, with a combination of institutional lacunae and behavioural inadequacies, we also have to think about how institutions should be set up here and now, to advance justice through enhancing the liberties and freedoms and well-being of people who live today and will be gone tomorrow. And this is exactly where a realistic reading

of behavioural norms and regularities becomes important for the choice
of institutions and the pursuit of justice. (*IJ*: 81)

Associated with this is his qualification of the kind of criticism
he mounts against 'transcendental institutionalism'. He is careful to
retain an emphasis on the importance of institutions but a different
one to that of Rawls and company. As he puts it, 'we have to seek
institutions that promote justice, rather than treating the institutions
as themselves manifestations of justice, which would reflect a kind
of institutionally fundamentalist view'. What he constructs and
defends, by contrast, are views on justice and social choice that 'take
extensive note of the social states that actually emerge in order to
assess how things are going and whether the arrangements can be
seen as unjust' (*IJ*: 82).

Although he is careful to say that rules, institutions and sanctions
have their role, he argues that social choice brings something to the
fore that has been too often forgotten: the feasibility 'of producing
good results through social ethics'. Concerning this, he puts a lot
of emphasis on the role of debate and discussion, arguing that the
'nature, robustness and reach of the theories proposed themselves
depend on contributions from discussion and discourse'. He focuses
on this not only because he has a very optimistic view of what he
calls 'public reason', that is, procedures of public deliberation and
accountability, about which more in chapter 5, but also because he
suggests that this is the way to include continuously a plurality of
reasons and judgements as regards justice, because there is also
an inherent 'incompleteness' in our views of theories of justice. As
has been discussed in chapter 1, social theory – that of the original contributions by Borda and Condorcet and the revitalization
of the discipline by Arrow – is concerned with the development
of a framework for rational and democratic decisions for a group,
paying attention to the preference and interests of all its members.
Both advances in thinking in these terms yielded pessimistic results.
The 'Condorcet paradox' was the 'proof' that majority rule can be
thoroughly inconsistent. What became known as Arrow's 'impossibility theorem' was the 'proof' that even mild sensitivity to the
social decisions of the members of a society cannot be simultaneously satisfied by any procedure that can be described as rational
and democratic (at least as Arrow characterized these). As Sen notes,
though, despite this evident gloom, these groundbreaking observations were intended as contributions to the discussion of (and sourced

in a belief in) the possibility of providing a framework for rational and democratic decisions, which may explain why Arrow actually gave his proof the much more cheerful name of 'general possibility theorem' (Sen 2014).

This faith in the possibility of this outcome, Sen suggests, is evidenced by two important developments, mostly thanks to his own work: (1) that if we relax at least one of Arrow's conditions – the impossibility of interpersonal comparisons of well-being – we not only avoid some of his pessimistic conclusions but we begin to see the importance of insisting on incompleteness of information, and the same is true of the information necessary for assessing relative advantages; and (2) given that social choice theory is concerned with the rational basis of social judgements and public decisions in choosing between alternatives, the outcome of the social choice procedure takes the form of ranking different states of affairs from a 'social point of view', that is, in light of the assessments of the people involved. As Sen notes, not only does this emphasize the plurality of judgements involved (regarding justice in this case), which makes a mockery of the single axiomatic view given by Rawls, but, moreover, it 'is very different from a search for the supreme alternative among all possible alternatives' (*IJ*: 87–95).

By reference to the example that we do not need (nor even normally can have) a conception of the perfect picture in the world in order to judge (decide) how we should rank a Picasso against a Van Gogh, Sen insists that the 'acceptability of evaluative incompleteness' is central to social choice theory and theories of justice. Indeed, 'persistent incompleteness may be a hardy feature of judgements of social justice.' While this may be a problem for the identification of a perfectly just society, thanks – in part – to social choice theory, this does not prevent us from 'making comparative judgements about justice in a great many cases – where there might be fair agreement on particular pairwise rankings – about how to enhance justice and reduce injustice' (*IJ*: 105). He calls this a relational – as opposed to a transcendental – approach to justice. Sen argues that this approach is advantageous as it focuses on 'the practical reason behind what is to be chosen and which decisions should be taken', and he seems to suggest that the advantage has got to do with the fact that, unlike in the case of transcendental justice, on which 'there may or may not be any agreement', the relational approach only requires 'fair agreement' on rankings. I return to this comment in chapter 5, but it is worth noting here that the assumption of agreement even at this lower threshold may be too much to ask of democratic politics.

In any case, he defends this approach, as I have noted, for four main reasons. The two I have discussed thus far are as follows. The first is the argument that his approach does a better job at recognizing 'the inescapable plurality of competing principles' and reasons, which may or may not conflict with one another, and lead to an impasse, or what social choice theorists call an 'impossibility result'. Concomitantly, as social choice theorizing has also brought to the fore, this allowance for plurality and impasse also facilitates re-examination, or reassessment and further scrutiny. As Sen notes, one of the main consequences of results like Arrow's impossibility theorem is to demonstrate that general principles about social decisions that initially look plausible can turn out to be problematic as they conflict with other plausible principles. The answer is not to throw up one's arms in resignation but to reassess the principles and reasons that lie behind the analysis. This, Sen suggests, is the inherent democratic form of this way of proceeding as regards questions of justice. The second reason he offers in defence of his approach to justice is, it therefore follows, that social choice theory allows the possibility that 'even a complete theory of justice can yield incomplete rankings of justice'. This can be an assertive incompleteness – that X and Y cannot be ranked in terms of justice – or a tentative incompleteness – an incompleteness that is tentatively accepted while working towards completion on the basis of, say, more information or more penetrating examination (*IJ*: 107). Sen's approach to justice takes both kinds of incompleteness on board. So these are the first two reasons Sen submits that comparison is so vital for a theory of justice and why social choice enables this kind of comparison best.

In the third of the four reasons given above, diversity of interpretation and partial resolution are listed separately by Sen, but it makes sense to summarize them together. The two kinds of incompleteness which Sen's approach to justice allows, indeed celebrates, are important as they highlight how his approach can work, that is, can be of practical use under non-ideal conditions. As has been established by means of studies on preference adaptation (Elster 1983), the formation and transformation of wants and needs (Hamilton 2003a) and bounded rationality (Simon 1957, 1979), tentative incompleteness may not reflect deep conceptual or valuational deadlock. They may simply be related to what Sen terms, reverting to economic terminology, 'operational problems', that is, limitations of knowledge, complexity of calculation and so on. However, it is important to note, Sen urges, that even when we are talking about these kinds of causes of incompleteness or partial resolutions, his

kind of approach supposes that it is a good thing that they be incor-
porated into a functioning theory of justice. This is important for
two reasons. First, it warrants drawing into the idea of justice room
for re-examination and possible extension; the partial nature of the
resolution here becomes integral to the conclusions advanced by a
theory of justice and to justification for that theory to remain open
to further scrutiny and revision. Second, it supports the associated
idea, which is itself supported by the structure of social choice theory,
that in the exploration of functional connections between individual
rankings and priorities on one side and social conclusions on the
other, it is vital to remain open to alternative interpretations. As we
have seen in chapter 2, with respect to the structure of Sen's view
of capabilities, a person's voice may count for one or both of two
main reasons: first because her interests are involved; and, second,
because her reasoning and judgement would enlighten a discussion.
This latter category can be further subdivided: a person's judgement
may be seen as important because she is one of the parties directly
involved; or a person's perspective and the reasons behind it bring
important insights to an evaluation, and there is thus a case for
listening to that assessment, whether or not the person is directly
involved. In other words, the insistence on structural incompleteness
within Sen's view of justice allows for a much greater and more
fruitful variety of judgements and forms of information than are
normally admitted into mainstream approaches to justice. Thus we
have more diverse means for making comparisons and more possibility for the inclusion and assessment of both plural views (inputs)
as well as plural interpretations (outputs).

Sen, in fact, goes even further. He suggests that these central features of what social choice theory foregrounds for a theory of justice
provide the bedrock for two further central planks of the account he
proposes. He submits that, in contrast to the Rawlsian world of justice
as fairness, where a person's direct involvement – membership of a
nation-state, or what Sen calls 'membership entitlement' – receives all
the attention (even if 'vested interests' are supposedly removed via
the 'original position'), the idea of justice he proposes as an alternative encourages a plurality of voices – including 'distant voices'. As
in the work of Adam Smith, Sen argues, 'distant voices' turn out
to be vital. This is the case for both versions of the 'Enlightenment'
reason noted above, which Sen calls 'Enlightenment relevance': that
is, they may enlighten a discussion irrespective of whence they come,
but they will often do so with greatest significance and impact if
they come from far away. These 'impartial spectators', Sen suggests,

following Smith, will be one of the main ways in which responses to injustice can avoid the 'parochialism of local perspectives' (*IJ*: 107–9). I discuss Sen's account of 'impartiality' below, and again in chapter 5, in the context of Sen's views on the role of global perspectives in public reason and human rights as central pillars in his account of democracy.

The second central plank of his insistence on incompleteness and plural voices, and the fourth component part of his emphasis on comparison in a theory of justice, is the role of public reasoning. Although I discuss this at greater length in chapter 5, it may be helpful to note here that, despite its mathematical and formal nature, social choice theory has had a close association with the championing of public reason. And this is not only, as I have already noted, due to its faith in rational and democratic discussion but also to its very structure, or so some suppose. The mathematical results, it is argued, can be inputs in public discussion in the sense that an impossibility theorem is designed to throw up a problem whose resolution is part and parcel of the public discussion, involving further scrutiny and contemplation. Sen even uses his own account of the 'impossibility of the Paretian liberal' as an exemplar of this. This theorem showed the incompatibility of a minimal insistence on the liberty of individuals over their personal lives, along with respect for unanimous preferences of all over any other choice (*CS*: ch. 6; Sen 1970). This formal contribution – this 'result' – led to a large literature and further critical scrutiny in a number of areas: the relevance of preference; the right way of capturing the value of liberty and liberalism in social choice; the need to respect one another's rights over their personal lives; reasons for cultivating tolerance; and so on. All told, a 'mere impossibility result' generates the 'need for re-examination of the norms of reasoning and behaviour' (*IJ*: 111).

This may well be true, but two obvious problems with this view rear their heads: given the small number of specialists capable of grasping these kinds of proofs and the extent of specialization necessary even to be part of this process of public reasoning, to what extent can it even be called 'public'? It has hardly been taken up in citizens' everyday political discussion, let alone in the corridors of power; and, given this, it would seem to be grist to the mill of those, including Sen himself, who criticize economics in particular for having removed itself – by means of over-specialization in general and the use of mathematics in particular – from the everyday world of public opinion, criticism, discussion and so on, and thus necessarily from the worlds of ethics and politics, something of which it was once part and parcel (Smith 1976 [1776]; Marx and Engels 1976 [1867]; Marx 1996 [1875]; Hirschman 1977, 1981, 1982, 1986; Chang 2003, 2015). If it is this arcane world of social choice theorizing that constitutes even part of Sen's model for public reasoning, we must surely have to question his view of public reason, and thus his view of justice and democracy. The beginning of an answer to this question is the subject of the second half of chapter 5.

Impartiality

Sen's view of public reasoning is in fact much broader than the above suggests. To see why, we have to be clear as to what he means by impartiality. This is the case because, as has been noted, from the perspective of the view of justice defended by Sen, impartiality is central to the evaluation of social justice and societal arrangements. He makes an important distinction between 'closed impartiality' and 'open impartiality'. He argues that Rawls's theory of justice propounds a view of 'closed impartiality', that is, a procedure of making impartial judgements that invokes only the members of a given society or nation (or what Rawls calls a given 'people') for whom the judgements are being made. Rawls's device of a social contract based on an original position among the citizens of a political community is clear that no outsider is party to such a contractarian procedure. This is not the place to go into the details of his criticism of this approach to impartiality; suffice it to say that he finds three main things wanting in it:

1 Given that justice is partly a relation in which ideas of obligation to each other are important, Sen submits that to argue 'that we do not really owe anything to others who are not in our neighbourhood, even though it would be very virtuous if we were to be kind and charitable to them' is to artificially and unhelpfully narrow the limits of our obligations;
2 Given that the actions of one country can seriously influence lives elsewhere both through direct use of force (e.g. the occupation of Iraq in 2003) and through the less direct influence of trade and commerce, 'should not the voices of affected people elsewhere count in some way in determining what is just or unjust in the way a society is organized?';
3 If we avoid all voices from elsewhere, we can easily invoke parochial – even if impartial – views and thus accounts of justice.

Objectivity in the assessment of justice, Sen suggests, requires us to use the 'eyes of mankind', it demands serious scrutiny and the taking note of different viewpoints from elsewhere, not just those parochial ones found within one's own society or polity (*IJ*: 123, 129, 130).

By contrast, a tradition of thinking about justice rooted in the works of Adam Smith, in particular his *The Theory of Moral Sentiments*, produces a different version of impartiality, which Sen describes as 'open impartiality'. Based on Smith's idea of the impartial spectator, that is, the requirement, when judging one's own conduct, to 'examine it as we imagine an impartial spectator would imagine it' or 'to examine our own conduct as we imagine any other fair and impartial spectator would imagine it', Sen defends a view of impartiality that not only admits but requires judgements that 'would be made by disinterested people from other societies as well – far as well as near' (Smith 1976 [1790], III, I, 2 [the extended version occurs in the sixth edition]; Raphael 1975; Rothschild 2001; *IJ*: 124–5). According to Sen, Smith invoked the reflective device of the impartial spectator to go beyond reasoning that may be constrained by local conventions, deliberately to examine what the accepted conventions would look like from the perspective of a 'spectator' at a distance. In Smith's words,

> We can never survey our own sentiments and motives, we can never form any judgement concerning them; unless we remove ourselves, as it were, from our natural station, and endeavour to view them as at a distance from us. But we can do this in no other way than by endeavouring to view them with the eyes of other people, or as other people are likely to view them. (Smith 1976 [1790]: III, i, 2)

The advantages of 'open impartiality' over 'closed impartiality' are manifold, suggests Sen, but he lists three 'immediate' ones. First, the insistence of 'open impartiality' accepts the legitimacy and importance of the 'Enlightenment relevance' (and not just 'membership entitlement') of views from others. (This distinction was introduced above, that is, between the enlightening role of views near and far as against the contractarian idea that only the views of members of the polity in question count.) Second, Sen highlights the comparative (and not just transcendental) focus of Smith's investigation, going beyond the search for a perfectly just society. Third, there is Smith's involvement with social realizations (going beyond the search only for just institutions). These differences are related to one another since 'the broadening of admissible voices beyond the confines of the local territory or polity can allow more non-congruent principles to be brought into consideration in answering a wide variety of justice related questions' (*IJ*: 134–5). Some may worry that this will open particular questions of justice up to a whole range of competing views. Sen, by contrast, celebrates this pluralism. He argues that 'open impartiality' will generate 'considerable divergence between different impartial views', but there is nothing to fear from this, especially if it is viewed through the lens of social choice theorizing. These different impartial views would yield an 'incomplete social ranking, based on congruently ranked pairs, and this incomplete ranking could be seen as being shared by all'. In other words, not only can this 'lack of agreement' be, as it were, 'owned' by all involved, but it will also motivate the kind of examination and scrutiny that Sen suggests enriches 'public reasoning on justice and injustice' (*IJ*: 135).

Sen, like Smith, is ultimately concerned to navigate the tricky path of actual moral and political judgement about justice in a way that is simultaneously sensitive to local conditions and concerns yet retains objectivity, that is, it navigates beyond relativism while acknowledging deep cultural diversity. As I have argued, in adopting Smith's idea of the 'impartial spectator' for these purposes, particularly as regards his views of 'open impartiality', he assumes that Smith is advancing an argument along these lines. However, it is not unambiguously clear that Smith is, in fact, doing so. In adopting Smith's account of the 'impartial spectator', Sen may not be standing on as firm ground as he confidently assumes he is, especially when the idea of the 'impartial spectator' is read in the context of Smith's overall position in *Moral Sentiments* and elsewhere. As Fonna Forman-Barzilai points out, although Sen's distinction between open and closed impartiality is very noble, hopeful and helpful, there is at the very least some doubt as to whether Smith's idea of the 'impartial spectator' amounts to a theory of open impartiality. This is the case for two main reasons. First, although Sen is right that Smith spoke occasionally in *Moral Sentiments* of the distant stranger-spectator, he overplays Smith's use of the distant spectator. Second, he under-emphasizes the importance in Smith's theory of intimacy and proximity for accurate and well-informed judgement.

Allow me a few words on the first of these in particular (for more on the second, see Forman-Barzilai 2010: 141–75). When he referred to the 'eyes of other people', something Sen repeatedly invokes as the key to Smith's 'openness', Smith was primarily concerned 'with

describing the effects of spectatorship on moral sentiment in relatively close quarters'. 'The eyes of other people' tended to be the
eyes of those with whom an individual came into contact most frequently: 'those he already knew, those he already loved, those with
whom he was already most inclined to agree on a variety of subjects'.
'Spectatorship was primarily a local, visual affair for Smith: he valued
it in a distinctly modern way for producing social harmony and
moral consensus without traditional forms of coercion.' Although
this is unlike Rawls's contractarian, procedural 'veil of ignorance',
the consensus it describes or yields tends to be similarly 'parochial'
and focused on single polities, something that Sen explicitly rejects
in Rawls. The stranger-spectator is, in fact, invoked by Smith very
specifically in the 'case of subduing intense factional (read: affective)
prejudice. Smith does not in any sense invoke the stranger-spectator
for purposes of cultural awareness, or in Sen's words, to scrutinize
"the impact of entrenched tradition and custom"' (Forman-Barzilai
2010: 180–1). (Forman-Barzilai is quoting from Sen 2002: 459 but, as
is obvious from the preceding discussion of Sen's *The Idea of Justice*,
he retains his faith in the supposed Smithian view of the critical,
scrutinizing effect of views of disinterested people far and near.) In
other words, there is at least quite a bit of interpretive justification
for suggesting that Smith's view is closer to a closed rather than an
open view of impartiality.

Sen may retort, as he does (Forman-Barzilai 2010: 249, fn. 53), that
he is less concerned with being faithful to Smith's theory and more
with what might be made of it for other purposes. This is all well
and good, but there are two associated problems with this response.
The first is that Sen – he assumes with Smith – suggests unequivocally that our moral judgements are likely to improve as our circle of
comparison broadens; the 'eyes of mankind' are better than simply
'the eyes of others'. But it is far from clear that this is true, or that
it is at least more often the case as not. It is at least as likely that
coming upon something strange, unfamiliar or perplexing without
a predisposition for openness, without a suspension of certitude and
a willingness to learn and broaden oneself, may actually reinforce
rather than break down local prejudice. It is just as likely that this sort
of situation would lead one stubbornly to reject the unfamiliar and
entrench one's own view or position, or even transform or destroy
what one encounters. One only need glance at European encounters in their imperial conquests for all too much evidence of this, a
subject Smith himself discussed at some length in part V of *Moral
Sentiments*. Smith castigated the hypocrisy of European civility for

condemning the 'barbarity' of Amerindian practices while Europeans themselves engaged in a host of barbarities, including slavery and the corseting of women (Forman-Barzilai 2010: 189). Whatever the substance of his response, Smith is absolutely clear about one thing: he did not believe that this 'encounter with the New World' would lead necessarily to openness and a broadening of one's perspective, and, needless to say, the subsequent history of colonialism, apartheid and imperialism bears out his doubts very well. We still struggle today with the distorted racial, caste, gender and class legacies – not to speak of the very large global imbalances of power – of these 'encounters'. Just to be clear, I am not suggesting that globalization in general is not a good thing or that we should not continue to break down cultural and other kinds of barriers. I am merely questioning Sen's optimistic faith in the idea that these sorts of processes will always, of necessity, improve our moral and political judgements as they will generate more, not less, open impartiality (cf. Hirschman 1981: 17, who makes a similar argument against J. S. Mill's belief that 'contact between dissimilar groups is always a source of all-around progress'). Moreover, this scepticism was shared by Smith, the very thinker that Sen marshals to make the opposite point.

The related, second point is that it is:

> not certain that Smith would have agreed with Sen that his system enables the 'forceful scrutiny of local values,' and 'adequately objective scrutiny of social conventions and parochial sentiments' – although if he did agree, it would not be because his sympathy mechanism produced 'open impartiality,' as Sen argues, but because of the instinctive revulsion towards human suffering that Smith connected with justice. (Forman-Barzilai 2010: 248–9)

However, for Smith, these are two very different processes. Given Smith's condemnation of European hypocrisy and barbarity, one might have expected him to be shocked by the Chinese foot-binding and Amerindian torture he describes in part V of *Moral Sentiments*. But he was not. Rather, he asserts something profound and too rarely noticed: he argues that 'nations' develop the general tendencies that are best suited to them, and that this phenomenon of 'cultural expediency' should diminish our sense of their perversion: 'Hardiness is the character most suitable to the character of a savage: sensibility to those of one who lives in a very civilized society' (Smith 1976 [1790], V, II, 13, quoted in Forman-Barzilai 2010: 249).

In other words, Smith is much more of a particularist, however troubled, than Sen suggests. At least as regards Smith, Sen may be guilty of transplanting the idea he finds central for his view of justice – the stranger-spectator – from one area of Smith's thought to another – from its role in subduing factional, affective prejudice to his overall view of justice – and thereby giving it a quite distinct role from the one that Smith gave it. Given the significance of 'open impartiality' for Sen's account of justice and the role of Smith's thought as an alternative basis for thinking about justice in general and about Sen's idea of justice in particular, this may be more problematic for Sen's overall account than he assumes when he claims that he is not concerned with being faithful to Smith's theory.

Whatever one thinks of these interpretive issues, Sen's defence of impartiality is even at odds with his own earlier arguments on sympathy and commitment. In his justly famous 'rational fools' argument, discussed on pp. 35–7, Sen mounts an important riposte to Harsanyi's attempt to answer Sen's critique of mainstream economics. From within the framework of utility, Harsanyi makes a distinction between 'ethical' preferences and 'subjective' preferences, where the former expresses what an individual prefers (or would prefer) on the basis of impartial, impersonal social considerations and the latter what is actually preferred, that is, the individual's conception of his own welfare (Harsanyi 1955: 315). Sen's response is as follows: '[b]ut what if he departs from his personal welfare maximization (including any sympathy), not through an impartial concern for all, but through a sense of commitment to some particular group, say to the neighbourhood or to the social class to which he belongs?' Harsanyi's move, according to Sen, does not get us very far, which is why the introduction of commitment is so central and telling in this article. In this early, famous piece, Sen is at pains to stress that the binary distinction mobilized by Harsanyi between utility and impartiality is unhelpful as it forgets the central significance of local commitment in human motivational structures. As he says at the end of the essay, '[g]roups intermediate between oneself and all, such as class and community, provide the focus of many actions involving commitment' (Sen 1977, reprinted in *CWM*: 106). In 1977, Sen defends local commitment against the idea of impartiality. In 2009, via a reinterpretation of Smith, impartiality is brought to the fore at the expense of further political analysis of class and group commitment.

Unlike some who search incessantly for coherence or any example of internal contradiction in the development of a thinker's idea, from my perspective, Sen can comfortably hold both positions, even if they prove somewhat contradictory. Thinkers change their minds as they develop their thought to meet new challenges and contexts. However, it would be at least helpful if we could have (or find) an answer regarding this shift, specifically as to why the important notion of commitment can (or cannot) be accommodated within Sen's supposedly Smith-inspired view of impartiality regarding questions of justice.

And, even if we lay these interpretive concerns and their consequences to one side, we are left with a major difficulty. Although Sen is clearly fusing the Smithian idea of the impartial spectator with social choice theory, he advances his idea of 'open impartiality' as a direct expression of Smith's idea of the 'impartial spectator' and notes that it is a device for critical scrutiny and public discussion. As I have already noted, it therefore need not, he suggests, seek unanimity or total agreement. Yet it is still action guiding. In fact, he thinks it is this characteristic of it that makes it a better action-guiding mechanism than the transcendental institutional approach suggested by Rawls. As he says,

> Any concurrence that may emerge need not go beyond a partial ordering with limited articulation, which can nevertheless make firm and useful statements ... [they] need not demand that some proposal is uniquely just, but perhaps only that it is plausibly just, or at least not manifestly unjust. Indeed, the demands of reasoned practice can, in one way or another, live with a good deal of incompleteness or unresolved conflicts. (*IJ*: 135)

This may well be true, and some outcomes of this impartial, plural, public procedure may very well be impartial and useful. But it is worth asking in what sense Sen is using the term 'useful'. What he seems to mean is that they are useful in some abstract action-guiding sense, but he steers well clear of what political theorists call the 'enforcement problem', that is, the notion that at least some kind of coercive authority is required to ensure that individual action follows the prescripts of justice, even if they are the result of only practical, 'plausibly just' injunctions that are the result of 'open impartiality'.

Sen is keen to avoid this question for two main reasons. First, as will be discussed at greater length in chapter 5, what he draws from his amalgamation of Smith, social choice theory, and his view of human rights, among other things, leaves him opposed to the idea of a global state as defended by Thomas Pogge (2002, 2007), Charles Beitz (1985), Brian Barry (1999), and others. While he is, of course, aware of the asymmetries between different groups of people that may be affected and involved in what he calls a cross-border 'global framework of thought', he thinks it unrealistic to imagine how the idea of one global exercise of social contract for the entire population could or would work 'now and in the foreseeable future' (*IJ*: 140–1). At this point, he alludes to the excellent knock-down argument advanced by Thomas Nagel, which refutes these arguments in their own contractarian terms (Nagel 2005). As Sen puts it, again citing Smith: 'The relevance and influence of global discussions are not conditional on the existence of a global state, or even a well-organized planetary forum for gigantic institutional agreements' (*IJ*: 141). He makes the associated important point that the partitioning of the global population into distinct 'nations' or 'peoples' is not the only line of division; and nor does the national partitioning have any pre-eminent priority over other categorizations. In fact, there are many more, within and across borders, and the artificial priority given to national partitioning can easily drown out the competing relevance of other partitions; and, related to that, the need to consider other identities and human beings across the world, as some of his own empirical work has investigated so well (Sen 2005, 2006a). National identity is only one among a whole manifold of identities and interpersonal relations. This point is well taken, as is the point that if the operations of transnational corporations are to be scrutinized, they have to be seen for what they are, namely corporations that operate without borders. Many of the examples of cross-border identity he uses – global commerce, global philanthropy, global protest – focus on real and important identities, and they link directly to the kinds of existing institutions upon which the kinds of obligations he has in mind would rest.

In today's world, global dialogue, which is vitally important for global justice, comes not only through institutions like the United Nations or the World Trade Organization, but much more broadly through the media, through political agitation, through the committed work of citizens' organizations and many NGOs, and through social work that draws not only on national identities but also on other commonalities, like trade union movements, cooperative operations, human rights campaigns and feminist activities. The cause of open impartiality is not entirely neglected in the contemporary world (*IJ*: 151).

However sanguine one is as regards the effectiveness of these different components of open impartial public reason, and however hopeful one might be as to how they may become more effective and powerful in their fights against injustice, it is important to remain a realist about the problem of enforcement. None of these institutions or practices carry with them means of enforcing compliance. They may all provide glimmers of hope – or nascent examples – of Sen's view of justice, but none of them come close to providing a means of situating the locus of duty bearer as regards the rights individuals may claim in line with Sen's view of justice. As we shall see in chapter 5, Sen thinks it unhelpful to be too rigid in insisting on a strict coordination between rights holders and duty bearers. This is the case, he argues, because a developed account of justice will show – as he claims his does – that, along with the power it brings to individuals, it invokes a set of responsibilities or duties. And, moreover, these can be spread across various forms of collective action institutions, locally and globally. But this still fails to confront the enforcement problem, that is, which or what agency has the means to enforce overcoming instances of injustice once we have identified them. As things stand, this still remains the state, and Sen does not think that this can be replaced by a global state. So much of what he argues begs the question: how or who would take the results of impartial scrutiny and enforce its outcomes?

In the absence of clear guidelines as to how exactly we could carry out the comparisons that Sen suggests lie at the heart of his account of justice, and also without clear guidelines as regards whose and which views from far and near would pass the important test of open impartiality – the closest we get is the notion of a kind of benevolent disinterestedness (Shapiro 2011) – coupled with an avoidance of the problem of enforcement, we are bereft of guidance. We are left with a distinct dilemma as regards Sen's view of justice. It fails to deliver on its promise. Its promise is a theory of justice that does not purport to answer the theoretical problems once and for all and yet provides practicable means of identifying and overcoming instances of injustice in the real world of politics and economics.

Conclusion

In this chapter, I have laid out the main components of Sen's original view of justice: a focus on instances of injustice, comparison and impartiality. I have argued that although Sen is drawing on ideas from across the globe, a performative act that neatly encompasses his own arguments as to how a social choice theory-inspired view of justice would operate with open impartiality, his views still sit squarely within the relatively recent turn in Anglo-American political philosophy. This turn places a specific view of justice – distributive justice – at the heart not just of our understanding of justice but also of how best we ought to understand politics.

It would not be too much of a stretch to think that, given Sen's account of justice, particularly his acceptance that justice is not exempt from the disagreement that pervades politics – 'there are many of us, and we disagree about justice' (Waldron 2000: 36) – and his associated allergy to accounts of justice that concern themselves only with the 'basic structure', or legal and political framework, of modern democracies, he would end up with an argument along the following lines. Institutions and outcomes, as well as the associated fair distribution of goods therein, depend not on pre-political and universally applicable legal structures but on representative and participative institutions that enable the articulation, identification and evaluation of actually existing needs directed towards overcoming domination. It is not clear from what I have outlined in this chapter that this is where he ends up. Why?

The short answer may be as follows. Sen's 'realization-based' or 'accomplishment-based' approach to justice does not go far enough. Even if articulated in pluralist, social choice outcomes of individual preferences and judgements, what we are left with is a strong and unrealistic role for what he calls 'public reason', based on rational deliberation as central to politics: that it can produce just outcomes agreeable to all from near and far. Contrary to what Sen suggests, his interpretation of Adam Smith's idea of an impartial spectator is not that far from the various pre-political ideals of agreement common in the political theoretical literature: that the fair distribution of goods depends upon agreement – via the heuristic device of a 'veil of ignorance' (Rawls 1973, 1993) or by means of deliberation that generates consensus (Habermas 1984, 1987, 1996a) or through pre-political, constitutional determinations that safeguard the common interests of 'the people' (Pettit 1997; Rousseau 1997). It would be odd to expect otherwise, despite Sen's evocation of, in particular, Indian intellectual history to support many of his novel moves and examples. This is the case because as a distinct view on how best to tackle interpersonal comparisons of advantage that takes issue with Rawls's account, Sen's view of justice still sits firmly in the predominant field of distributive justice (Robeyns 2017: 147; cf. 149).

The long answer is, in part, the subject of the next chapter and the book's main conclusion: that Sen's faith in 'public reason' leaves him blind to the fact that the problem may not just be 'valuational plurality' and associated stubborn conflict, even despite the 'confrontation with reason', but that conflict may have its source in irrevocably partisan interests that undermine the very idea of impartiality that lies at the heart of Sen's account of justice. Moreover, if this is the case, then Sen's lack of attention to what is known in political theory as the 'enforcement problem' becomes even more problematic. If discussion and deliberation can get us to a point where we more or less agree on the impartiality of incomplete rankings, and yet we fail to agree on whose rankings or interests to prioritize, the need for a final, enforcing arbiter becomes ever more urgent. A world of deliberation and discussion represented by the UN, NGOs, labour movements, feminist activists and anti-globalization activists, to name but a few, all solving pressing questions of justice and injustice may be a world that many hold up as an ideal, but it may also be a world in which very little effectively gets done. It behoves social and political theorists and philosophers to think beyond the mere dynamics of collective judgement and decision making. There is a need also to think harder about the institutional dynamics of how to act on our decisions, however incomplete, and work out mechanisms for making these decisions both enforceable and legitimate. Is that not what lies at the heart of democracy?

5

Democracy

From the very beginning of his interest in social choice theory, both in its contemporary form and early articulations, through his concern for development, capability and his views on freedom, and explicitly in his work on justice, Amartya Sen has been a vocal and articulate advocate for democracy. Of late, too, he has made many important public, critical contributions to democracy in India, Europe and the United States. He has been a champion for democracy. He has articulated the virtues of democracy in many contexts and as against many sceptics. He has done so with great courage and erudition against those within the field of economics generally, and development economics in particular, who suggest that for less-developed countries, democracy is somehow a luxury: that they have to choose between democracy or development. And he has spoken truth to power in India in particular, but also in Europe and the United States, especially since the 2008 financial crisis (Sen 2012a, 2012b; Basu 2015; Sen 2016).

Speaking very broadly and at the risk of oversimplification, there are at least three main views or approaches to the question of democracy under conditions of modern representative democracy. Laying to one side for a moment the various ancient and other precedents and ideas that have contributed to our democratic ideas and institutions, the first is what has become known as the 'minimalist' or 'elite' view of democracy. Best articulated in the work of Joseph Schumpeter, in this view democracy is the mechanism for competition between leaders. Periodic elections enable elite groups to compete with one another for the electorate's vote, based in part on what they propose to do if elected; and, once in power, the chosen elites carry out their policies with little or no participation by citizens. The role of citizens is simply to legitimize, via periodic election, a group of elites in government to carry out policy (Schumpeter 1942).

The second version is similar to the first in the sense that it accepts – or at least identifies – a central role for public representatives and representative institutions and agrees that in representative democracy, the representatives in question gain legitimacy for their actions primarily through elections. This view, though, is not as stark as the elite account since theorists here identify various ways in which individual citizens, via specific institutions and rights, can participate in and thus influence the process of determining the interests of the polity and citizens in question and hold representatives accountable: citizens are equal before the law, forming critical views on issues they deem important for their representatives to address, and organizing and mobilizing around these, safeguarded by individual rights to speech, free press, academic freedom, freedom of religion, association, movement, assembly, peaceful protest and so on; specified institutions ensure that electoral outcomes reflect the real choice of the majority of voters; and there exists constitutional or judicial oversight of new laws and policies decided upon by representatives (Dahl 1961, 1973, 1989; Dunn 2006, 2014; Shapiro 2006). Depending upon the way these different component parts are inflected, this second account of democracy is either termed the 'liberal' or the 'realist' view of democracy.

A third approach to democracy incorporates a broader range of theories and views, but all have in common the identification or prescription that democracy is (or ought to be) about the participation of citizens in public deliberation or discussion to determine the common good (or, in some versions, the interests of citizens) in a way that either assumes or aims at broad consensus and thereby legitimizes public action to meet this good (or set of interests). This is commonly called 'deliberative democracy' (Rawls 1973, 1993; Habermas 1984, 1987, 1996a, 1996b; Cohen 1989; Benhabib 1996; Gutmann and Thompson 2004).

In this chapter, I describe the main components of Sen's view of democracy: ancient and medieval global precedents, discussion, public reason, impartiality and human rights. I argue that Sen's view of democracy fits neatly into the third of the categories noted above, that is, that he propounds a version of 'deliberative democracy' with particular emphasis on the role of discussion, dialogue and public reason. I then end by suggesting that, as a consequence, we are left with an approach to democracy that lacks realism. What it lacks in realism, some suggest, it makes up for in hope and its interlinking of democracy with global discussion, justice and a realistic view of human rights. I remain unconvinced of this take on Sen's view of democracy. It is not clear that the assumptions made as regards discussion, reason and rights can provide the 'security' and 'motivations' necessary to secure the kind of democracy Sen has in mind.

Public reason

Sen positions himself dextrously as regards various traditions of democracy. He combines some recent advances in North Atlantic political philosophy with older, varied traditions of thought around the idea of democracy. Both share the idea that democracy is first and foremost a matter of 'government by discussion' (*IJ*: 324, 318). He situates his view on democracy as an heir to two disconnected but complementary traditions of thinking about democracy. The first has its origins in what John Rawls calls 'the exercise of public reason' and is part and parcel of a large shift in the understanding of democracy that has been brought about by the works of John Rawls, Jürgen Habermas, Bruce Ackerman, Seyla Benhabib, Joshua Cohen and Ronald Dworkin, among others. Sen focuses, in particular, on the work of Rawls and Habermas, quoting from both at various points, as well as building on their ideas. For example, he repeatedly cites Rawls's claim that 'the definitive idea for deliberative democracy is the idea of deliberation itself, [the] exchange of views and debate [of] supporting reasons concerning public political questions'. And the same is true of the positive appraisal of the way Habermas situates as central to democracy the broad reach of public reasoning, in particular the dual presence in political discourse of both 'moral questions of justice' and 'instrumental questions of power and coercion' (Rawls 1999: 579–80; Habermas 1984, 1987, 1996a, 1996b; for representative examples, see *IJ*: 324–5; Drèze and Sen 2014: 258).

Taken together, Sen suggests, these advances in thinking about democracy bring about the general recognition that the central issues in a broader understanding of democracy are political participation, dialogue and public interaction. Moreover, and crucially for Sen's own views on democracy, public reason and justice, '[t]he crucial role of public reasoning in the practice of democracy makes the entire subject of democracy relate closely with the topic that is central to this work, namely justice' (*IJ*: 326; cf. Dunn 2006, 2014). In contrast to what Sen calls 'political institutionalists' and those with a 'narrow' view of the history of democracy, whom he suggests focus particularly on the procedure of balloting and elections, this alternative view of 'government by discussion' is a noble attempt to give greater weight to deliberative dialogue in politics. This idea, which from one perspective has its roots in ancient Athens in general and in the work of Aristotle in particular, focuses on attempting to prescribe how a community of human beings should wish for its public decisions to be taken. The focus, invariably, is on groups of human beings who can communicate with one another, where deliberation would ideally become a common enquiry and an exercise in public reasoning, that is, the group in question should take (or be able to take) these decisions reflectively, attentively, in good faith and as regards the public good (and not as calculations as to what would be personally advantageous) (Dunn 2006: 178). Sen argues that not only is this view central to democracy in and of itself, the reasons for which I outline below, but it is also central to the very ballots and elections that 'political institutionalists' emphasize. Balloting can be thoroughly inadequate on its own, as is obvious in the astounding electoral victories of a whole array of authoritarian regimes, such as North Korea, Russia, Angola and Zimbabwe, among many others. As Sen notes, the problem is not simply about the punitive pressure brought to bear on voters in the balloting process itself, 'but in the way the expressions of public views are thwarted by censorship, informational exclusion and a climate of fear, along with the suppression of political opposition and the independence of the media, and the absence of basic civil rights and political liberties'. All of this makes direct coercion unnecessary; dictators often get away with 'gigantic electoral victories' without any overt coercion in the process of voting. In other words, as Sen puts it, the 'effectiveness of ballots themselves depends crucially on what goes with balloting, such as free speech, access to information and freedom of dissent' (*IJ*: 327).

This view of democracy is supported both by typical Eurocentric claims to a classical Greek tradition, but also by a varied tradition in thinking, including a whole series of cases Sen takes from Indian and African history, or more exactly what he calls the 'global origins of democracy'. While Sen doffs his cap to Ancient Greece, acknowledging that in terms of the idea and practice of democracy it was indeed unique (Dunn 2006; Ober 2008, 2017; Cartledge 2016), he argues convincingly that it does not follow from this – as some have suggested – that democracy is a quintessentially 'European' or 'western' idea. While Athens was certainly a pioneer in combining a tradition of public discussion with balloting, Sen draws attention to a whole array of other examples that, for whatever reason, have received less attention. These include the fact that many Asian regions used balloting in the centuries that followed, largely under Greek influence, particularly in Iran, Bactria and India, with the city of Shushan, or Susa, in South-West Iran a great exemplar: for several centuries it had an elected council, a popular assembly and magistrates who were elected by the assembly. See also the various Indian examples of local democratic governance that Sen points to in the works of Radhakumud Mookerji (1958 [1919]) and Bhimrao Ramji Ambedkar (2002), though the latter would eventually see little merit in drawing on these experiences for devising a constitution for modern Indian democracy.

Also, for contemporary political reasons, it is important to set the historical record straight by emphasizing, as Sen does, that it is in the Middle East that we find a distinguished past as regards democracy, especially if in search of democratic precedents we keep to the fore public reasoning and tolerance of different points of view. While it may be true that democracy as an institutional system has not been prominent in the recent past of the Middle East, Sen points to Maimonides's ideas and experience of seeking shelter not in Europe but in a tolerant Muslim kingdom in the Arab world, that of Emperor Saladin in Cairo, after being forced to emigrate from intolerant Spain in the twelfth century. In fact, there are many examples of public discussion and political participation through dialogues (and tolerance in general) in Middle Eastern history and the history of Muslim people: Muslim-ruled Spain in the tenth century; Muslim kingdoms centred around Cairo, Baghdad and Istanbul, and in Iran and India. The extent of toleration of diversity of views was, for example, exceptional in comparison with Europe at the time of the great Mughal emperor Akhbar (Sen 2006a; *IJ*: 334).

So there are many examples of the co-dependence between balloting and democracy as public discussion in non-western societies. Moreover, Sen also goes on to show that if we adopt the broader view of democracy – democracy understood in terms of public reasoning – we can easily identify a large number of independent forms of democracy as open deliberation in several parts of the Muslim world and other ancient civilizations besides Ancient Greece. For example, some of the 'earliest open general meetings aimed specifically at settling disputes between different points of view, on social and religious matters, took place in India in the so-called Buddhist "councils"'. In these, which began in the sixth century BCE, adherents of different points of view could argue out their differences. The first of these met in Rajagriha (modern Rajgir) shortly after Gautama Buddha's death, and the second was held, about a hundred years later, in Vaisali (*IJ*: 330–1). Sen goes on to list many others, including a famous one hosted by Emperor Ashoka in the third century BCE, where there was an attempt to codify the rules for public discussion, as there was in early seventh-century Japan, under the Buddhist prince Shotoku, who produced the so-called 'constitution of seven articles' in 604 CE (Sen 2005).

Sen also quotes from Nelson Mandela's autobiography, *Long Walk to Freedom*, where Mandela describes how impressed and influenced he was as a young boy by seeing the democratic nature of the proceedings of the local meetings that were held in the regent's house in Mqhekezwini, which Mandela calls 'democracy in its purest form', where everyone was allowed to speak, and where the 'foundation of self-government was that all men were free to voice their opinions and equal in their value as citizens' (Mandela 1994: 21, cited in *IJ*: 332). Mandela's views about democracy were hardly aided by the practices and ideas of the apartheid state that, as he grew up, tightened its grip on all aspects of life in South Africa in defence of the interests of 'Europeans' in South Africa and run by people of European origin. Sen correctly notes that in this context the cultural term 'European' as opposed to just 'white' was the term of self-description among this colonial and then apartheid dominating power. 'Pretoria had little to contribute to Mandela's comprehension of democracy. His discernment of democracy came, … from his general ideas about political and social equality, which had global roots, and from his observations of the practice of participatory public discussion that he found in his local town' (*IJ*: 332).

Sen's point is not that our path in or to democracy depends on these histories (or depends on us being born into a country with a long democratic history); rather, established traditions are an important influence on ideas, whether we are moved by them, 'wish to resist and transcend them' or '(as the Indian poet Rabindranath Tagore discussed with compelling clarity) want to examine and scrutinize what we should take from the past and what we must reject, in the light of our contemporary concerns and priorities' (*IJ*: 332). Although, as in much of his later work, Sen is keen to resuscitate a lot of forgotten and important non-western literature on ideas on freedom, justice and democracy, the main point in all this is to show that there is a broader view of democracy that has a long history (and is not simply the consequence of recent political philo-sophical debate in the North Atlantic). Moreover, and this it seems to me is central, we can see this only if we are willing to broaden our view of democracy to the kind of view Sen is defending: democ-racy as discussion, dialogue, deliberation, that is, as public reasoning. As he puts it himself, '[w]hen democracy is seen in the broader perspective of public reasoning, going well beyond the specific insti-tutional features that have emerged particularly strongly in Europe and America over the last few centuries, we have to reassess the intellectual history of participatory governance in different countries in many parts of the world – not just those in Europe and North America' (*IJ*: 328).

This is an important and welcome counterbalance to many assump-tions within, in particular, the history of western political thought as regards democracy (see also Keane 2009; Isakhan and Stockwell 2011; Hamilton 2015). It is important, however, to dig a little deeper into what exactly Sen means by democracy as public reasoning. There are at least two central parts to his position: first, his more concrete ideas on examples of public reasoning within existing insti-tutional forms of representative democracy; and, second, his important argument as to why no democracy with these elements of public reason has ever succumbed to famine.

First, Sen is very clear that one of the central features of democra-cies which advance public reasoning in the world is support for a free and independent press. Unrestrained and healthy media are, he argues, important for five main reasons, the first four of which are:

1   The most elementary connection concerns the 'direct contribution of free speech in general and of press freedom in particular to the quality of lives'. Media freedom is critically important for us to have the capability to do something we have reason to want: 'to communicate with each other and to understand better the world in which we live'. Without free media, the quality of human life drops or is reduced, 'even if the authoritarian country that imposes such suppression happens to be very rich in terms of gross national product' (*IJ*: 335–6).
2   The press has a major informational role in disseminating knowl-edge and allowing critical scrutiny. This is true of both investi-gative journalism and more everyday journalism. The former is vital in unearthing information that otherwise might not have been revealed – to take a very recent example, the important

role played by amaBhungane, the investigative arm of the *Mail & Guardian* newspaper in South Africa, in enabling the demise of the venal regime of Jacob Zuma by revealing the extent and depth of corruption under his rule. The latter – everyday journalism – is also crucial as more 'mundane' matters and information also play an important role in keeping the citizenry generally informed.

3 Relatedly, the media provides an important 'protective function in giving voice to the neglected and disadvantaged, which can greatly contribute to human security'; the media forces rulers to face the misery of common people, however insulated the former would like to remain.

4 'Informed and unregimented formation of values requires openness of communication and argument'; in other words, the freedom of the press, and the fact that it helps spread new norms and priorities, is vital for the interactive process of value formation. In this instance, Sen makes particular reference to the role of the press as regards tolerance and how important that value is in the protection of minority rights within majority rule (*IJ*: 335–7).

As will be clear, these four functions of the media help us identify the four main component parts of public reason: unhindered communication; critical scrutiny; human security; and value formation. Then, in sum, Sen points out the fifth main function of a free and independent press in enabling democracy as public reasoning: 'a well-functioning media can play a critically important role in facilitating public reasoning in general ... [that is] the evaluation needed for the assessment of justice is not just a solitary exercise but one that is inescapably discursive' (*IJ*: 337). In other words, due to the very nature of the intersubjective or interrelational view of justice defended by Sen, the media become a central means of enacting the choices and processes of value formation that his realization-focused view of justice requires. It is therefore clear that for Sen the pursuit of democracy and justice are deeply interlinked and that democracy understood as public reasoning, especially by means of media that are safeguarded from censorship, regulation, suppression of dissent, banning of oppositional voices and the incarceration (or worse) of dissidents, is a *sine qua non* of justice. Democracy understood in these terms both requires and helps undermine these sorts of barriers to freedom of expression and free media and thus is centrally important to the pursuit of justice. Or as Sen puts it, in scare quotes, '"Discussionless justice" can be an incarcerating idea' (*IJ*: 337).

This then brings us to the second point noted above: why no democracy understood in terms of these elements of public reasoning has ever succumbed to famine. In part, Sen's emphasis on democracy as public reasoning emerges from his earlier work on famines, and what is crystal clear is that this is one of the empirical realities of human misery that Sen convincingly suggests best supports his claims as regards democracy. Sen's original argument, re-elaborated a number of times, is as follows: 'no major famine has ever occurred in a functioning democracy with regular elections, opposition parties, basic freedom of speech and a relatively free media (even when the country is very poor and in a seriously adverse food situation)' (*IJ*: 342; see *PF* for Sen's original argument). He focuses a great deal of attention on the Bengal famine of 1943, which he witnessed as a child, and argues that it was

> made viable not only by the lack of democracy in colonial India, but also by severe restrictions on reporting and criticism imposed on the Indian press and the voluntary practice of 'silence' on the famine that the British-owned media chose to follow (as part of the alleged 'war effort', for fear of aiding the Japanese military that were at the door of India, in Burma). (*IJ*: 339)

Governmental policy exacerbated the famine: even more damning than the lack of any official famine relief over the many months in which thousands were dying every week, the famine was aggravated by the fact that the British India Government in New Delhi had suspended the trade in rice and food grains between the Indian provinces. This meant that, despite the much higher price of food in Bengal, food could not move through legitimate channels of private trade to reach Bengal. In other words, had this intervention not occurred, the demand in Bengal (represented via higher prices) would have been better met. Moreover, rather than trying to get more food into Bengal, the official policy was to look to get food exports out of Bengal in that period. Finally, the government bought food at high prices from rural Bengal to run a selective rationing system at controlled prices, specifically for the resident population of Calcutta, part of the war effort 'intended to lessen urban discontent'. This then further exacerbated exploding food prices in Bengal, leaving the rural population, with their low and stationary incomes, unable to purchase food. All of these measures would not have occurred, Sen argues, in a situation of a democracy constituted by the various components of public reasoning noted above. None of these empirical problems on the ground and the terrible responses to them came into parliamentary discussion in any substantive way during the period of news and editorial blackout. 'A democratic system with public criticism and parliamentary pressure would not have allowed the officials ... to think the way they did' (*IJ*: 339–41).

Sen argues that this is a simple but important illustration of the most 'elementary aspect of the protective power of political liberty' expressed best, he claims, if we view democracy as public reasoning in which we not only have periodic election but a free and independent press. To drive home this point, he makes two important comparisons. The first is the fact that, despite many other failings and imperfections, Indian democracy since independence has 'been adequate to eliminate major famines'. The Bengal famine was the last substantial famine in India, and it occurred only four years before the Empire ended; famines, which had been a persistent feature of the British Indian Empire, ended abruptly with the establishment of democracy after independence. The second is that independence – or self-government – is not in itself sufficient to avoid famines; Sen's point is to emphasize the causal significance of democracy in the avoidance of famine and so he compares democratic India with China. Despite China's greater success than India's in many economic fields, China had the largest famine in recorded history in 1958–61, with a mortality rate estimated at close to 30 million. Although this famine in China raged for three years, the government was not pressed to change its disastrous policies: 'there was, in China, no parliament open for critical dissent, no opposition parties and no free press' (*IJ*: 342). Sen's major critical point is that the history of famines more generally has had a peculiarly close connection with authoritarian rule, whether that be under colonialism (in India and Ireland), one-party states (as in the USSR in the 1930s, or in China and Cambodia later in the century) or military dictatorships (as in Ethiopia and Somalia).

In fact, Sen's point here is twofold. First, although the rulers never starve, when a government is accountable to the public, particularly by means of a free press and uncensored public criticism, then the government too has an 'excellent incentive to do its best to eradicate famines'. Famines normally affect much less than 10 per cent of the population. So, if democracy was only a numbers game at election time, and assuming that the remnants of any famine-ravaged group would then vote against the existing government, this would not, on its own, be a strong incentive to avoid or eradicate famine. The point is that a famine becomes a political disaster for a ruling government due to the reach of public reasoning, 'which moves and energizes a very large proportion of the general public to protest and shout about the "uncaring" government and to try to bring it down'. In other words, one of the great advantages of democracy is 'the ability to make people take an interest, through public discussion, in each other's predicaments, and to have a better understanding of the lives of others' (*IJ*: 343).

The second point is the informational role played by democracy. As one of the tragic consequences of China's 'Great Leap Forward', the famine of 1958–61, shows, in situations where there is little public knowledge of the consequences of government policy, government can easily be misled. The vast number of communes and cooperatives which had failed to produce enough grain were, of course, aware of their own problem, but this information never reached Beijing; in fact, due to a variety of reasons, Chinese authorities mistakenly believed that they had 100 million more metric tons of grain than they actually had – the reasons include the fact that no collective farm wanted to acknowledge that it had failed; failures were kept a closely guarded secret by local party officials competing for credit in Beijing; rosy reports; and simply a lack of knowledge (*IJ*: 343–4). As Sen reminds us, even Chairman Mao – much too late – recognized that, without the right kind of democracy, you are 'unable to collect sufficient opinions from all sides; there can be no communication between top and bottom' (Tse-tung 1974: 277–8). As Sen notes, Mao's view of democracy is clearly one-sided here, as he is only concerned with the informational side. The reality is a little more complex. Despite the fact that China was committed to eliminating hunger, it did not substantially revise its disastrous policies due to lack both of information and incentive to do so, and this was due mainly to not enabling democracy as public reasoning.

Sen also provides support for his view of democracy as public reasoning with regard to at least three further important imperatives: development; human security; and minority rights.

As discussed in the introduction to this book, development is one overriding concern of all of Sen's voluminous work. At the risk of repetition, however, allow me to make clear why he sees democracy and development as closely interrelated and complementary. Many sceptics and critics have tended, at best, to think that democracy and development, while both important, are different goals and, at worst, to argue that there are serious tensions between the two and that developing countries in particular need to make up their minds and work out what they want – democracy or development. This latter position in particular came from, or at least seemed reinforced by, a series of East Asian countries who were immensely successful through the 1970s and 1980s in promoting economic growth without pursuing democracy. Take a look at South Korea, Singapore, Taiwan and Hong Kong: at least initially, did they not achieve astonishingly fast economic progress without fulfilling the basic requirements of democratic governance? This then led to a general theory: 'democracies do quite badly in facilitating development, compared with what authoritarian regimes can achieve' (*IJ*: 346).

Sen counters this vehemently. He does so by paying attention both to the content of what is called development and to the interpretation of democracy, as has been discussed at length in this chapter already. As regards development, he stresses that: 'The assessment of development cannot be divorced from the lives that people can lead and the real freedoms that people can enjoy' (*IJ*: 346). As has been discussed throughout this book, Sen's capability approach provides a means of doing this – as opposed to viewing development in terms of rise in GNP (or in personal incomes) or industrialization, 'important as they may be as means to the real ends'. If development is viewed in this way, then it becomes immediately clear that the relation between development and democracy has to be seen partly in terms of their constitutive connection, in particular the 'recognition that political liberties and democratic rights are among the "constituent components" of development' (*IJ*: 346). Yet, as Sen notes, it is also important to subject democracy to consequential analysis, that is, to assess it in terms other than these political liberties and civil rights, for example, how it deals with economic poverty. So, economic growth, even if measured in the limited terms of growth of GNP or GDP per head, remains vital since raising real income not only clears the way to some really important achievements but also expands public revenue, which provides government with the opportunity to make the process of economic expansion more equitably shared. India, which until relatively recently was cited as living proof that democratic countries are destined to grow much more slowly than authoritarian ones, now (or, rather, beginning in the 1980s and consolidated in the economic reforms of the 1990s) provides a perfect exemplar of the exact opposite: India has had rapid economic growth for nearly four decades and is no less democratic now than it was in the 1960s or 1970s (*IJ*: 345–8).

As has already been noted, in moving beyond mere economic growth, it is possible to identify another component of development that democracy as public reasoning enables: human security. Here the argument is quite simple, though not uncontroversial. Democracy provides a voice to the deprived and the vulnerable. Using a series of examples drawn from South Korea, Indonesia and India, Sen puts it succinctly when he says: 'Democracy gives an opportunity to the opposition to press for policy change even when the problem is chronic and has had a long history, rather than being acute and sudden, as in the case of famines' (*IJ*: 349). Here the politicization of chronic problems is often the only means of raising the problem to a level of concern sufficient enough for rulers to listen, as the important example of political activism around universal education, basic health care, elementary gender equity and land reform in the Indian state of Kerala shows well. For Sen, this is but one example of the role of a broader view of democracy in empowering citizens to help advance development and affect public choice. Although democratic freedom can be used to enhance social justice, the process is not automatic and requires activism on the part of politically engaged citizens. As Sen puts it: 'It is hard to escape the general conclusion that economic performance, social opportunity, political voice and public reasoning are all deeply interrelated' (*IJ*: 350).

Finally, Sen argues that his view of democracy as public reasoning provides a way out of a persistently sticky issue: it must be concerned with majority rule and the rights of minorities. Sen suggests that his view has the advantage of enabling the formation of 'tolerant values', which turn out to be central to the smooth functioning of democracy in general but particularly as regards the consistently thorny problem of the possibility in a democracy that a ruthless majority can eliminate minority rights. He links this to the potential danger of sectarian and communal thinking, which is the subject of some of his more recent work (Sen 2005, 2006a). He argues that the '[r]ole of democracy in preventing community-based violence depends on the ability of inclusive and interactive political processes to subdue the poisonous fanaticism of divisive communal thinking'. As he has noted in various places, this has been an important task in independent, democratic India, and he celebrates it for having remained inclusive as regards a whole range of identities and nationalities, including Hindu, Muslim, Sikh and Christian, following the well-documented tragedy of Partition. He argues that after the murderous attacks in Mumbai in 2008 by terrorists from a Muslim background, the fact that 'the much-feared reaction against Indian Muslims did not emerge was to a great extent due to the public discussions that followed the attacks' (*IJ*: 353).

I wonder whether he is as sanguine now, in the face of years of sectarian Hindu nationalism, driven, or at least stoked, by the Modi government in India. In fact, the answer is obviously to hand; he isn't, as regards the effect of the Modi government both on Hindu nationalism and on academic freedom, and the public spat between himself and Prime Minister Modi – or at least Modi's supporters – rages on. (See the very large number of press releases and reports of the various components of this public spat all over the media, especially on the internet.) But has this changed his very optimistic view of the role of public reasoning in safeguarding minority rights and ensuring against sectarian thinking and violence?

We do not have the definitive answer to hand, but it does highlight a line of critique of this view of democracy that is worth noting now. Sen's point about the link between democracy and the prevention of famine is the most important and historically astute of all his contributions on the subject of democracy (*PF*; *IJ*: 342–5; Shapiro 2011). However, two parts of his broader claim fail to stand up to scrutiny. The first is that, as he himself notes (*DF*; Drèze and Sen 1999 [1989], 2014; cf. *IJ*: 389), his account of the link between democracy and famine prevention cannot be stretched to include democracy and the prevention of chronic poverty. In fact, the record speaks to a completely contrary picture: democracies do not have a good record on poverty alleviation or the best means of equitably sharing economic expansion. Sen himself makes this point unambiguously in his China–India comparisons: India's democracy is not able to address chronic malnourishment, poverty and stubborn class, caste and gender inequalities (Drèze and Sen 2014: 244, 254ff). As Ian Shapiro puts it, 'democratic responsiveness to famine has not carried over, for example, to alleviating chronic poverty or reducing extreme inequalities – despite the expectations of many nineteenth- and twentieth-century thinkers to the contrary' (Shapiro 2011: 1260). More exactly, Shapiro reminds us of two things. First, classical liberals such as John Stuart Mill, a thinker who is eulogized throughout Sen's *The Idea of Justice*, and Alexis de Tocqueville feared that a universal franchise would lead to majority tyranny through which the masses would expropriate the assets of the few. Second, Shapiro reaffirms two more modern views: the shortcomings of the particular prediction found in the medium voter theorem – that the imposition of majority rule in capitalist democracies would generate significant downward redistribution – and the more general failure of democracy to alleviate chronic poverty (Shapiro 2006; Banik 2007).

If Shapiro (and Sen) are right on these two points, and there is no reason to think they are not, then Sen's other claims as regards why it is best to conceive of democracy as public reason – the

associated arguments around human security and minority rights
– start to look a little shaky. It seems to me that one of the main
reasons for this scepticism has to do with the fact that more realist
thinkers and commentators on democracy identify something that
Sen's system does not just ignore but positively disavows: the idea
that it is necessary to lay greater weight on institutions not so much
because it is possible (or even necessary) to provide a once-and-for-
all institutional blueprint, *à la* Rawls, but more prosaically because
institutions are part and parcel of a view of human behaviour in
two important senses. First, humans always act within an institutional structure; although they can choose to change it, they start
from a particular institutional configuration. Second, well-constructed
institutions can often channel even self-interested behaviour in a
way that aids or abets public interests. Sen's strong stress on behaviour, via social choice, comes from a deep-seated optimism as regards
the potentially good ways in which humans can behave, and in so
doing it underplays the importance of institutions in the formation
and regulation of behaviour, that is, in the formation of preferences,
choices and values (*IJ*: 354 and *passim*).

The second part of Sen's broader claim that does not stand up to
realist scrutiny involves his strong emphasis on and elaboration of
the supposed actual empirical power of the media. The media are
not, and are never likely to be, the sorts of entity that can secure,
ensure and enable the kind of public reason that Sen has in mind.
John Dunn puts it as follows.

> In the Assembly at Athens any fully adult male with the good fortune
> to have been born a citizen, if they happened also to be present on
> the occasion and wished to do so, had an equal right to address the
> people on what was to be done. They could, if only they had the
> courage, defend their interests in person with their own judgement
> and in their own voice. In the law-making (and still the war-making)
> decisions of a modern democracy, nothing vaguely similar is ever
> now true. Ordinary citizens are never present in their personal capac-
> ity within a legislative assembly. Still less do they ever hold executive
> authority as ordinary citizens within a modern state. In most democ-
> racies, most of the time and on most issues, ordinary citizens are
> almost certainly freer to speak or think than the Athenians ever were.
> The penalties they face for voicing views which most of their con-
> temporaries dislike or find scandalous are far less harsh and altogether
> less public. But most also have little chance to make themselves at
> all widely audible; and none at all, except by resolute and extremely
> successful competitive effort, has an effective right of direct access to

legislative deliberation. The newspaper press, which John Stuart Mill offered to mid-nineteenth-century Britain as an effective substitute for the political immediacy of the Athens Assembly, still does something to offset the lobbying power of great economic interests. But most of it, in many different parts of the world, belongs to a very small number of private individuals; and the ways in which it operates cannot be said to seriously modify the evident political impotence of the great majority of citizens at most times and over almost all issues. (Dunn 2006: 174–5)

Sen lays a great deal at the door of the media to engender public reason but, even if with the best of intentions, it is not structured either to be held properly to account by citizens or to influence them as much as Sen supposes; this is the case as regards both private and public media houses. And Sen himself suggests as much. In his more recent, empirical work, he is a lot less idealistic about the actual role of the media in India, accusing them of doing little more than mirroring – and reinforcing – entrenched class, caste and gender inequalities and deprivations that stubbornly continue to obtain in India despite 80 years of democracy (Drèze and Sen 2014: 243–87). Moreover, even if the media houses were better structured as regards public accountability, all that it would do (and has done) is incentivize those who hold a great deal of private power to gain control over large parts of the media. Sen celebrates the South African media post-apartheid, but this is belied by the reality on the ground: most of it is still controlled by a small number of very powerful individuals and corporations. The same, of course, is true of the very powerful media houses that dominate the politics of the United States, despite Donald Trump (or, rather, that should probably read, 'a distorted picture now in the process of being worsened and entrenched by Donald Trump').

Human rights

Sen's appeal to discussion and impartial scrutiny that generates public reasoning as the constitutive component of democracy is also central to his view of human rights. He has an optimistic and open view of rights as ethical claims that generate perfect and imperfect obligations and yet are not reducible to legislated law. They are forceful means for promoting a series of moral claims that we all have reason to value, or so he argues. His conception of human rights links back to his view of freedom – in particular the opportunity and process aspects of freedom as discussed in chapter 3 – and the development and demands of deliberative democracy. He situates this process of public reasoning 'beyond the legislative route', that is, mainly in global and local NGOs that actively defend the freedoms of individuals around the world, for example, Human Rights Watch, Amnesty International, OXFAM, Médecins sans Frontières, Save the Children, the Red Cross and so on (*IJ*: 355–87). In fact, it is not too much of an exaggeration to suggest that, for Sen, the activism that surrounds the promotion and safeguarding of human rights exemplifies the richest form of democracy as public reason. One of many quotes could be taken from a series of works (*IJ*; Sen 2004b, 2006b), but this should suffice: 'In the approach pursued in this work, human rights are ethical claims constitutively linked with the importance of human freedom, and the robustness of an argument that a particular claim can be seen as a human right has to be assessed through the scrutiny of public reasoning, involving open impartiality' (*IJ*: 365–6).

In a great deal of theoretical work on rights and human rights, it has become the norm to make a distinction between natural, moral and human rights, on the one hand, and legal (or positive) rights on the other (Geuss 2001; Griffin 2009). Alongside these distinctions, there has been the long-standing – and important – discussion of the need, when thinking of a right, to identify the correlative (or corresponding) duty, and thus the agent (natural or fictive person) who bears the obligation to carry out the correlative duty. Sen is well aware of these theoretical debates, but he makes a convincing point when he suggests that some theorists and philosophers find it too easy to dismiss human rights in a manner reminiscent of Bentham's famous quip that 'natural rights' are 'nonsense upon stilts' (Bentham 1843 [1792]). Bentham, of course, wanted to show how the moral theory he had refined – utilitarianism – was a better alternative to thinking through public policy than the seemingly loaded historical notion of natural rights, that is, rights given by God or nature. As soon as the belief in an omnipotent deity becomes outdated, so does this notion. However, like even non-utilitarian critics of human rights, Bentham's main point was that the problem with natural rights was that they were not linked to any 'real' positive rights, as found in the legislation of any particular nation-state. Sen makes the important point that when these critiques compare natural rights (and then, later, human rights) with legal rights, they are not comparing like with like. While it is of course true, Sen notes, that human rights will not have the same direct link to specified duty bearers in other individuals or the state, that is not the point of human rights.

As national and international proclamations have shown for centuries – in the late eighteenth century the 'inalienable rights' of the American Declaration of Independence and the French revolutionary declaration of 'the rights of man', and more recently the adoption by the United Nations of the Universal Declaration of Human Rights in 1948 – the practices of utilizing the concept are all linked not to positive law but 'are really strong ethical pronouncements as to what should be done' (*IJ*: 357). They demand acknowledgement of imperatives, argues Sen, and indicate that something needs to be done for the realization of certain recognized freedoms that are identified, now, through the notion of human rights. 'One thing they are not are claims that these human rights are already established legal rights, enshrined through legislation or common law' (*IJ*: 358). Sen therefore suggests that Bentham (and many modern critics) confound these two issues – they confuse the fact that human rights can have moral and political force in the world without being part of any positive legal code.

Against these critics – who would then turn around and say, 'Well, if they do not even have pretensions to become legal rights, what practical, political good are they for us now?' – he has two main answers. First, he makes a distinction between their link to certain freedoms that we have reason to value and, second, he suggests that their very nature allows them to be central to the public and open process of informed scrutiny. In other words, the declaration of a human right focuses attention on the critical importance of certain freedoms (such as the freedom from torture or the freedom to escape starvation); and 'there is an implicit presumption in making pronouncements on human rights that the underlying ethical claims will survive open and informed scrutiny' (*IJ*: 358). While he also admits that human rights as ethical assertions are often invitations to initiate some fresh legislation, rather than relying on what is already in place in the existing legal structure, not all human rights are of this kind. While some will motivate specific legislation, will be parents of law, as Herbert Hart (1955) suggested we ought to view rights (as opposed to Bentham's view of rights as a 'child of law'), others will remain simple ethical assertions that we agree are human rights but would not want the state to enforce or regulate. For example, we may all agree that the young have a moral obligation to ensure the well-being of their elderly, and that the notion of the human rights of the elderly captures this best, without thinking that it necessarily be regulated by any form of positive law.

Sen argues that the importance of freedoms 'provides a foundational reason not only for affirming our rights and liberties, but also for taking an interest in the freedoms and rights of others – going well beyond the pleasures and desire-fulfilment on which utilitarians concentrate'. For a freedom to be included as a human right, Sen suggests, it must (1) be important enough to provide reasons for others to pay serious attention to it; and (2) meet certain 'threshold conditions', in particular, the 'social importance' of the freedom and the 'possibility of influencing its realization' (*IJ*: 367). The first of these 'threshold conditions' would seem to leave a great deal of room for what we determine as 'social' and 'important'; and the second would seem to be too reliant on existing means of responding to the rights claim, something you would assume, given the view of human rights Sen defends, that he would want to avoid. In other words, Sen sees human rights as part and parcel of his freedom-based ethics and his thoroughgoing critique of utilitarianism. They are not trumps, as supposed by rights thinkers as diverse as Nozick and Dworkin, but rather one among a variety of competing ethical claims. We must allow other competing claims based on well-being or freedom that may take us in a contrary direction or, as the great founders of the idea of human rights put it, we must not attribute unconditional all-conquering pretensions to the rights of human beings (Paine 1906 [1791]; Wollstonecraft 1995 [1790, 1792]).

In order to help move beyond the two broad and vague claims regarding 'threshold conditions', Sen returns to two central pillars of his view of justice: 'sympathy' and 'perfect and imperfect obligations'. As in his analysis of capabilities, Sen shows how both the opportunity and process aspects of freedom figure in human rights. In the example where someone decides to go out for an evening, 'choosing freely to go out' and 'being forced to go out' presents an important distinction. Even if the latter ends up in the same 'realization' that would have been chosen – going out – it involves an immediate violation of the process aspect of freedom since an action is being forced on the person, even though it is an action she would have freely chosen. The opportunity aspect would be violated if she were forced to do something other than she would have chosen, that is, if she were forced to stay in. As regards human rights, the opportunity aspect of freedom might well be fully captured by the idea of 'capability' – the real opportunity to achieve valuable functionings – but matters related to the process aspect of freedom demand that we go beyond seeing freedoms only in terms of capabilities. 'A denial of "due process" in being, say, imprisoned without a proper trial can be the subject matter of human rights – no matter whether the outcome of the trial could be expected to be any different or not' (*IJ*: 371).

This distinction becomes important as regards Sen's related points about the role of imperfect and perfect obligations in thinking about human rights. When we link these opportunity and process aspects of freedom (as human rights) to obligations that others may bear, it becomes important to distinguish between the move from having a reason for action (to help another person) to having an actual duty to undertake that action. For example, having sympathy for the plight of others is not a sufficient reason for a duty to obtain. The basic general obligation comes, in fact, from elsewhere: what one can 'reasonably do to help the realization of another person's freedom, taking note of its importance and influenceability, and of one's own circumstances and likely effectiveness' (*IJ*: 372–3). Sen is keen to avoid the assumption that we owe nothing to each other but, at the same time, given any person's limited abilities and reach and the existence of various competing priorities, he wants to provide a realistic mechanism to judge best how one's various obligations (including imperfect obligations) figure. This is a matter of 'serious practical reasoning'. Its origins lie in an inherent, unavoidable but still cogent ambiguity at the heart of human rights.

> The recognition of human rights is not an insistence that everyone rises to prevent any violation of any human right no matter where it occurs. It is, rather, an acknowledgement that if one is in a position to do something effective in preventing the violation of such a right, then one does have good reason to do just that – a reason that must be taken into account when deciding what should be done. (*IJ*: 373)

There may well be other obligations or non-obligational concerns that end up overriding the reason for this action in question; and this fact, plus the realities of choice priorities, weights and diversity in causal analysis, may generate some ambiguity in the specification of duties; but Sen is keen to insist that, as with many of his other arguments, the presence of some ambiguity in an idea is not a reason for dismissing the cogency of it (for more on this, see *IR*). In contrast to those who think that without a clear perfect correlative obligation, evidenced in legal rights and the correlative duties that thereby inhere in individuals and the state, no obligations obtain, Sen maintains that loosely specified obligations, such as those that human rights create, must not be confused with no obligations at all (*IJ*: 374). They simply belong to an important category of duties that Immanuel Kant called 'imperfect obligations', which can coexist with other – more fully specified – 'perfect obligations' (Kant 1997 [1788], 1998 [1785]; *IJ*: 372–4).

Sen's point is that while it may make sense for legal rights to exempt those not directly involved, the same cannot be said for human rights. There is no real case for such impunity for the rest of humanity to do what they reasonably can do to help in the broader ethical domain in which human rights reside.

It is obvious to see why this approach to the question of human rights is so central for understanding Sen's view of the world and the nature of democracy: he is less concerned with the matter of enforcement – that actually existing legal rights and duties be connected via perfect obligations and the means to enforce them – than he is with the idea that change and the realization of opportunity comes about through ethical claims in terms of human rights. He uses the example of second-generation rights and how the notion of human rights has enabled the transformation of some legal systems to incorporate them into legislation and thus 'to integrate ethical issues underlying general ideas of global development with the demands of deliberative democracy' (*IJ*: 381). Global development and deliberative democracy, he asserts, 'connect with human rights and quite often with an understanding of the importance of advancing human capabilities'. Even more explicitly, as regards public discussion and public reason, '[t]he viability of ethical claims in the form of a declaration of human rights is ultimately dependent on the presumption of the claims' survivability in unobstructed discussion … The force of a claim for a human right would indeed be seriously undermined if it were possible to show that it is unlikely to survive public scrutiny' (*IJ*: 381, 386). For more realist political thinkers, it seems obvious to ask where and how does this 'unobstructed discussion' and reasoned 'public scrutiny' occur?

Global imperatives?

In a sense, Sen's instinct in answering this question is to go global rather than local. He does not dissect the power relations of everyday human existence, marked as it is – mostly – by local and national concerns and affiliations. No, he moves outwards to the world of global NGOs and the activism they supposedly exemplify. Relatedly, his main card is to push hard with the idea that much of the criticism around the idea of human rights rests on a confusion: 'a not fully realized right is still a right, calling for remedial action' (*IJ*: 384). Unlike some cosmopolitan-inclined thinkers, Sen suggests that the idea of a global state is a futile idea, but it does not follow from this that we cannot impose obligations and remedial action on global actors (*IJ*: 408). We do so, he suggests, by means, again, of the idea of human rights, alongside Sen's version of Smith's idea of the 'impartial spectator' and the significance of the 'eyes of the rest of mankind' (*IJ*: 406). The resulting public reason gives rise to global imperatives, about which there does not need to be full consensus, that may not be enforced in the way that rights captured in positive law may be but which remain effective components of 'global democracy', 'even without waiting for the global state' (*IJ*: 410). These global imperatives are ethical claims with imperfect obligations as opposed to claims for global versions of existing legal arrangements at national level that, through legislation and enforcement, create perfect obligations.

As discussed in chapter 4, Sen submits that a global perspective which is as central to democracy as public reasoning is important for two main reasons: the 'relevance of other people's interests for the sake of avoiding bias and being fair to others'; and 'the pertinence of other people's perspectives to broaden our own investigation of relevant principles'. In other words, taken together, and supposedly in line with Smith's reasoning, a global perspective – a perspective from 'far or near' – avoids 'under-scrutinized parochialism of values and presumptions in the local community' (*IJ*: 402, 404). These ideas were discussed in chapter 4 so there is no need to rehash them here, apart from the important point that, due to our increasing global interdependence, this is an important ethical point and one that becomes more and more of an imperative itself, something that Sen reminds us Dr Martin Luther King, Jr pointed out so poignantly in April 1963 in a letter from Birmingham jail: 'Injustice anywhere is a threat to justice everywhere' (*IJ*: 403).

Using a variety of examples, from slavery to the subjection of women, and infanticide to capital punishment, in various places and times, Sen identifies examples of the importance of examining the justificatory arguments for and against particular comparative questions of justice that are used elsewhere. Keen to draw on the authority of Smith for this, Sen suggests that 'distant judgements are particularly important to consider and scrutinize in order to avoid being trapped in local or national parochialism ... Scrutiny from "a distance" can be very useful in order to arrive at grounded but open-minded judgements, taking note of questions that consideration of non-local perspectives can help to generate (as Smith discussed in some detail)' (*IJ*: 406–7).

Then, in a similar move to the one he makes as regards his more general view of democracy – as public reasoning, discussion and dialogue as opposed to other alternatives – Sen argues that the lack of plausibility of a global state on the horizon should not deter those who are keen to see justice done globally by means of a global democracy. '[I]f democracy is seen in terms of public reasoning, then the practice of global democracy need not be put in indefinite cold storage. Voices of global democracy that can make a difference come from several sources, including global institutions as well as less formal communications and exchanges' (*IJ*: 408). Sen has in mind here the UN and associated institutions, citizens' organizations, NGOs, the news media, activist coalitions and even 'anti-globalization' protest, which, as Sen points out, is one of the most globalized movements in the world today. While he admits that these global entities and their articulations are not perfect for the purpose of 'global arguments', they do exist and actually operate with some effectiveness, 'and they can be made more effective through supporting the institutions that help the dissemination of information and enhance the opportunities for discussions across borders'. Moreover, far from being a problem, as has already been discussed, '[t]he plurality of sources enriches the reach of global democracy seen in this light' (*IJ*: 408).

Two characteristics are obvious from Sen's view of global democracy via the creation and defence of global imperatives. The first is Sen's view of global democracy as global dialogue: his strong belief that all the major issues of global politics are 'eminently discussable issues which could be fruitful subjects for global dialogue, including criticisms coming from far as well as near' (*IJ*: 409). As has been noted already in the discussion of his views on democracy in general, this assumption flies in the face of history under non-democratic and democratic conditions. Some problems – often the most important problems – do not lend themselves to resolution via public discussion. The two examples Sen uses most often to support his case – slavery and the subjugation of women – can in fact be shown to be instances of the exact opposite of what he suggests: neither has been successfully eradicated worldwide, despite centuries of debate and global pressures; and both, where they have been overcome, involved and required much more than public reasoning, often open conflict (in the United States, for example, the abolition of slavery required a civil war; in the United Kingdom, for example, women's emancipation – yet to be fully achieved – required the suffragettes to resist in ways well outside of Sen's conception of public reasoning).

The second characteristic is that the creation and defence of global imperatives rest on Sen's particular interpretation of Smith's account of the 'impartial spectator', which, as I have already argued, contradicts one of the main claims in his earlier works, has been subjected to substantial criticism and may not even play the kind of role in an account of justice that Sen gives it, let alone an account of 'global democracy'.

Moreover, it has been convincingly argued that Sen's focus on the impartial spectator and his view of democracy are at odds with each other. This is the case for two main reasons. First, there is no reason to think that democratic publics will take the advice of impartial spectators – Sen himself provides a number of examples of exactly this phenomenon (see, e.g., *IJ*: 406). Second, Sen's view of democracy is one of public reason and discussion, an academic seminar writ large, where the best argument wins, but in real democracies outsiders are usually portrayed as stooges to some unacknowledged local interest or as having agendas of their own. Think of the 'impartial' development plans handed out by the International Monetary Fund and the World Bank, the Quartet's roadmap for Palestinian–Israeli peace or the climate control policies recommended by the Intergovernmental Panel on Climate Change. As Shapiro puts it, '[i]f one is going to be committed to both impartiality and to democracy as vehicles for advancing justice, some attention is needed to the ways in which they conflict' (Shapiro 2011: 1259). Sen seems either not to notice the problem or to ignore it. This leaves us with a lack of realism as regards his view of global democracy and democracy, a theme taken up in this book's concluding chapter.

Conclusion

In this chapter, I have laid out, in as much detail as space provides, Sen's view of democracy: public reasoning through discussion, dialogue and impartiality. I have argued that his view fits neatly into the third of the categories I outlined in the introduction to the chapter, that is, that he propounds a version of 'deliberative democracy' with particular emphasis on the role of discussion, dialogue and public reasoning. I have shown that Sen gives an important – if not a central – role to the media within this view of democracy. He also emphasizes a whole series of other local and global institutions and movements that provide the avenues and spaces for public reasoning, that is, dialogue over the centrally important substantive issues that lie at the heart of national and global democracy.

In his own words, Sen is absolutely clear about the main components of his view of democracy.

> Much will depend on the vigour of democratic politics in generating tolerant values, and there is no automatic guarantee of success by the mere existence of democratic institutions. Here an active and energetic media can play an extremely important part in making the problems, predicaments and humanity of certain groups more understood by other groups. The success of democracy is not merely a matter of having the most perfect institutional structure that we can think of. It depends inescapably on our actual behaviour patterns and the working of political and social interactions … Understanding the demands of justice is not any more of a solitarist exercise than any other discipline of human understanding … communication and discourse have significant roles to play in the understanding and assessment of moral and political claims. (*IJ*: 354, 392 [citing Habermas 1993])

The first thing to point out is that Sen's eulogizing of a Habermasian view of democracy is at odds with his clearly articulated position regarding capabilities and incompleteness, as outlined in chapter 2. The reader will recall that there I noted the following. At the level of political decision making, Sen takes issue with the typical extension of the Kantian argument that holds that if theory fails, there is the transcendental rationality of practical discourse exemplified by the Habermasian position: a universal 'ideal speech situation' which assumes agreement. At this point, Sen argued that Rawls's and Habermas's arguments rest on a metaphysical assumption that falls short of the reality of politics. However, in this chapter we have seen that when it comes to analysing one of the most central concepts in real modern politics – democracy – Sen discards this earlier scepticism regarding the Kantian idealism of Rawls's and Habermas's views. He goes even further. He embraces Habermas's deliberative democracy, with all its associated idealistic assumptions regarding the centrality of dialogue and public reason in the way we do – or at least ought to – conceive of democracy. This is not intended as a deep criticism, as theorists would not be human if they did not change their minds. I merely point this out to highlight that it is a change of mind that requires Sen to say a little bit more about how this change would map onto his earlier thoughts, especially as regards social choice and capabilities.

Besides this shift, and the fact that Sen does not seem to identify the contradiction it may involve, there are two big related questions that arise. First, how do we ensure the right kind of behaviour by the media or ordinary citizens? And more generally, how do we ensure that existing or new power relations do not repress some voices, exclude certain forms of discourse or set the agenda (Lukes 2005; Hamilton 2014a)? Sen never seems to address these questions of regulation, and this may be because, from his perspective, the decision-making processes for regulation occur within democratic institutions, and so, for Sen, much of the focus of his interconnected account of justice and democracy is on realizations and social choice, not on the determinants of the power relations that may require regulation.

While it is true that Sen's focus on public action, especially in his empirical, collaborative work, goes some way towards identifying the important relationship between participation – cooperative and adversarial – and public delivery and state initiative (Drèze and Sen (1999 [1989], 2014), ultimately it is not clear exactly what follows from this as regards regulation and the extent of state control and incentive. In early work, for example Sen (1981), the term 'public action' still stood largely for state action, but that changed soon thereafter. By the late 1980s, his view of public action was a mix of state initiative and 'participation by the public in the process of social change', where the latter was seen to be 'an indispensable ingredient of public health campaigns, literacy drives, land reforms, famine relief operations [and so on]' (Drèze and Sen (1999 [1989]: 259). This is then taken even further in later work by reference to various social movements in India whose actions are used as examples of public action that has helped to drive change, more of which may be necessary to overcome India's deeply entrenched class, caste and gender inequalities and deprivations – there is a 'need for impatience' in Indian democracy today (Drèze and Sen 2014: 276–87 and *passim*). This important focus on public action avoids the dichotomy between state and market in mainstream economics. It is also, arguably, a natural corollary of many of the ideas presented in this book (in particular his 'concern for capabilities').

In the context of India, in the works just cited and in others, Sen displays awareness of the institutional background of power relations and their link to entrenched, multidimensional inequalities in a way that brings to vivid life all of his novel conceptual work. In the end, though, what does it mean, in practical terms, for democracy and development? The answer seems to be that Sen has retreated from viewing the state as the agent of change to viewing public action circumscribed by public reason as the agent of change. In the case of India, as complex and deeply unequal as it is, this amounts to the plea that the 'voice' of the excluded – the majority of impoverished and deprived Indians – be given greater space and power. This has its source in clear and understandable moral outrage as regards the 'pervasive disregard for the interests of the underprivileged in public policy' (Drèze and Sen 2014: 286); it is not, however, part and parcel of a diagnosis of the institutions and power relations that have given rise to this distorted status quo.

Out of this concern about a lack of focus on or interest in the background power relations within which extant public reasoning is played out, that is, historical diagnosis of the institutional framework, there have been various critiques aimed at Sen's ideas around democracy that can be captured, or at least outlined, in a paragraph or two.

In thinking about democracy, Sen lays a lot at the door of the 'impartial spectator' and 'public reasoning' and either ignores or downplays the role of power and partiality in democratic politics. This has the concomitant effect of reducing the centrality of conflict (or at least the potential for conflict) in politics, despite what Sen has to say about the importance of plural interests, concerns, values and judgements and – sometimes – adversarial participation. Given the inherent partiality of interests in every form of politics, this seems like a rosy view of how best to recognize and resolve concerns from various quarters in democratic politics. The priority Sen gives to impartiality and public reasoning is in danger of having the effect of brushing under the carpet the main matters of dispute in any particular time and place. The answer for questions of justice, injustice and associated democratic norms and practices may rather lie in a view of politics that directly confronts and incorporates this conflict by means of partisan institutions that would enable citizens to participate more actively in the determination of their needs, give their representatives greater autonomy in the process of identifying and evaluating existing needs and interests, and provide citizens with the means meaningfully to control, critique and veto the decisions of their political representatives. (For more on this view of politics and some institutional proposals that may thus enhance representative democracy, see Shapiro 2006, 2016; Geuss 2008; McCormick 2011; Dunn 2014; Hamilton 2014a, 2016.)

So, at least as regards the power dynamics that are unlikely ever to be cleansed from the real world of democracy, the centrality that Sen gives to public reasoning in much of his later work, or at least the manner in which he links justice to democracy via the notion of public reasoning and impartial scrutiny, is, ironically, idealistic. As he puts it: 'Indeed, the basic connection between public reasoning, on the one hand, and the demands of participatory social decisions, on the other, is central not just to the practical challenge of making democracy more effective, but also to the conceptual problem of basing an adequately articulated idea of social justice on the demands of social choice and fairness' (*IJ*: 112–13). This leaves out large swathes of concepts and concerns that cannot but lie at the heart of democracy in theory and practice, in particular the roles of representation, power and institutions in democratic politics.

Conclusion

In the introduction to this book, I suggested that, if there is one animating core to Sen's wide-ranging and important contributions to our understanding of our social, economic and political world, it lies in his deep and abiding dedication to development. In doing so, I introduced his life, his life's works and some of his life's major contributions: some life. Including his important contributions regarding how best to understand famines, Sen is most famous for developing a substantive, broad view of development based on his conception of capability, or what he prefers to call his 'concern for capabilities'. As I argue in the introduction, this is important for a number of reasons. First, he presents a philosophical alternative to the utilitarianism that underpins so much of economics. Second, he delivers an alternative development objective, where development becomes 'a process of expanding the real freedoms that people enjoy' (*DF*: 3, 74). This transforms the 'evaluative space' for determining development issues. This is an important advance on a number of narrower views of development proposed by those that identify development with the growth of gross national product (GNP), or with the rise (or maximization) in personal incomes, or with industrialization, or with technological advance, or with social modernization. As he argues, all of these can be very important as means to expanding the freedoms enjoyed by members of a society. But freedoms and quality of life depend also on other determinants, such as social and economic facilities for education and health care as well as political and civil rights. If freedom and quality of life is what development advances – if that is the goal of development

– 'then there is a major argument for concentrating on that overarching objective, rather than on some particular means, or some specially chosen list of instruments' (*DF*: 3).

This alternative development objective not only informs a wide range of issues, from markets to gender, democracy to poverty and freedom to justice; it also meets head-on an enduring problem within the theory and practice of development: paternalism. As I discuss in the main introduction to this book, from a variety of different ideological perspectives, development has been unable to escape a top-down method of proceeding, where ideas and institutions from afar are given licence to dictate to the poor how best to develop without reference to their needs, values and conditions. Sen's starting point is different. As he puts it in *Development as Freedom*, his approach to development investigates various contributions 'to enhancing and guaranteeing the substantive freedoms of individuals, seen as active agents of change, rather than as passive recipients of dispensed benefits' (*DF*: xiii). Sen's theoretical and practical proposals based on his version of capability value the agency of individuals in and of itself – as constitutive of lives worth living – and because they tend to produce better overall effects in the measurement of well-being, quality of life and so on. As I hope has become obvious in this book, agency, and the requirements for it, lie at the very heart of most of Sen's work. Agency, too, drives his major conceptual innovation for development but also for assessments of standards of living in all contexts: his capability approach. The whole point of Sen's capability approach is to shift focus from goods themselves to what goods do for the lives of humans, that is, what goods enable humans to be and do. Against the grain of most of development economics, Sen argues that the 'process of economic development can be seen as a process of expanding the capabilities of people' (Sen 1983c: 755).

In chapter 1, I began where Sen really starts to take the academic world by storm: revolutionizing social choice theory. I outlined how, by relaxing some of the formal constraints imposed by Arrow, Sen was able to inspire a whole series of similar moves that helped to slacken the rigidity of social choice theory and to realize some of the democratic inspirations and assumptions that had always underpinned it. The substance of the chapter is also important in the sense that it identifies the central role of 'choice' in Sen's thinking, especially as regards how he convincingly expands our theoretical conceptions of choice in order to escape the possibility of further damaging our understanding of motivations and reasons for choice (as, he suggests, the 'rational fools' of mainstream welfarist economic theory exemplify). To help us avoid the then common mistake of assuming we are always self-interested utility maximizers, he draws on, in particular, a subtle account of 'commitment' to belie the reality of the 'social moron' underlying welfare economics.

This, though, is just one of a series of influential, searching critiques that Sen develops into the main foundations of welfarism: 'interpersonal comparison'; 'revealed preference'; 'utility'; 'rationality'; 'poverty'; 'inequality'; and 'welfare' itself. Moreover, a constant concern of his is the informational basis for measurement in economics in general and the assessment of living standards in particular – income, primary goods and resources. Sen casts damning doubt on all three. In doing so, he helps set the agenda for a series of searing criticisms of the two main foundations of modern economics: that individuals are always the best judges of their own preferences or wants; and that what is produced and consumed should be determined by the private consumption and work preferences of individuals. These assume, inter alia, that all individuals have 'given and complete preference functions' and that all seek to maximize their utility. (These and further critiques are also summarized and advanced in Elster 1983; Hamilton 2003a; Hodgson 2013; Gough 2017.) As becomes clear in chapter 2, Sen does eventually leave the language of preferences behind, even if he rightly argues that individual preferences must always remain morally and informationally important. However, as has been obvious throughout this book, Sen never completely discards some of the main tenets of social choice theory. His expansion of how we conceive of choice and reason, still tied to social choice mechanisms, proves vitally important in his work around freedom, justice and democracy.

The first chapter then moves on to Sen's various early ways of conceiving of deprivation, with particular emphasis on famine, poverty and inequality. In this section, it is possible to see Sen as a kind of forerunner to analyses of what are now called 'intersectional inequalities', that is, inequality is not just a matter of one form of inequality, say, class inequality, but has constitutive components based on race and gender that sometimes reinforce class inequalities and sometimes cut across them. In other words, just as inequality cannot be reduced to inequality of income or any other single measure, it cannot be reduced to one of a series of other broader kinds of inequality. I suggest that this highlights that Sen's early work on famine, poverty and inequality is all about bringing to the fore these, and other, disparities and forms of deprivation in complex, diverse and interdependent societies. The reason for this, moreover, is to show that the disparities and deprivations about which we are most concerned are not ultimately about income or primary goods or resources (though these may be important) but about the power or means to transform income (or primary goods or resources) into lives without deprivation. The notion of well-being, which includes subjective and objective components within an objective account, is also introduced via Sen's graceful critique of Atkinson's famous inequality measure. This paves the way for the development of what he comes to call his 'concern for capabilities'.

In chapter 2, I outlined and clarified Sen's version of the capability approach. I say 'Sen's version' as there are now a number of competing versions of it, as discussed in the chapter, but it is Sen's version that still draws the greatest attention. Moreover, lest it be forgotten amid the rush to hang onto his coat-tails, it was Sen who coined the admittedly rather clunky term 'capabilities', along with the equally unwieldy 'functionings'. Welded together, though, they constitute a novel and rich alternative to a series of ideas in economics and political philosophy that have predominated for more than a century. Sen's conceptual innovations, especially combined with a subtle view of objectivity and objective illusion, and an assertive incompleteness as regards the role of theory in practice, provide an important way around a number of problems within the two main competing philosophical positions in the modern era: utilitarianism and Kantianism.

In particular, Sen refocuses economic and political theory onto what goods do for humans, that is, how they enable (or disable) humans to lead the lives they would choose to lead. This provides economics and politics with a more substantive and less truncated view of how to determine what to do in any particular context and in response to a set of existing policies or set of proposed policies. In particular, Sen provides a conceptual reorientation and a means of evaluating those things that really matter to humans: well-being, agency, quality of life and standard of living. And yet he manages to resist the temptation to lay down a series of substantive goods that always, everywhere, will, as it were, fill the evaluative spaces. He remains assertively incomplete in his theorizing, particularly as regards laying down a list of valuable functionings and capabilities. This is a great strength, but it does lead him to leave a lot to what he calls the social choice processes of evaluation that would have to be carried out in each and every context, especially given the seemingly idealistic – or, at least, optimistic – view he has of human rationality in democratically determining social choice outcomes. This conceptual advance on utility, primary goods and resources situates freedom at the centre of any capabilities-oriented assessment of that which is valuable. What, then, does Sen mean by freedom?

As demonstrated in chapter 3, Sen capaciously includes elements of the three main dominant accounts of freedom – negative, positive and republican freedom – into a fourth view of freedom as effective power. To see this, it was necessary to emphasize, again, the central role played by choice. Freedom, for Sen, is based on an account of effective choice or the power to make and scrutinize the whole range of choices that makes up a human's life. That humans have these choices and the power to bring them about and to provide and assess the reasons for having them is central to his view of freedom as effective power. In sum, I suggested that, while Sen positions himself closest to a positive view of freedom, when viewed over the last half-century or so, we see the development of, at the very least, the basis of a fourth conception of freedom, what I have called elsewhere 'freedom as power' (Hamilton 2014a). The resultant position is important as Sen has spent some time rejecting the tendency in Pettit, for example, to incorporate Sen's advances in analysing freedom within a republican account of freedom as non-domination, particularly the idea that non-freedom is always defined by being under the control of another agent. Sen argues astutely that, given the complexity and interdependence of human life within and between modern polities and economies, it is more helpful to conceive of freedom as power, even if that power may only be indirectly under the control of the agent in question or may not even be under their control at all. This is an important insight for the realities of modern democracies that, as discussed in chapter 5, Sen does not seem to fully realize.

This third chapter also develops two possible lines of critique of Sen's account of freedom. I merely summarize them in this main conclusion.

The first line of criticism is that Sen does not think hard enough – at least thus far – about how freedom will play out in the world of politics, where power and representation are central. Sen avoids the most important political questions around the relationship between power, politics and the formation of agents' capabilities for freedom: the capacities (or powers) to determine what is deemed feasible. This is the power both to set the political agenda and to determine what is deemed a preference at all. Without a concomitant framework for dealing with how existing power relations secrete around themselves justifying practices, institutions and forms of rationality, it becomes difficult to see how Sen's contextually bound 'concern for capabilities' on its own can helpfully untangle these power relations. More specifically, which forms of political and economic representation would have to be under constant scrutiny for individual agents to retain the freedom Sen defends? Without an institutional analysis sensitive to existing power relations, it is difficult to see how Sen's account of freedom as power can address this question (cf. Hamilton 2014a, 2014b).

A second line of criticism has to do with the centrality of choice (and thus preference) in Sen's view of freedom. It runs as follows. Although Sen places a great deal of emphasis on the normal preferences, and the normal reasons individuals might have for holding them, he also places a lot of emphasis on discipline, the preferences individuals might have about their preferences, meta-rankings of preferences and the role of what he calls 'preference revision'. He holds to what he takes to be an important distinction between a person's actual desires and what would be her 'scrutinized' desires. This, he suggests, points to the volitional possibility of changing one's preferences, which he suggests is particularly important in the analysis of 'cultural freedom' and 'the role of cultivation in being able to enjoy music and the fine arts'. In doing so, he champions John Stuart Mill's famous (and infamous) distinction between 'higher' and 'lower' pleasures and argues that the 'scrutiny and cultivation of preferences' are central to his, that is Sen's, account of freedom and opportunity (*RF*: 618). In chapter 3, I suggested that, if this is the kind of distinction Sen has in mind when he refers to 'reasoned scrutiny' and, by extension, 'things we have reason to value', this may be too much of an assumption, given the plurality of human life that he points to over and over again. It may be too much of an assumption in three senses. He, like Mill, may simply be wrong about humans and pigs, who knows? How can we be sure of any kind of consensus around these 'higher pleasures'? If a scenario of disagreement even around 'higher pleasures' obtains, which history tells us is the norm, who will determine whose pleasures are the 'higher pleasures'? The answer, for Sen, is 'public reason' combined with a reconstruction of Adam Smith's idea of the 'impartial spectator', which brings us to the subject of justice, the concern of the book's fourth chapter.

In chapter 4, I laid out the main components of Sen's original view of justice: a focus on instances of injustice, comparison and impartiality as against a tendency, particularly in the analytical political philosophical circles of the North Atlantic, which have been his main stomping ground, to focus on what he calls 'transcendental justice' or fully worked-out conceptions of an ideally just society. To counter this predominant way of conceiving of justice, Sen draws on ideas from across the globe, neatly exemplifying his own arguments as to how a social choice theory-inspired view of justice would operate with open impartiality. He also develops a series of arguments for why we do not need a complete account of a just society in order to tackle instances of injustice in the world, in the same way that we do not need a conception of the ideal painting to choose between a Picasso and a Van Gogh. Here, his arguments around comparison and impartiality are central to his endeavour to provide an account of justice that is more practicable and applicable to overcoming practical instances of injustice.

Yet, as I argue in the chapter, his view of justice does not distance itself as much from the Rawlsian mainstream of Anglo-American political philosophy as Sen supposes. This is the case because, first, most of the mainstream analytical views on justice place a specific view of justice – distributive justice – at the heart of not just our understanding of justice but also how we ought best to understand politics, as does Sen. Second, Sen's 'realization-based' or 'accomplishment-based' approach to justice does not go far enough: even if articulated in pluralist, social choice outcomes of individual preferences and judgements, what we are left with is a strong and unrealistic role for what he calls 'public reason' based on rational deliberation as central to politics; and the idea that it can produce just outcomes agreeable to all from near and far. Third, Sen's faith in 'public reason' leaves him blind to the fact that the problem may not just be 'valuational plurality' and associated stubborn conflict, even despite the 'confrontation with reason', but that conflict may have its source in irrevocably partisan interests that undermine the very idea of impartiality that lies at the heart of Sen's account of justice. Given that all three of these criticisms are outlined at greater length below, I will desist here from any further comment on them.

In chapter 5, I analysed the main components of Sen's view of democracy: public reason, discussion, dialogue and impartiality. I argued that his view fits neatly into the third of the three views on democracy outlined in the chapter's introduction, that is, that he propounds a version of 'deliberative democracy' with particular emphasis on the role of discussion and public reason. I show that Sen gives a central role to the media within this view of democracy.

He also emphasizes a whole series of other local and global institutions and movements that provide the avenues and spaces for public reasoning, that is, dialogue over the centrally important substantive issues that lie at the heart of national and global democracy. In other words, despite Sen's earlier criticisms of the idealist assumptions of Rawls's and Habermas's view of democratic politics, under the broad theme of justice, Sen celebrates and adopts particularly Habermas's deliberative view of democracy.

As I argue in the chapter, Sen's overall account of democracy leaves unanswered two big, related questions. How can we – as citizens – ensure the right kind of behaviour by the media? And, more generally, how can we ensure that existing or new power relations do not repress some voices, exclude certain forms of discourse, set the agenda or preclude certain preferences by determining them unreasonable (Lukes 2005; Hamilton 2014a)? These questions remain unanswered, I submit, because of Sen's lack of focus on or interest in the background power relations within which public reasoning is played out, that is, the institutional framework or political economy of democracy. Two main critiques have therefore been aimed at Sen's ideas around democracy. I list them here and return to them in detail below (see pp. 161–4). First, in thinking about democracy, Sen lays a lot at the door of the 'impartial spectator' and 'public reasoning' and either ignores or downplays the role of power and partiality in democratic politics. Second, at least as regards the power dynamics that are unlikely ever to be cleansed from the real world of democracy, the centrality that Sen gives to public reasoning in much of his later work, or at least the manner in which he links justice to democracy via the notion of public reasoning and impartial scrutiny, is, ironically, idealistic.

Even when theorizing about democracy, Sen fails to address questions of regulation of the media, regulation of the participants in deliberations regarding conditions, values, priorities, needs and justice, the NGOs he has in mind and so on; nor does he propose how and who would or ought to control these processes of regulation, that is, to whom and how ought they be accountable. This may be because, from the perspective of the world he defends (capability expansion via social choice), the decision-making processes for regulation occur within democratic institutions, which he assumes are deliberative in nature and structure. Thus, for Sen, much of the focus of his interconnected account of justice and democracy is on realizations and social choice, not on the determinants of the power relations that may require regulation.

If this is a fair description, then Sen's lack of attention to what is known in political theory as the 'enforcement problem' becomes deeply problematic. As has already been noted at the end of chapter 4, if discussion and deliberation can get us to a point where we more or less agree on the impartiality of incomplete rankings, and yet we fail to agree on whose rankings or interests to prioritize, the need for a final, enforcing arbiter becomes ever more urgent. It is important therefore to think harder about the institutional dynamics of how to act on our decisions, however incomplete, and work out mechanisms for making these decisions enforceable, accountable and legitimate: the heart of democracy.

I end this book with three broad critiques of Sen's work, at least two of which speak directly to some of the lines of criticism already outlined in this conclusion.

First, as has been noted frequently, there are many problems with the idea of capabilities as a means of indexing or formatting how we conceive of some of the central problems in politics and economics. Up front, there is the supposed problem with their generality or the 'fuzziness' of the concept and its associated concepts, which makes them difficult to index, something Sen noted from the very outset (EW: 219). I will refrain from taking up this criticism at length, partly because Robeyns (2017) covers it so well and partly because it seems to me that the success of the practical application of indexes, such as the Human Development Index, constitutes enough of a retort. An equally practical concern, but one that has been dealt with most at a highly theoretical level, is the question of whether the capability approach is inherently paternalistic (Carter 2014). My position on this last concern has already been made clear: I think Sen's capability approach escapes this charge, but other capability theorists, such as Nussbaum, cannot so easily do so. To be clear, I think this is a different – if related – point to the one around developing lists of capabilities that can (and ought) to be applied anywhere, anytime, giving licence to external intervention and top-down views of development. However, one important matter does merit comment: the capability approach is now something of an industry, and it is important not to conflate the possibility of the existence of 'the capability approach' with Sen's 'concern for capabilities'; in fact, given this 'industry' and proliferation of capability approaches, I would go so far as to suggest that talk of 'the capability approach' is not particularly helpful at all (cf. Robeyns 2017).

Second, as noted in chapter 4, there exists an important critique of the tendency in analytical political philosophy to reduce the myriad of values and concerns in politics to one particular social ideal, the ideal of justice (and, moreover, distributive justice). This is not directed, first and foremost, at Sen's work but, given that he does not deviate from this norm, it is one that his work must confront (Hamilton 2016). This tendency in analytical political philosophy eviscerates both the concept of justice and our understanding of politics. If 'justice' is used in the third sense stipulated at the start of chapter 4 – that 'justice' is 'all the human excellences together', what Aristotle called 'universal justice' (Aristotle 1980: 1129b–30a) – then of course it comes as no surprise that all politics is about justice. It is no surprise because it is a tautology. The problem arises – as is clearly the case in Rawls and Sen, among others – when a theorist moves, as it is easy to do, from the tautology that 'justice' is about what is socially desirable to something that is by no means a tautology, 'namely to the claim that all politics is appropriately construed as the equitable or proportional distribution of pre-existing goods and benefits' (Geuss 2014: 158).

There are four problems with this now very prevalent slippage. First, as many have argued in the history of political thought and expressed during real struggles for liberation from domination under colonialism, imperialism, apartheid and patriarchy (among others), not all politics is about justice. Politics is also at least about freedom, security, the coordination of action, the exercise of influence, the regulation of power relations, the overcoming of domination, the control of the use of force and so on (Hamilton 2003a, 2014a, 2015; Geuss 2014; Shapiro 2016).

Second, this unique focus on distributive justice presumes that justice will have something to do with rules (and principles) and conformity to such existing rules or with conformity to a better set of ideal rules. In other words, there is also conceptual slippage back to the first two senses of 'just' described in chapter 4: (1) 'just' designates that which accords with existing legal codes; and (2) 'just' accords with what we – which 'we'? – think ought to be the enforced legal code.

Third, the distributive view of justice always associates justice with the distribution of goods that are considered to exist antecedently. In other words, as Marx pointed out regarding justice-centred theories of this kind propagated in his time, the goods in question are taken at face value as objects that come into existence in ways that are irrelevant to discuss (Marx 1976–8 [1867]). Marx thought it more important for political theory to scrutinize the activities through which such goods were produced and the social relations that structured these productive processes. For Marx, these were the most important features of any society, and justice in the sense of rules of distribution, in the sense of conformity to a legal code or some more desirable scheme of distribution, were secondary (Marx 1973 [1939–41]). Although Sen is crucially interested not just in goods but in how goods are converted (differentially) by humans into improving their powers and capacities as humans, he cannot escape this criticism as he is much less concerned with how goods are produced and what effect they have on our lives and preferences (and conceptions of justice).

Fourth, the predominant claims about justice refer to equal (or proportional) distribution of goods fundamental to our social order or to an ideally 'good' social order: but, 'what is so special about "our" notions of social order? [...] [and why assume that] societal order is good in itself?' (Geuss 2014: 160). Despite Sen's disavowal of requiring a conception of an 'ideally good social order', he is also susceptible to this critique as there is nothing in his account of justice that is aimed at questioning the basic foundations of our existing local and global social orders.

Conceiving of justice as central to politics may be the result of a number of understandable phenomena. Two are worth mentioning here. First, justice has historically been linked with the concepts of rationality and reasonableness, which in its extreme form (Plato, Kant, Rawls) leaves no room for actual political judgement and the conflict that might arise out of it (Hampshire 2000: 15–22); but, even in its most subtle form (as in the work of Sen), where consequentialism, real plurality of views and outcomes-oriented deliberation is made central, it is difficult to see how real judgement and dispute is admissible. This is the case because it falls back on a conception of public reason that requires all claims to pass before the reasoned assessment of the public via the notion of an impartial spectator who would assess them from near and far (to avoid parochialism and to include all the necessary, global information in the assessment). Besides the criticisms of this interpretation mounted in chapter 4, it is also important to ask a related question: How? How would we actualize or institutionalize this prescription? As Smith and Sen both admit, this idea of an impartial spectator is another form of heuristic, as this 'position' is not that of the actual views of those near and far but in fact the capacity for individuals to stand back and judge theirs and others' values, judgements and claims based on the 'as if' assumption of adopting the position of the impartial spectator *(IJ:* 121–5; Smith 1976 [1790]: III, I, 2). This is asking too

much of the capacity for impartiality among citizens as they struggle
to have their needs and interests heard and met. Also, why assume
that all needs and interests could only be admissible were they to
pass the full test of public reason? As I'll suggest below, there may
be partisan, legitimate needs that 'the public' in general would not
view as reasonable or rational.

Judgement is crucial, too, to the second phenomenon: given our
horror at the uncertainty and indeterminacy of human life, and our
anxiety at having to exercise judgement to decide in each case how
to act in the world, 'justice' provides us with a two-pronged exit
out of this state of horror. It enables us to cling to theories we have
once committed ourselves to, even if they have revealed themselves
as flawed; and it upholds the objectivity and determinacy we seek
– to start from 'justice' gives us the illusion that all the indetermina-
cies of our forms of valuation can be reduced to one objective, rational
ideal. We therefore do not need to exercise judgement, or so the
illusion is created (Geuss 2014).

Even if there are understandable motivations for us to cling to
justice as central to politics, they are seriously flawed as attempts
to understand and judge how best to act in the world of politics.
What is needed is the courage to jettison some of the main underpinnings of the received views on justice: (1) that a fully rational
and objective account of justice, existing a priori or following deliberation, is necessary for humans to act in the world; that is, justice
might always involve irreducible conflict (Hampshire 2000); (2) that
evaluation of the effects of social choice, individual behaviour (*IJ*)
and the formative role of existing institutions lies at the heart of
justice (Hamilton 2003a, 2016); and (3) that an assessment of existing
power relations in terms of whether they generate states of domination cannot be avoided in assessments of justice and injustice. In
order to right this ship of justice, theorists need to take more seriously two related and under-emphasized components of justice.
First, judgement, power relations and overcoming domination are
central to achieving practical justice – justice on the ground, not
aimed at castles in the air. Second, it is necessary to combine an
account of freedom with the identification, satisfaction and evaluation of needs and to show how a politics of needs is not first and
foremost aimed at resolving conflict but is rather about justifying
partisan institutions of representation that may help institutionalize
and control (class and other) conflicts.

As I have suggested elsewhere, in Sen's case an important hint
as regards why he has not been so energetic in pursuing these

realities of politics may lie in the obfuscation created by the language of capabilities and functionings itself. It is not clear why this language is necessary when there is a lot of evidence, especially in Sen's earlier work, but also throughout his corpus, that his account of capabilities is explicitly based in a contextual and subtle view of needs (EW: 218; Hamilton 1999; cf. Hamilton 2003a). What is wrong with the more everyday language of needs and interests, subtly and contextually conceived? Sen argues against the supposedly blunt instrument of needs, assuming they must always be a dangerous substitute for rights (Sen 1994). It is not clear that needs are as blunt or as unconnected to rights as he suggests (Hamilton 2003a). More tellingly, might it be the case that the technocratic language of capabilities and functionings effectively removes the politics and requirement to assess power relations that sit at the heart of the kind of critical framework Sen proposes?

This relates to the substance of the third broad critique of Sen's work: that its lack of politics, that is, its lack of interest in or mechanisms for assessing and criticizing existing power relations and the associated forms of domination that may obtain in the associated economic and political institutions, make it much less of a realist and more of an idealist project than Sen suggests. Sen himself submits repeatedly that his work is an example of a realistic approach to economic, political and social theory that may be useful for resolving a series of practical deprivations related to development, poverty, famine, inequality, freedom, democracy and justice, as he stresses in many places (*IJ*: 81, 105; but see also various examples in *OEI*; *OEE*; *DF*). Given its lack of politics, does it follow from this and his own assertions that Sen's work is an example of realistic or realist social and political theory?

Surely a realist is realistic, so if Sen's work is an example of the latter it is an example of the former. No, not exactly. In order to see why, we need first to clear up a confusion and then to be clear as to the characteristics of a realist political theory. To be realistic is not the same as being a realist in political theory. Someone who is 'realistic' accepts the existing framework for defining what is possible and impossible, and 'tries to cut his desires to fit the cloth that his particular society has made available'. What is possible and impossible is context dependent: it is both highly variable and a social construct in the sense that to some extent it always reflects the distribution of powers and interests, generally articulated through given laws. A realist who understands this 'will refuse to take this distinction as it is socially defined at any given moment to be the final and unquestioned framework for thought or action' (Geuss 2016: 43). In other words, while a realistic political agent will not strive for the impossible beyond the given laws of her society, a realist will; she will, without problem, be utopian in thought or action, however much of a contradiction in terms this may seem to some. So, while Sen may be realistic, he may not be a realist, at least in the sense of striving and resisting in a realist fashion, that is, in a way that thinks beyond the existing basic structure and laws of 'ordered' societies.

In order properly to characterize his contributions, we need to be crystal clear as to the characteristics of a realist political theory. First, a realist political theory must start from and be concerned in the first instance not with how people ought ideally (or ought 'rationally') to act, what they ought to desire or value and so on, but rather with the way the social, economic, political or other institutions actually operate in some society at a given time, and what really does move humans to act in given circumstances. Second, a realist political theory recognizes that politics is in the first instance about action and the contexts of action, not about mere beliefs or propositions, contending with a world in which conflict is a fact of life. Third, politics is historically located. Politics has to do with the interaction of humans in institutional contexts that change over time, and the study of politics must reflect this fact. In other words, although this is no objection to generalizing, if one wants understanding or any guidance to action, one has to take specific cultural and historical circumstances into consideration. Political theory cannot escape history and context. Fourth, given that the circumstances are always changing (that is, genuinely different and unexpected), politics is not about applying or mastering certain theories; it is more like a craft, art or skill; there is no axiomatic, universal theory that can guide action in every context and circumstance (Philp 2007; Geuss 2008).

If we take this to be the now relatively settled view of realism in political theory, it is far from clear that Sen can be described as a realist, both in terms of the utopian component to realism in political theory and these four theses. Despite Sen's criticism of Rawls and other proponents of what he calls 'transcendental justice', that is, theories of justice that aim at identifying perfectly just social arrangements, what he proposes in their stead still relies on a series of universal assumptions and an optimistic belief in the inherent rationality of modern, liberal societies. Recall that Sen is concerned with behaviour and social choice mechanisms to resolve distributional questions of justice; he is not concerned to critique the basic institutional structure of modern polities. In other words, although his sustained argument for the sufficiency of a partial and comparative view of justice in dealing with injustices provides an important corrective to the mainstream of normative political theory, particularly by showing how we might deal with injustices without the necessity for agreement on a full theory of justice focused on ideal institutional configurations, he falls back onto a series of universal injunctions that are not intended to reach beyond the existing basic order of our polities: 'open impartiality', 'plural reasons' and democratic deliberation guided by 'public reason' (Sen 2006c; *IJ*).

As I have argued, the 'open impartiality' he defends is taken explicitly, if not a little controversially, from Adam Smith's idea of the 'impartial spectator' as a means of locating the process of assessing injustices in actual sentiments – not just ones that are drawn from parochial contexts alone but also actual sentiments located far away. This, submits Sen, gives his account of justice a more global character or reach. However, there is a drawback to this move. In contrast to Rawls's idea of the 'original position', for example, the idea of the 'impartial spectator' – at least in Sen – does not depend on asking people to affirm what they would have chosen in principle but what they have chosen, and why they have chosen it: the centrally important role of existing 'plural reasons' and how they are played out in the various deliberative democratic fora he has in mind. There are a couple of problems that follow from this but, for my purposes here, I will focus on only one. As discussed in chapter 4, in drawing on the reasons actual people give for their views, Sen has to shoulder the burden that there is in fact an overlapping consensus in support of the principles of justice that we want to sustain in these cases. Even his own examples – tackling slavery and the subjugation of women – are not very encouraging, especially if viewed from a global perspective: slavery, for example, has been practised all over the world for millennia (Shapiro 2011); and it is far from true that the subjugation of women has been eradicated, even in rich democracies.

Moreover, it is not even clear that the main components of his theory of justice are central to the instances of injustice that concern him. Sen draws a great deal on Indian and other accounts of justice when making his theoretical points, but when he discusses concrete cases we see that something other than impartial, 'external' reason is doing the heavy lifting: objection to practices that are obvious instances of forms of domination. By contrast to, for example, Amilcar Cabral's insistence on circumstance, action and resistance as necessary to overcome instances of domination (in his case colonial rule), the lack of reference to actual motivations, institutions and power dynamics, forms of political action and historical circumstance gives Sen's views insufficient realism to be convincing as an account of justice that can supposedly include plural reasons, impartial orderings and so on (Cabral 1974).

This is an important criticism of Sen's account of justice. Realist thinkers tend to view the political world in more stark terms than we find in Sen. Unlike in the work of Sen, freedom as capability (or effective power) in Marx, Cabral or Fanon, to name but a few, is the result not of impartiality of deliberation based on public reason but on partial resistance to domination. Realists who have a similar view of freedom as effective power tend to focus on concrete forms of domination and how best to overcome them.

Sen does not think about democratic participation and resistance in these terms. His view is informed by a more idealistic faith in the role of public reason and social choice. As he puts it himself: 'Indeed, the basic connection between public reasoning, on the one hand, and the demands of participatory social decisions, on the other, is central not just to the practical challenge of making democracy more effective, but also to the conceptual problem of basing an adequately articulated idea of social justice on the demands of social choice and fairness' (*IJ*: 112–13).

In other words, Sen aims for capaciousness, while realists think capaciousness in political theory is the wrong way of proceeding. This may, ultimately, come down to the question of how much work you think political theory can do in the real world in informing our 'judgement' of how best to proceed, and, perhaps even more importantly, to this question: how do we know what is most important for our processes of judgement in modern politics? In concrete terms, that bring us back to one of the perennial divisions in development economics, Sen et al. view the role of NGOs, the media, theorists and so on positively partly because they see them as the best means of shining a light on the prevalent issues of the day, while realists tend to have little truck with what they see to be potentially biased and toothless entities. Realists, as I have suggested, are more concerned with how we best focus on and overcome forms of domination, class, power and so on. Perhaps we need to recognize the need for both points of view, but there is little doubt that too much emphasis on NGOs, the media and theorists, in a way that remains blind to their lack of formal democratic accountability, leaves out large swathes of concepts and concerns that cannot but lie at the heart of democracy in theory and practice, in particular the role of representation, accountability and power in democratic politics.

Moreover, Sen's view of justice and democracy has the concomitant effect of excluding artificially the centrality of conflict (or at least the potential for conflict) in politics, despite what Sen has to say about the importance of plural interests, concerns, values and judgements. Given the inherent partiality of interests in every form of politics, this seems like a rosy view of how best to recognize and resolve concerns from various quarters in democratic politics. The priority that Sen gives to impartiality and public reasoning is in danger of having the effect of brushing under the carpet the main matters of dispute in any particular time and place. Rather, the answer for questions of justice, injustice and associated democratic norms and practices may lie in a view of politics that directly confronts and incorporates this conflict by means of partisan institutions that would enable citizens both to participate more actively in the determination of their needs, give their representatives greater autonomy in the process of identifying and evaluating existing needs and interests, and provide citizens with the means meaningfully to control, critique and veto the decisions of their political representatives (Shapiro 2006, 2016; Geuss 2008; McCormick 2011; Dunn 2014; Hamilton 2014a, 2016).

As I have argued in relation to freedom in general elsewhere (Hamilton 2014a), in order to be more realist, and thus helpful in political terms – that is, provide theoretical insights aimed at guiding political action – Sen's work on capability, freedom, justice and democracy would need also to include the means to criticize existing economic and political institutions. In other words, it would need to provide citizens with the real means, power or capabilities to: (1) overcome obstacles in their everyday lives; (2) resist social convention; (3) choose their representatives; and (4), by means of their representatives, influence their social and economic environment. In other words, although Sen provides us with the substantive ingredients for a distinct conceptual schema to the one that still predominates in our highly unequal and impoverished world, he does not do so in typically realist fashion. In assertively ignoring institutions and power, what Sen leaves us with is not a theory that guides political judgement in the real world of politics but, ironically, an *ideal* theory of what we would marshal in a deliberative democratic exercise aimed at decreasing deprivations.

Notes

Introduction

1 Needless to say, Sen's emphasis on agency does *not* align him with the post-development school (see Escobar 1992, 1995, 1997). This is a relativist position where the rejection of a top-down approach involves the complete rejection of indicators and a fetishization of the micro, giving complete autonomy to local movements, which only bolsters the already highly idealized world of contemporary 'civil society' practitioners and theorists (Hamilton 2003b).

2 Hirschman's critique was focused on the common assumption in development economics that 'underdevelopment' everywhere and anywhere could be resolved via the same technical mechanism or solution, irrespective of context and the politics of the place in question. It is worth quoting him at length.

> At an earlier time, contempt for the countries designated as 'rude and barbarous' in the eighteenth century, as 'backward' in the nineteenth and as 'underdeveloped' in the twentieth had taken the form of relegating them to permanent lowly status, in terms of economic and other prospects, on account of unchangeable factors such as hostile climate, poor resources, or inferior race. With the new doctrine of economic growth, contempt took a more sophisticated form: suddenly it was taken for granted that progress of these countries would be smoothly linear if only they adopted the right kind of integrated development program! Given what was seen as their overwhelming problem of poverty, the underdeveloped countries were expected to develop like wind-up toys and to 'lumber through' the various stages of development single-mindedly; their reactions to change were not to be nearly as traumatic or aberrant as those of the Europeans, with their feudal residues, psychological complexes and exquisite high culture. In sum, like the 'innocent' and *doux* trader of the eighteenth century, these countries were perceived to have only *interests* and *no passions*. Once again, we have learned otherwise. (Hirschman 1981: 24)

Chapter 1 Choice

1 Transitivity is simply the idea that if I prefer apples to pears and pears to oranges, I prefer apples to oranges. The four conditions as stated in the text are Sen's elegant reduction of the more complex five found in Arrow's original formulation: (1) 'universal domain' (Sen's 'unrestricted domain'), or the set of all logically possible profiles of complete and transitive individual preference orderings, thus requiring the aggregation rule to cope with any level of *pluralism* in its inputs; (2) 'ordering', or 'transitivity', that is, that the social welfare function gives a consistent ordering of all feasible alternatives (included in (1) by Sen); (3) 'weak Pareto principle', or 'unanimity', the axiom that if everybody in the society strictly prefers a social state X to another social state Y, then X is strictly better than Y for the society, or, in other words, when all individuals strictly prefer alternative X to alternative Y, so does society; (4) 'non-dictatorship', that there is no 'dictator, who always determines the social preferences, regardless of other individuals' preferences'; (5) 'independence of irrelevant alternatives', which requires that the social choice between any two alternatives must depend 'only on the orderings of the individuals over these two alternatives, and not on their orderings over other alternatives' (Arrow 1951; *CWM*: 10; Sen 1999: 183; Mueller 2003: 583; Maskin and Sen 2014).
2 Ordinal utility ranks choices by order of preference (it does not try to give a magnitude to the choice in question, that is, how much it is liked). Cardinal utility gives specific choices a specific utility value (it ranks the magnitude of how much one good is preferred to another).
3 As Sen notes, this does not deny that the differential earning power of women vis-à-vis men may affect the status of women, or influence economic calculations underlying child care, and so on. For more on this, and associated references, see *IR*: 124.

Chapter 2 Capability

1 Sen himself says as much, though tucked away in one of his very many long footnotes: CW: 30, fn. 2. As he says there, a direct link between 'capabilities' and 'potential' goes all the way back to Aristotle: the Greek word *dunamin* (from the Greek *dunamis*, or 'capacity'; for more, see Ober 2017) is used by Aristotle to discuss an aspect of the human good. It is sometimes translated as 'potentiality' and can be translated as 'capability of existing or acting' (Liddell and Scott 1977: 452). Nussbaum takes this inadvertent link to Aristotle to its logical and rather uncomfortable conclusion (Nussbaum 1988; and for explication of the discomfort, Hamilton 2003a).

2 As I have said, primary goods are 'things which it is supposed a rational man wants whatever else he wants' and include 'income and wealth', the 'basic liberties', 'freedom of movement and choice of occupation', 'powers and prerogatives of offices and positions of responsibility' and 'the social bases of self-respect' (Rawls 1973: 92; further elaborated in Rawls 1982: 162 and Rawls 1988: 256–7).
3 This does not have to emerge from a thesis concerning the 'possibility of altruism' (e.g. Nagel 1970) because the cause could be one that has little, or nothing, to do with the well-being of others but still endangers personal well-being, like some obsessive sporting quests.
4 This and what follows comes from personal communication with Amartya Sen in 1998.

Chapter 3 Freedom

1 Contrary to the lineage traced by Berlin and his followers, it is Hobbes, with his relentlessly negative conception of freedom, who provides an account of the state that has the clearest totalitarian conclusions.
2 Producing what he famously calls a modelling of the individual as a 'rational fool', who cannot distinguish between choice rankings, interest orderings and valuational judgements. See chapter 1 above and Sen 1977.
3 This is closely linked to his defence of a subtle version of consequential-ism, the details of which, for reasons of space and meta-ethical complexity, I leave to one side here.

References

Ambedkar, B. R. (2002), *The Essential Writings of B. R. Ambedkar*, ed. V. Rodrigues (Delhi: Oxford University Press).

Anand, P., Pattanaik, P. and Puppe, C. (2009), *The Handbook of Rational and Social Choice* (Oxford: Oxford University Press).

Anand, P., Santos, C. and Smith, R. (2009), 'The Measurement of Capabilities', in K. Basu and R. Kanbur, *Arguments for a Better World: Essays in Honor of Amartya Sen* (Oxford and New York: Oxford University Press), pp. 283–310.

Anand, P., Hunter, G., Carter, I., Dowding, K., Guala, F. and van Hees, M. (2009), 'The Development of Capability Indicators', *Journal of Human Development and Capabilities* 10(1): 125–52.

Aristotle (1980), *The Nicomachean Ethics*, trans. D. Ross (Oxford: Oxford University Press).

Arrow, K. J. (1951), *Social Choice and Individual Values* (New York: Wiley).

Arrow, K. J. and Hahn, F. H. (1971), *General Competitive Analysis* (San Francisco: Holden-Day). (Reprinted Amsterdam: North-Holland, 1980.)

Atkinson, A. B. (1970a), *Poverty in Britain and the Reform of Social Security* (Cambridge: Cambridge University Press).

Atkinson, A. B. (1970b), 'On the Measurement of Inequality', *Journal of Economic Theory* 2: 244–63.

Atkinson, A. B. (1983), *Social Justice and Public Policy* (Cambridge, MA: MIT Press).

Banik, D. (2007), *Starvation and India's Democracy* (London: Routledge).

Barry, B. (1995), *Justice as Impartiality* (Oxford: Clarendon Press).

Barry, B. (1999), 'Statism and Nationalism: A Cosmopolitan Critique', in I. Shapiro and L. Brilmayer (eds), *Global Justice* (New York: New York University Press).

Basu, I. (2015), 'The Amartya Sen Interview: "The Failure of the State is Continuing in India"', *Huffington Post*, at: https://www.huffingtonpost.in/2015/02/20/amartya-sen-interview_n_6720062.html

Basu, K. and López-Calva, L. (2011), 'Functionings and Capabilities', in K. J. Arrow, A. K. Sen and K. Suzumura (eds), *Handbook of Social Choice and Welfare* (Amsterdam: Elsevier), pp. 153–87.

Becker, G. S. and Stigler, G. J. (1977), 'De gustibus non est disputandum', *American Economic Review* 67(2): 76–90.

Beitz, C. (ed.) (1985), *International Ethics* (Princeton: Princeton University Press).

Benhabib, S. (1996) (ed.), *Democracy and Difference: Contesting the Boundaries of the Political* (Princeton: Princeton University Press).

Bentham, J. (1843 [1792]), *Anarchical Fallacies*, in J. Bowring (ed.), *The Works of Jeremy Bentham*, Vol. II (Edinburgh: William Tait).

Bentham, J. (1970 [1781]), *Introduction to the Principles of Morals and Legislation* (London: Athlone).

Bentham, J. (1970 [c. 1782]), *Of Laws in General*, ed. H. L. A. Hart (Oxford: Oxford University Press).

Bergson, A. (1938), 'A Reformulation of Certain Aspects of Welfare Economics', *Quarterly Journal of Economics* 52(2): 310–34.

Berlin, I. (1996 [1969]), 'Two Concepts of Liberty', in *Four Essays on Liberty* (Oxford: Oxford University Press).

Borda, J.-C. de (1781), 'Mémoire sur les élections au scrutin', *Histoire de l'Académie Royale des Sciences* (Paris: Imprimerie Royale).

Buchanan, J. (1954), 'Social Choice, Democracy, and Free Markets', *Journal of Political Economy* 62(2): 114–23.

Buchanan, J. and Tullock, G. (1962), *The Calculus of Consent: Logical Foundations of Constitutional Democracy* (Ann Arbor, MI: University of Michigan Press).

Burke, E. (2004 [1790]), *Reflections on the Revolution in France*, ed. Conor Cruise O'Brien (London: Penguin).

Cabral, A. (1974), 'Análise de alguns Tipos de Resistência', in *Colecção de Leste a Oeste* (Lisbon: Seara Nova).

Carter, I. (2014), 'Is the Capability Approach Paternalist?', *Economics and Philosophy* 30 (March): 75–98.

Cartledge, P. (2016), *Democracy: A Life* (Oxford: Oxford University Press).

Chang, H.-J. (2003), *Rethinking Development Economics* (London: Anthem Press).

Chang, H.-J. (2015), *Economics: The User's Guide* (London: Bloomsbury).

Chenery, H., Ahluwalia, M. S., Bell, C. L. G., Duloy, J. H. and Jolly, R. (1979), *Redistribution with Growth: Policies to Improve Income Distribution in Developing Countries in the Context of Economic Growth* (London: Oxford University Press).

Cohen, G. A. (1993), 'Equality of What? On Welfare, Goods and Capabilities', in M. Nussbaum and A. K. Sen (eds), *The Quality of Life* (Oxford: Clarendon Press), pp. 9–29.

Cohen, G. A. (2008), *Rescuing Justice and Equality* (Cambridge, MA: Harvard University Press).

Cohen, J. (1989), 'Deliberative Democracy and Democratic Legitimacy', in A. Hamlin and P. Pettit (eds), *The Good Polity* (Oxford: Blackwell).

Cohen, J. (1995), 'Book Review of Inequality Reexamined', *Journal of Philosophy* 92: 275–88.

Comim, F., Qizilbash, M. and Alkire, S. (2008), *The Capability Approach: Concepts, Measures, and Applications* (Cambridge: Cambridge University Press).

Condorcet, Marquis de (1785), *Essai sur l'application de l'analyse à la probabilité des décisions rendues à la pluralité de voix* (Paris: L'Imprimerie Royale).

Dahl, R. (1961), *Who Governs? Democracy and Power in an American City* (New Haven: Yale University Press).

Dahl, R. (1973), *Polyarchy: Participation and Opposition* (New Haven: Yale University Press).

Dahl, R. (1989), *Democracy and its Critics* (New Haven: Yale University Press).

Davidson, D. (1986), 'Judging Interpersonal Interests', in J. Elster and A. Hyllan (eds), *Foundations of Social Choice Theory* (Cambridge: Cambridge University Press).

Debreu, G. (1959), *Theory of Value* (New York: Wiley).

Deneulin, S. and Shahani, L. (eds) (2009), *An Introduction to the Human Development and Capability Approach: Freedom and Development* (Sterling, VA: Earthscan).

Dodgson, C. L. (1874), *Facts, Figures, and Fancies: Relating to the Elections to the Hebdomadal Council, the Offer of the Clarendon Trustees, and the Proposal to Convert the Parks into Cricket Grounds* (Oxford: Parker).

Dodgson, C. L. (1884), *The Principles of Parliamentary Representation* (London: Harrison and Sons).

Drèze, J. and Sen, A. K. (1999 [1989]), 'Hunger and Public Action', in *The Amartya Sen and Jean Drèze Omnibus* (New Delhi: Oxford University Press).

Drèze, J. and Sen, A. K. (1999 [1995]), 'India: Economic Development and Social Opportunity', in *The Amartya Sen and Jean Drèze Omnibus* (New Delhi: Oxford University Press).

Drèze, J. and Sen, A. K. (2002), *India: Development and Participation*, 2nd edn (Oxford: Oxford University Press).

Drèze, J. and Sen, A. K. (2014), *An Uncertain Glory: India and Its Contradictions* (London: Penguin).

Dunn, J. (2006), *Setting the People Free: The Story of Democracy* (London: Atlantic Books).

Dunn, J. (2014), *Breaking Democracy's Spell* (New Haven and London: Yale University Press).

Dworkin, R. (1981), 'What is Equality? Part 2: Equality of Resources', *Philosophy & Public Affairs* 10(4): 283–345.

Dworkin, R. (2000), *Sovereign Virtue: The Theory and Practice of Equality* (Cambridge, MA: Harvard University Press).

Edgeworth, F. (1881), *Mathematical Physics: An Essay on the Application of Mathematics to the Moral Sciences* (London: Kegan Paul).

Elster, J. (1983), *Sour Grapes: Studies in the Subversion of Rationality* (Cambridge: Cambridge University Press).

Encyclopedia Britannica Online (2018), Lancelot Brown, at: https://www.britannica.com/biography/Lancelot-Brown

Escobar, A. (1992), 'Imagining a Post-Development Era? Critical Thought, Development and Social Movements', *Social Text* 31/32: 20–56.

Escobar, A. (1995), *Encountering Development: The Making and Unmaking of the Third World* (Princeton: Princeton University Press).

Escobar, A. (1997), 'The Making and Unmaking of the Third World through Development', in M. Rahnema and V. Bawtree (eds), *The Post-Development Reader* (London: Zed Books).

Fanon, F. (2008 [1952]), *Black Skin, White Masks*, ed. Homi K. Bhabha and Ziauddin Sardar (London: Pluto Press).

Forman-Barzilai, F. (2010), *Adam Smith and the Circles of Sympathy: Cosmopolitanism and Moral Theory* (Cambridge: Cambridge University Press).

Fukuda-Parr, S. (2003), 'The Human Development Paradigm: Operationalizing Sen's Ideas on Capabilities', *Feminist Economics* 9(2–3): 301–17.

Fukuda-Parr, S. and Kumar, A. K. S. (2009), *Handbook of Human Development: Concepts, Measures, and Policies* (New York: Oxford University Press).

Geuss, R. (1995), 'Freedom as an Ideal', *Proceedings of the Aristotelian Society, Supplementary Volume* 69(1): 87–112.

Geuss, R. (2001), *History and Illusion in Politics* (Cambridge: Cambridge University Press).

Geuss, R. (2008), *Philosophy and Real Politics* (Princeton: Princeton University Press).

Geuss, R. (2010), 'On the Very Idea of a Metaphysics of Right', in *Politics and the Imagination* (Princeton: Princeton University Press).

Geuss, R. (2014), 'Politics and Architecture', in *A World Without Why* (Princeton: Princeton University Press).

Geuss, R. (2016), 'Realism and the Relativity of Judgement', in *Reality and Its Dreams* (Cambridge, MA: Harvard University Press), pp. 25–50.

Geuss, R. (2017), *Changing the Subject: Philosophy from Socrates to Adorno* (Cambridge, MA: Harvard University Press).

Gough, I. (2017), *Heat, Greed and Human Need* (Cheltenham: Edward Elgar).

Green, T. H. (1881), 'Liberal Legislation and Freedom of Contract', in R. L. Nettleship (ed.), *Works of Thomas Hill Green, III* (London: Longmans, Green), pp. 365–86.

Griffin, J. (2009), *On Human Rights* (Oxford: Oxford University Press).

Gutmann, A. and Thompson, D. (2004) (eds), *Why Deliberative Democracy?* (Princeton: Princeton University Press).

Habermas, J. (1984), *The Theory of Communicative Action, Volume 1: Reason and the Rationalization of Society*, trans. T. McCarthy (Boston: Beacon Press).

Habermas, J. (1987), *The Theory of Communicative Action, Volume 2: Lifeworld and System: A Critique of Functionalist Reason*, trans. T. McCarthy (Boston: Beacon Press).

Habermas, J. (1993), *Justification and Application: Remarks on Discourse Ethics*, trans. C. Cronin (Cambridge, MA: MIT Press).

Habermas, J. (1996a), *Between Facts and Norms: Contributions to a Discourse Theory of Law and Democracy*, trans. W. Rehg (Cambridge: Polity).

Habermas, J. (1996b), 'Three Normative Models of Democracy', in S. Benhabib (ed.), *Democracy and Difference: Contesting the Boundaries of the Political* (Princeton: Princeton University Press).

Hamilton, L. (1999), 'A Theory of True Interests in the Work of Amartya Sen', *Government and Opposition* 34(4): 516–46.

Hamilton, L. (2003a), *The Political Philosophy of Needs* (Cambridge: Cambridge University Press).

Hamilton, L. (2003b), '"Civil Society": Critique and Alternative', in S. Halperin and G. Laxer (eds), *Global Civil Society and Its Limits* (London: Palgrave).

Hamilton, L. (2014a), *Freedom is Power: Liberty through Political Representation* (Cambridge: Cambridge University Press).

Hamilton, L. (2014b), *Are South Africans Free?* (London: Bloomsbury).

Hamilton, L. (2015), 'Democratic Theory: The South African Crucible', *Democratic Theory* 2(2): 41–58.

Hamilton, L. (2016), 'Justice and Real Politics: Freedom, Needs and Representation', in C. Boisen and M. C. Murray (eds), *Distributive Justice Debates in Political and Social Thought: Perspectives on Finding a Fair Share* (London: Routledge).

Hamilton, L. (2018), 'Freedom in the Decolonizing Republic', *The Good Society* 26(1): 120–34.

Hampshire, S. (2000), *Justice is Conflict* (Princeton: Princeton University Press).

Hare, R. M. (1982), 'Ethical Theory and Utilitarianism', in A. Sen and B. Williams (eds), *Utilitarianism and Beyond* (Cambridge: Cambridge University Press), pp. 23–38.

Harsanyi, J. (1955), 'Cardinal Welfare, Individualistic Ethics, and Interpersonal Comparisons of Utility', *Journal of Political Economy* 63(4): 309–21.

Harsanyi, J. (1977), 'Non-Linear Social Welfare Functions: A Rejoinder to Professor Sen', in R. E. Butts and J. Hintikka (eds), *Foundational Problems in the Special Sciences* (Dordrecht: Reidel), pp. 294–5.

Hart, H. L. A. (1955), 'Are There Any Natural Rights?', *The Philosophical Review* 64(2) (April): 175–91. (Reprinted in J. Waldron, 1984, *Theories of Rights*, Oxford: Oxford University Press.)

Hicks, J. R. (1939), *Value and Capital* (Oxford: Clarendon Press).

Hicks, J. R. (1956), *A Revision of Demand Theory* (Oxford: Oxford University Press).

Hirschman, A. O. (1977), *The Passions and the Interests: Political Arguments for Capitalism Before Its Triumph* (Princeton: Princeton University Press).

Hirschman, A. O. (1981), 'The Rise and Decline of Development Economics', in *Essays in Trespassing: Economics to Politics and Beyond* (Cambridge: Cambridge University Press).

Hirschman, A. O. (1982), *Shifting Involvements: Private Interest and Public Action* (Princeton: Princeton University Press).

Hirschman, A. O. (1986), *Rival Views of Market Society and Other Recent Essays* (London: Viking Penguin).

Hobbes, T. (1996 [1651]), *Leviathan*, ed. R. Tuck (Cambridge: Cambridge University Press).

Hodgson, G. M. (2013), *From Pleasure Machines to Moral Communities: An Evolutionary Economics without Homo Economicus* (Chicago: University of Chicago Press).

Holland, E. (2014), *Allocating the Earth: A Distributional Framework for Protecting Capabilities in Environmental Law and Policy* (Oxford: Oxford University Press).

ILO (International Labour Organization) (1976), *Employment, Growth and Basic Needs: A One-World Problem* (Geneva: ILO).

Isakhan, B. and Stockwell, S. (eds) (2011), *The Secret History of Democracy* (London: Palgrave Macmillan).

Kant, I. (1997 [1788]), *Critique of Practical Reason* (Cambridge: Cambridge University Press).

Kant, I. (1998 [1785]), *Groundwork of the Metaphysics of Morals* (Cambridge: Cambridge University Press).

Keane, J. (2009), *The Life and Death of Democracy* (New York: W. W. Norton).

Kuklys, W. (2005), *Amartya Sen's Capability Approach: Theoretical Insights and Empirical Applications* (New York: Springer).

Liddell, H. G. and Scott, R. (1977), *A Greek–English Lexicon, extended by H. S. Jones and R. McKenzie* (Oxford: Clarendon Press).

Livy, T. (2005), *Ab Urbe Condita [History of Rome from its Foundation: Rome and the Mediterranean]*, trans. Henry Bettenson (London: Penguin).

Lovett, F. (2010), *A General Theory of Domination and Justice* (Cambridge: Cambridge University Press).

Lukes, S. (2005), *Power: A Radical View*, 2nd edn (New York: Palgrave Macmillan).

Mandela, N. (1994), *Long Walk to Freedom* (London: Little, Brown & Co.).

Marshall, A. (1890), *Principles of Economics* (London: Macmillan).

Marx, K. (1973 [1939–41]), *Grundrisse*, trans. M. Nicolaus (Harmondsworth: Penguin).

Marx, K. (1976–8 [1867]), *Capital*, 3 vols, trans. D. Fernbach, intro. E. Mandel (Harmondsworth: Penguin).

Marx, K. (1996 [1875]), *Critique of the Gotha Programme*, in T. Carver (ed.), *Marx: Later Political Writings* (Cambridge: Cambridge University Press).

Marx, K. and Engels, F. (1976 [1867]), *The German Ideology*, in *Marx, Engels: Collected Works (MECW)*, Vol. 5 (London: Lawrence and Wishart).

Maskin, E. (2014), 'The Arrow Impossibility Theorem: Where Do We Go from Here?', in E. Maskin and A. Sen, *The Arrow Impossibility Theorem* (New York: Columbia University Press), pp. 43–55.

Maskin, E. and Sen, A. (2014), *The Arrow Impossibility Theorem* (New York: Columbia University Press).

McCormick, J. P. (2011), *Machiavellian Democracy* (Cambridge: Cambridge University Press).

Meeks, J. G. (2017), 'Amartya Sen (1933–)', in R. Cord (ed.), *The Palgrave Companion to Cambridge Economics*, Vol. 2 (Basingstoke: Palgrave Macmillan), pp. 1045–78.

Meeks, J. G. (2018), 'On Sen on the Capability of Capabilities: the Evolution of an Enterprise', in P. B. Anand, F. V. Comim and S. Fennell (eds), *New Frontiers of the Capability Approach* (Cambridge: Cambridge University Press).

Menger, C. (1981 [1871]), *Principles of Economics*, trans. J. Dingwall and B. F. Hoselitz (New York: New York University Press).

Mill, J. S. (2008 [1859]), *On Liberty*, in John Gray (ed.), *On Liberty and Other Essays* (Oxford: Oxford University Press).

Mills, C. W. (2015), 'Decolonizing Western Political Philosophy', *New Political Science* 37(1): 1–24.

Mookerji, R. (1958 [1919]), *Local Government in Ancient India* (Delhi: Motilal Banarsidas).

Morris, M. D. (1979), *Measuring the Condition of the World's Poor: The Physical Quality of Life Index* (New York: Pergamon).

Mueller, D. C. (2003), *Public Choice III* (Cambridge: Cambridge University Press).

Nagel, T. (1970), *The Possibility of Altruism* (Oxford: Oxford University Press).

Nagel, T. (1986), *The View from Nowhere* (Oxford: Oxford University Press).

Nagel, T. (2005), 'The Problem of Global Justice', *Philosophy and Public Affairs* 33(2): 113–47.

Nobel (1998), The Official Web Site of the Nobel Prize, at: https://www.nobelprize.org/nobel_prizes/economic-sciences/laureates/1998/press.html

Nozick, R. (1974), *Anarchy, State, and Utopia* (Oxford: Basil Blackwell).

Nozick, R. (1993), *The Nature of Rationality* (Princeton: Princeton University Press).

Nussbaum, M. (1988), 'Nature, Function, and Capability: Aristotle on Political Distribution', in *Oxford Studies in Ancient Philosophy* (supplementary volume) (Oxford: Oxford University Press).

Nussbaum, M. (1993), 'Non-Relative Virtues: An Aristotelian Approach', in M. Nussbaum and A. K. Sen (eds), *The Quality of Life* (Oxford: Clarendon Press), pp. 242–69.

Nussbaum, M. (2000), *Women and Human Development: A Study in Human Capabilities* (Cambridge: Cambridge University Press).

Nussbaum, M. and Sen, A. K. (1989), 'Internal Criticism and Indian Rationalist Traditions', in M. Krausz (ed.), *Relativism: Interpretation and Confrontation* (Notre Dame: University of Notre Dame Press).

Ober, J. (2008), 'The Original "Meaning" of Democracy: The Capacity to Do Things, Not Majority Rule', *Constellations* 15(1): 1–9.

Ober, J. (2017), *Demopolis: Democracy before Liberalism in Theory and Practice* (Cambridge: Cambridge University Press).

Paine, T. (1906 [1791]), *The Rights of Man* (London: Dent).

Pareto, V. (1906), *Manuale di Economia Politica con una introduzione alla scienza sociale* (Milan: Societa Editrice Libraria) [Pareto, V. (2014), *Manual of Political Economy: A Critical and Variorum Edition*, ed. A. Montesano et al. (Oxford: Oxford University Press)].

Pattanaik, P. K. (2014), 'Introduction', in E. Maskin and A. Sen (eds), *The Arrow Impossibility Theorem* (New York: Columbia University Press), pp. 1–21.

Pettit, P. (1997), *Republicanism: A Theory of Freedom and Government* (Oxford: Oxford University Press).

Pettit, P. (2001), 'Capability and Freedom: A Defence of Sen', *Economics and Philosophy* 17(1): 1–20.

Philp, M. (2007), *Political Conduct* (Cambridge, MA: Harvard University Press).

Pigou, A. (1920), *The Economics of Welfare* (London: Macmillan).

Piketty, T. (2014 [2013]), *Capital in the Twenty-First Century* (Cambridge, MA: Harvard University Press).

Pitkin, H. (1988), 'Are Freedom and Liberty Twins?', *Political Theory* 16(4): 523–52.

Pogge, T. (2002), *World Poverty and Human Rights: Cosmopolitan Responsibilities and Reforms* (Cambridge: Polity Press).

Pogge, T. (2007), *Freedom from Poverty as a Human Right* (Oxford: Oxford University Press).

Putnam, H. (1987), *The Many Faces of Realism* (LaSalle, IL: Open Court).

Raphael, D. D. (1975), 'The Impartial Spectator', in A. S. Skinner and T. Wilson (eds), *Essays on Adam Smith* (Oxford: Clarendon Press).

Rawls, J. (1973), *A Theory of Justice* (Oxford: Oxford University Press).

Rawls, J. (1982), 'Social Unity and Primary Goods', in A. K. Sen and B. Williams (eds), *Utilitarianism and Beyond* (Cambridge: Cambridge University Press).

Rawls, J. (1988), 'Priority of Right and Ideas of the Good', *Philosophy and Public Affairs* 17(4): 251–76.

Rawls, J. (1993), *Political Liberalism* (New York: Columbia University Press).

Rawls, J. (1999), *Collected Papers* (Cambridge, MA: Harvard University Press).

Riker, W. (1982), *Liberalism Against Populism* (San Francisco: W. H. Freeman & Co.).

Robbins, L. (1938), 'Interpersonal Comparisons of Utility: A Comment', *Economic Journal* 48(192): 635–41.

Roberts, W. C. (2016), *Marx's Inferno: The Political Theory of Capital* (Princeton: Princeton University Press).

Robertson, J. (2015), *The Enlightenment: A Very Short Introduction* (Oxford: Oxford University Press).

Robeyns, I. (2017), *Wellbeing, Freedom and Social Justice: The Capability Approach Re-Examined* (Cambridge: Open Book Publishers).

Robinson, R. and Johnston, O. (1971), *Prospects for Employment in the 1970s* (London: Her Majesty's Stationery Office).

Rothschild, E. (2001), *Economic Sentiments: Smith, Condorcet and the Enlightenment* (Cambridge, MA: Harvard University Press).

Rousseau, J.-J. (1997 [1762]), 'The Social Contract', in Victor Gourevitch (ed.), *The Social Contract and Other Later Political Writings* (Cambridge: Cambridge University Press).

Samuelson, P. A. (1938a), 'A Note on the Pure Theory of Consumer's Behaviour', *Economica* 5(17): 61–71.

Samuelson, P. A. (1938b), 'A Note on the Pure Theory of Consumer's Behaviour: An Addendum', *Economica* 5(17): 61–71.

Samuelson, P. (1947), *Foundations of Economic Analysis* (Cambridge, MA: Harvard University Press).

Samuelson, P. A. (1948), 'Consumption Theory in Terms of Revealed Preference', *Economica* 15(60): 243–53.

Sandel, M. (1982), *Liberalism and the Limits of Justice* (Cambridge: Cambridge University Press).

Sandel, M. (2009), *Justice: What's the Right Thing to Do?* (New York: Farrar, Straus and Giroux).

Schlosberg, D. (2012), 'Climate Justice and Capabilities: A Framework for Adaptation Policy', *Ethics & International Affairs* 26(4): 445–61.

Schokkaert, E. (2009), 'The Capabilities Approach', in P. Anand, P. Pattanaik and C. Puppe (eds), *The Handbook of Rational and Social Choice* (Oxford: Oxford University Press), pp. 542–66.

Schumpeter, J. (1942), *Socialism, Capitalism and Democracy* (New York: Harper and Brothers).

Scitovsky, T. (1976), *The Joyless Economy: The Psychology of Human Satisfaction* (Oxford: Oxford University Press).

Sellar, A. (1994), 'Should the Feminist Philosopher Stay at Home?', in K. Lennon and M. Whitford (eds), *Knowing the Difference: Feminist Perspectives in Epistemology* (London and New York: Routledge).

Sen, A. K. (1960), *Choice of Techniques: An Aspect of the Theory of Planned Economic Development* (Oxford: Basil Blackwell).

Sen, A. K. (1970), 'The Impossibility of a Paretian Liberal', *Journal of Political Economy* 78(1): 152–7.

Sen, A. K. (1973), 'Behaviour and the Concept of Preference', *Economica* 40 (159): 241–59.

Sen, A. K. (1976), 'Liberty, Unanimity and Rights', *Economica* 43(171): 217–45.

Sen, A. K. (1977), 'Rational Fools: A Critique of the Behavioural Foundations of Economic Theory', *Philosophy and Public Affairs* 6: 317–44. (Reprinted in various places including *CWM*, pp. 84–106.)

Sen, A. K. (1979), 'Utilitarianism and Welfarism', *Journal of Philosophy* 76(9): 463–89.

Sen, A. K. (1981), 'Public Action and the Quality of Life in Developing Countries', *Oxford Bulletin of Economics and Statistics* 43: 287–319.

Sen, A. K. (1982a), 'Rights and Agency', *Philosophy and Public Affairs* 11(1): 3–39. (Reprinted in S. Scheffler [ed.], 1988, *Consequentialism and Its Critics*, Oxford: Oxford University Press.)

Sen, A. K. (1982b), 'Liberty as Control: An Appraisal', *Midwest Studies in Philosophy* 7(1): 207–21.

Sen, A. K. (1983a), 'Liberty and Social Choice', *Journal of Philosophy* 80(1) (January): 5–28.

Sen, A. K. (1983b), 'Evaluator Relativity and Consequential Evaluation', *Philosophy and Public Affairs* 12(2) (Spring): 113–32.

Sen, A. K. (1983c), 'Development: Which Way Now?', *The Economic Journal* 93(372): 745–62.

Sen, A. K. (1983d), 'Poor, Relatively Speaking', *Oxford Economic Papers* 35(2): 153–69.

Sen, A. K. (1985), 'Women, Technology and Sexual Divisions', *Trade and Development* 6: 195–223.

Sen, A. K. (1989), 'Development as Capability Expansion', *Journal of Development Planning* 19: 42–58.

Sen, A. K. (1990a [1989]), 'More Than 100 Million Women are Missing', *New York Review of Books*, 20 December.

Sen, A. K. (1990b), 'Gender and Cooperative Conflicts', in I. Tinker (ed.), *Persistent Inequalities* (New York: Oxford University Press).

Sen, A. K. (1990c), 'Justice: Means versus Freedoms', *Philosophy and Public Affairs* 19(2): 111–21.

Sen, A. K. (1994), 'Freedoms and Needs: An Argument for the Primacy of Political Rights', *The New Republic*, 10 and 17 January.

Sen, A. K. (1995), 'Rationality and Social Choice', *American Economic Review* 85(1): 1–24.

Sen, A. K. (1999), 'The Possibility of Social Choice', *American Economic Review* 89(3): 349–78.

Sen, A. K. (2000), 'A Decade of Human Development', *The Journal of Human Development* 1(1): 17–23.

Sen, A. K. (2002), 'Open and Closed Impartiality', *Journal of Philosophy* 99(9): 445–69.

Sen, A. K. (2004a), 'Dialogue: Capabilities, Lists, and Public Reason: Continuing the Conversation', *Feminist Economics* 10(3): 77–80.

Sen, A. K. (2004b), 'Elements of a Theory of Human Rights', *Philosophy and Public Affairs* 32(4): 315–56.

Sen, A. K. (2005), *The Argumentative Indian* (London and Delhi: Penguin).

Sen, A. K. (2006a), *Identity and Violence: The Illusion of Destiny* (London and Delhi: Penguin).

Sen, A. K. (2006b), 'Human Rights and the Limits of Law', *Cardozo Law Journal* 27 (April).

Sen, A. K. (2006c), 'What Do We Want from a Theory of Justice', *The Journal of Philosophy* 103(5): 215–38.

Sen, A. K. (2012a), 'The Crisis of European Democracy', *New York Times*, 22 May, at: https://www.nytimes.com/2012/05/23/opinion/the-crisis-of-european-democracy.html

Sen, A. K. (2012b), 'What Happened to Europe? Democracy and the Decision of Bankers', *The New Republic*, at: https://www.nytimes.com/2012/05/23/opinion/the-crisis-of-european-democracy.html

Sen, A. K. (2014), 'Arrow and the Impossibility Theorem', in E. Maskin and A. Sen, *The Arrow Impossibility Theorem* (New York: Columbia University Press), pp. 29–42.

Sen, A. K. (2015), *The Country of First Boys and Other Essays* (New Delhi: Oxford University Press).

Sen, A. K. (2016), 'Don't Want Modi as My PM: Amartya Sen', 8 June, at: http://www.thehindu.com/news/national/dont-want-modi-as-my-pm-amartya-sen/article4941075.ece

Sen, A. K. and Williams, B. (1982), *Utilitarianism and Beyond* (Cambridge: Cambridge University Press).

Shapiro, I. (2006), *The State of Democratic Theory* (Princeton: Princeton University Press).

Shapiro, I. (2011), 'Review of Sen's *The Idea of Justice*', *Journal of Economic Literature* 49(4) (December): 1251–63.

Shapiro, I. (2016), *Politics Against Domination* (Cambridge, MA: Harvard University Press).

Simon, H. (1957), *Models of Man* (New York: Wiley).

Simon, H. (1979), *Models of Thought* (New Haven: Yale University Press).

Skinner, Q. (1997), *Liberty before Liberalism* (Cambridge: Cambridge University Press).

Skinner, Q. (2002), 'The Idea of Negative Liberty: Machiavellian and Modern Perspectives', in *Visions of Politics, Vol. II: Renaissance Virtues* (Cambridge: Cambridge University Press).

Smith, A. (1976 [1776]), *An Inquiry into the Nature and Causes of the Wealth of Nations*, 2 vols, ed. R. H. Campbell, A. S. Skinner and W. B. Todd (eds) (Oxford: Clarendon Press).

Smith, A. (1976 [1790]), *The Theory of Moral Sentiments*, ed. D. D. Raphael and A. A. Mackie (Oxford: Clarendon Press).

Stewart, F. (1985), *Planning to Meet Basic Needs* (London: Macmillan).

Stewart, F. and Deneulin, S. (2002), 'Amartya Sen's Contribution to Development Thinking', *Studies in Comparative International Development* 37(2): 61–70.

Streeten, P. P., Burki, S. J., ul Haq, M., Hicks, N. and Stewart, F. (1981), *First Things First: Meeting Basic Needs in Developing Countries* (New York: Oxford University Press).

Sugden, R. (1998), 'The Metric of Opportunity', *Economics and Philosophy* 14(2): 307–13.

Taylor, C. (1985), *Philosophy and the Human Sciences: Philosophical Papers 2* (Cambridge: Cambridge University Press).

Tse-tung, M. (1974), *Mao Tse-tung Unrehearsed, Talks and Letters: 1956–71*, ed. S. Schram (Harmondsworth: Penguin).

Van Parijs, P. (1995), *Real Freedom for All: What (If Anything) Can Justify Capitalism?* (Oxford: Oxford University Press).

Venkatapuram, S. (2011), *Health Justice: An Argument from the Capabilities Approach* (Cambridge: Polity Press).

Waldron, J. (2000), *The Dignity of Legislation* (Cambridge: Cambridge University Press).

Walras, L. (1899), *Éléments d'économie politique pure*, 4th edn (1954, *Elements of Pure Economics*, trans. W. Jaffé, London: George Allen and Unwin).

Walzer, M. (1983), *Spheres of Justice: A Defense of Pluralism and Equality* (New York: Basic Books).

Weber, M. (1978 [1922]), *Economy and Society*, Vol. I, ed. G. Roth and C. Wittich (Berkeley, CA: University of California Press).

Williams, B. (1985), *Ethics and the Limits of Philosophy* (Cambridge, MA: Harvard University Press).

Williams, B. (2001), 'From Freedom to Liberty: The Construction of a Political Value', *Philosophy and Public Affairs* 30(1): 3–26.

Williams, M. (2014), *The End of the Developmental State?* (London: Routledge).

Wold, H. O. A. (1963), *Demand Analysis* (New York: Wiley).

Wolin, S. (1982), 'What Revolutionary Action Means Today', *Democracy: A Journal of Political Renewal and Radical Change* 2(4) (Fall): 17–28.

Wolin, S. (1994), 'Fugitive Democracy', *Constellations* 1(1): 13–25.

Wollstonecraft, M. (1995 [1790, 1792]), *A Vindication of the Rights of Men and a Vindication of the Rights of Woman*, ed. S. Tomaselli (Cambridge: Cambridge University Press).

Further Reading

Alkire, S. (2002), *Valuing Freedoms: Sen's Capability Approach and Poverty Reduction* (Oxford and New York: Oxford University Press). Illuminating and wide-ranging introduction to Sen's capability approach; does not include coverage of *IJ*, obviously.

Morris, C. (ed.) (2010), *Amartya Sen* (Cambridge: Cambridge University Press). An edited volume with some excellent essays and good coverage; focuses on the more philosophical side of Sen's ideas.

Reiko, G. and Dumouchel, P. (eds) (2009), *Against Injustice: The New Economics of Amartya Sen* (Cambridge: Cambridge University Press). On the importance of focusing on the identification of specific cases of injustice rather than trying to construct a theory of a uniquely specified 'just society'.

Robeyns, I. (2017), *Wellbeing, Freedom and Social Justice: The Capability Approach Re-Examined* (Cambridge: Open Book Publishers). Excellent introduction to the capability approach in all its variants, with a preference for Sen's approach, but not much about other parts of Sen's work.

Index